WOMEN ARTISTS

ON THE LEADING EDGE

VISUAL ARTS AT DOUGLASS COLLEGE

JOAN MARTER

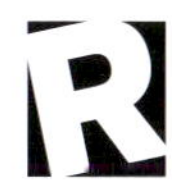

RUTGERS UNIVERSITY PRESS

NEW BRUNSWICK • CAMDEN • NEWARK, NEW JERSEY
LONDON

WOMEN ARTISTS
ON THE LEADING EDGE

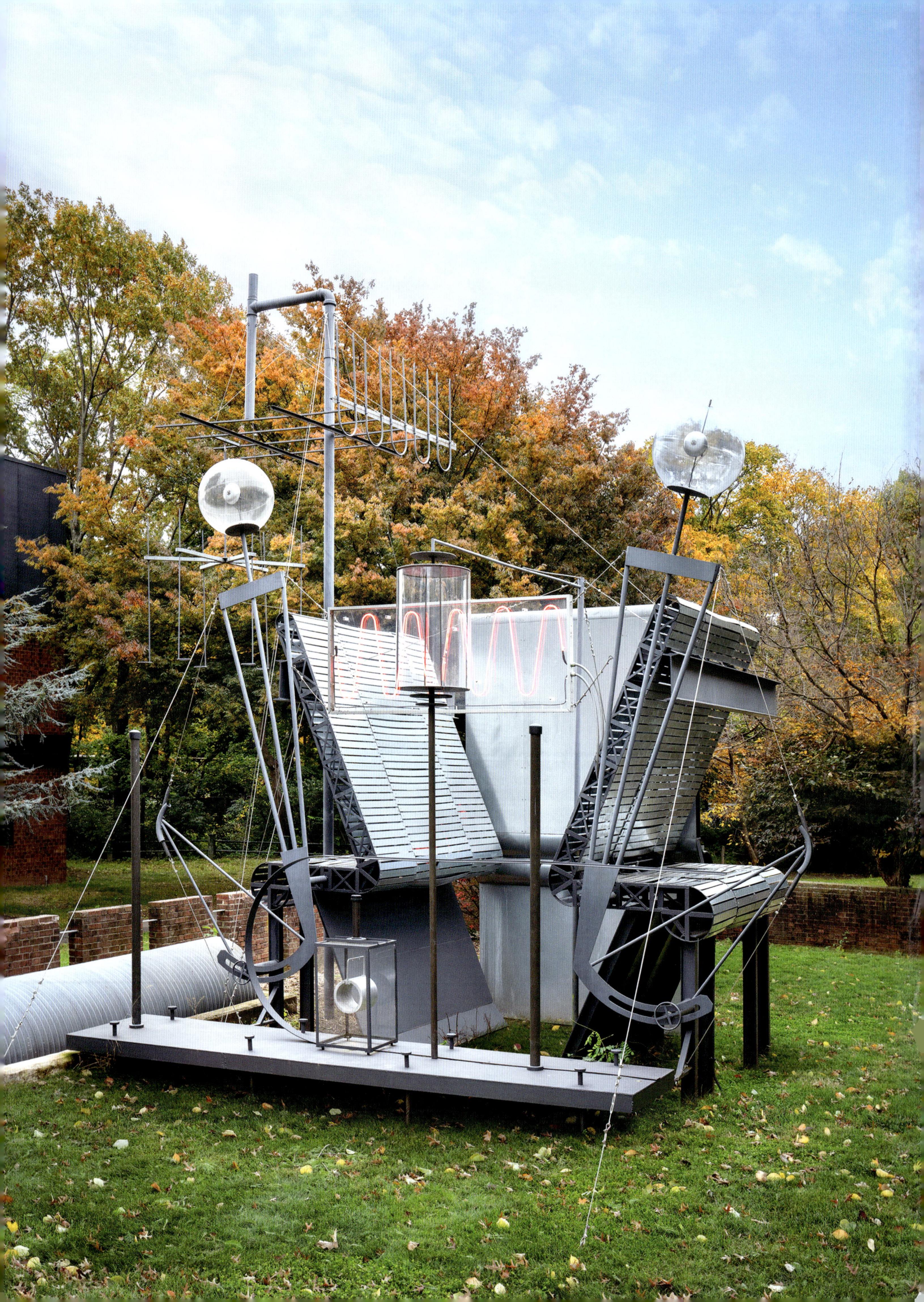

Library of Congress Cataloging-in-Publication Data

Names: Marter, Joan M., author, interviewer.
Title: Women artists on the leading edge : visual arts at Douglass College / Joan Marter.
Description: New Brunswick : Rutgers University Press, 2019. | Includes bibliographical references and index.
Identifiers: LCCN 2019002218 | ISBN 9780813593340 (cloth)
Subjects: LCSH: Women art students—New Jersey—New Brunswick. | Art—Study and teaching (Higher)—New Jersey—New Brunswick. | Douglass College—Faculty—Interviews. | Douglass College—Students—Interviews.
Classification: LCC N330.N2952 D686 2019 | DDC 700.71/1097151--dc23
LC record available at https://lccn.loc.gov/2019002218

A British Cataloging-in-Publication record for this book is available from the British Library.

Frontispiece: Alice Aycock. *Miraculating Machine in the Garden (Tower of the Winds)*, 1980-82. Glass, concrete, steel sheet metal, copper, neon light, and vegetation, 30' × 30' × 20' deep. Douglass College. Photo: Mike Van Tassell.

Cover and text design by Studiolo Secondari.

♾ The paper used in this publication meets the requirements of the American National Standard for Information Sciences—Permanence of Paper for Printed Library Materials, ANSI Z39.48-1992.

www.rutgersuniversitypress.org

Manufactured in the United States of America

CONTENTS

Art Programs at Douglass College

This publication begins with faculty and students active in the 1950s, when the New Jersey College for Women officially becomes Douglass College. Previous to the 1950s, the teaching of studio art adhered to a traditional curriculum with study from plaster versions of statuary from the ancient world, studies of the human figure, and paintings and drawings of still life and landscape subjects. The 1950s ushered in a new curriculum, and Dean Mary Bunting, who supported avant-garde developments in the creative arts.

From the progressive agenda of Dean Mary Bunting and the faculty, who explored a range of new ideas and approaches to artmaking, to the avant-garde events presented by the Voorhees Assembly Board, the women's college at Rutgers found itself on the leading edge of midcentury art world events. Initially there were prominent members of the Pop Art and Fluxus movements who were instructors in the visual arts. Happenings and art installations took place on campus. As Douglass quickly recognized a burgeoning feminist involvement among the students, programs were initiated, lectures were arranged, and distinguished initiators of the women's art movement, such as Judy Chicago and Faith Ringgold, were invited to campus. Later the Guerrilla Girls, Karen Finley, and other artists performed at Douglass.

Undergraduates began curating exhibitions of women artists to be shown in the Douglass College Art Gallery and in the Douglass Library. For example, in 1979 an exhibition entitled *Expressions of Self: Women and Autobiography* was organized by undergraduates in Professor Marter's Workshop in Curatorial Practices. A 1980 exhibition, *Fragments of Myself/the Women*, organized by students for the Douglass College Art Gallery, included African American artists Emma Amos, Camille Billops, Howardena Pindell, and Faith Ringgold, among others.

Among the renowned artists who were undergraduates at Douglass College are Alice Aycock, Rita Myers, and Joan Snyder. Recollections by these artists about their time on campus, and reminiscences of other graduates are included in this book.

The Master of Fine Arts Program

It was 1962 when the first students completed the master of fine arts degree at Douglass College. Among the early graduates of the MFA program were Mimi Smith, Jackie Winsor,

Joan Snyder, Rita Myers, Loretta Dunkelman, Ann Tsubota, and Marion Levinston Munk. Based in part on the pedagogy of Black Mountain College, and heavily indebted to John Cage's media course at the New School, the curriculum at Douglass emphasized artistic innovation and links to everyday experience: the cutting edge of a new Art. Although there were differences in methods, materials, and approaches to artmaking, similar themes and goals characterize the MFA pedagogy at Douglass. As Mimi Smith has often expressed it, "I was taught that anything could be art." And anything *was* art for many faculty and students alike. Art could be derived from the ordinary world of experience (as in household items), and art could incorporate state-of-the-art media (film and photography combined). Art could be related to the body, or it could have a phenomenological reference. It could be a combination of performance and environment; it could be ephemeral or lasting. The faculty opened up a full range of possibilities for the students. The book includes essays based on interviews with distinguished graduates, who consider the importance of their study with the art faculty of Douglass College. A full range of art will be featured here: painting, sculpture, photography, and multimedia works. Mason Gross School of the Visual and Performing Arts was established at Rutgers in 1975. Before that time the graduate program in visual arts was centered at Douglass College, and many of the Douglass art faculty were involved in the MFA curriculum.

After the Mason Gross School formed, the graduate students moved to a downtown location. Some classes were taught at Douglass, but the curriculum and the administration were separate from the Douglass College program.

The Women Artists Series (Later the Mary H. Dana Women Artists Series)

From its inception in 1971, the shows of the Women Artists Series were installed in the Mabel Smith Douglass Library, where all students and faculty would be informed of the achievements of women. In addition to providing role models of gifted women for the Douglass students, the Women Artists Series served as an important political milestone. Initiated at a time when critical attention to women's work was negligible, the series continues now in a period of greater, but still limited, acceptance of women in commercial galleries and museums. Still today, when there are more exciting and talented women artists than ever before, there remains a need to celebrate the accomplishments of outstanding women professionals. At Douglass, this series continues as a model of support for women by women. These shows both inform and enrich the campus community. It is evident that many women artists benefited from their exhibitions at Douglass College. For some, inclusion in the series provided their first opportunity for a solo exhibition. The artists were able to reach a different audience from those who frequent New York galleries—initially the Women Artists Series was an important source of role models for aspiring art students. The history of the series, and key moments in the decades of commitment to contemporary women artists are part of the history of Douglass College. Joan Snyder, the initiator of this well-recognized project, addresses its importance and legacy in her discussion of the Women Artist Series and its history.

PART ONE

VISUAL ARTS FACULTY AT DOUGLASS COLLEGE

When Douglass College expanded the visual arts offerings in earnest, it was the 1950s, a time when many exciting changes were happening on the campus. Mary Ingraham Bunting became the dean,[1] and she was eager to promote avant-garde approaches to the visual and performing arts. Was it just coincidental that Robert Watts, who had been hired for the engineering program in 1952, transferred to the art department the following year to teach sculpture and ceramics? By the fall semester Watts was showing abstract paintings at the Douglass College Art Gallery. Also in 1953 Allan Kaprow was hired at Rutgers College (the all-male undergraduate college) to teach art history and art. A remarkable interaction of faculty and students commenced on both campuses. At Douglass, the students were introduced to a whole range of new approaches to artmaking. From the introductory courses on, students were urged to experiment with new methods and materials. The Rutgers College art department was located in a small house on College Avenue. Students were permitted to take courses on both campuses, and occasionally Douglass students walked across town to take a class with Kaprow.

Following the example of Black Mountain College in North Carolina, which closed in 1957, the Douglass faculty introduced students to various new trends combining art creation with performance.[2] Robert Rauschenberg, who had studied at Black Mountain, was lionized by the faculty, who urged students to see his New York exhibitions.[3] In the summer of 1952, Rauschenberg had participated in an event at Black Mountain that combined art, poetry, and dance, known later as *Theatre Piece No. 1*. Eventually this interdisciplinary approach to the visual and performing arts was to spawn notable developments at Douglass College. John Cage offered a class at the New School for Social Research in New York City, attended by Kaprow, George Brecht, Al Hansen, and others, which was another connection with the intermedia approach of Black Mountain College.

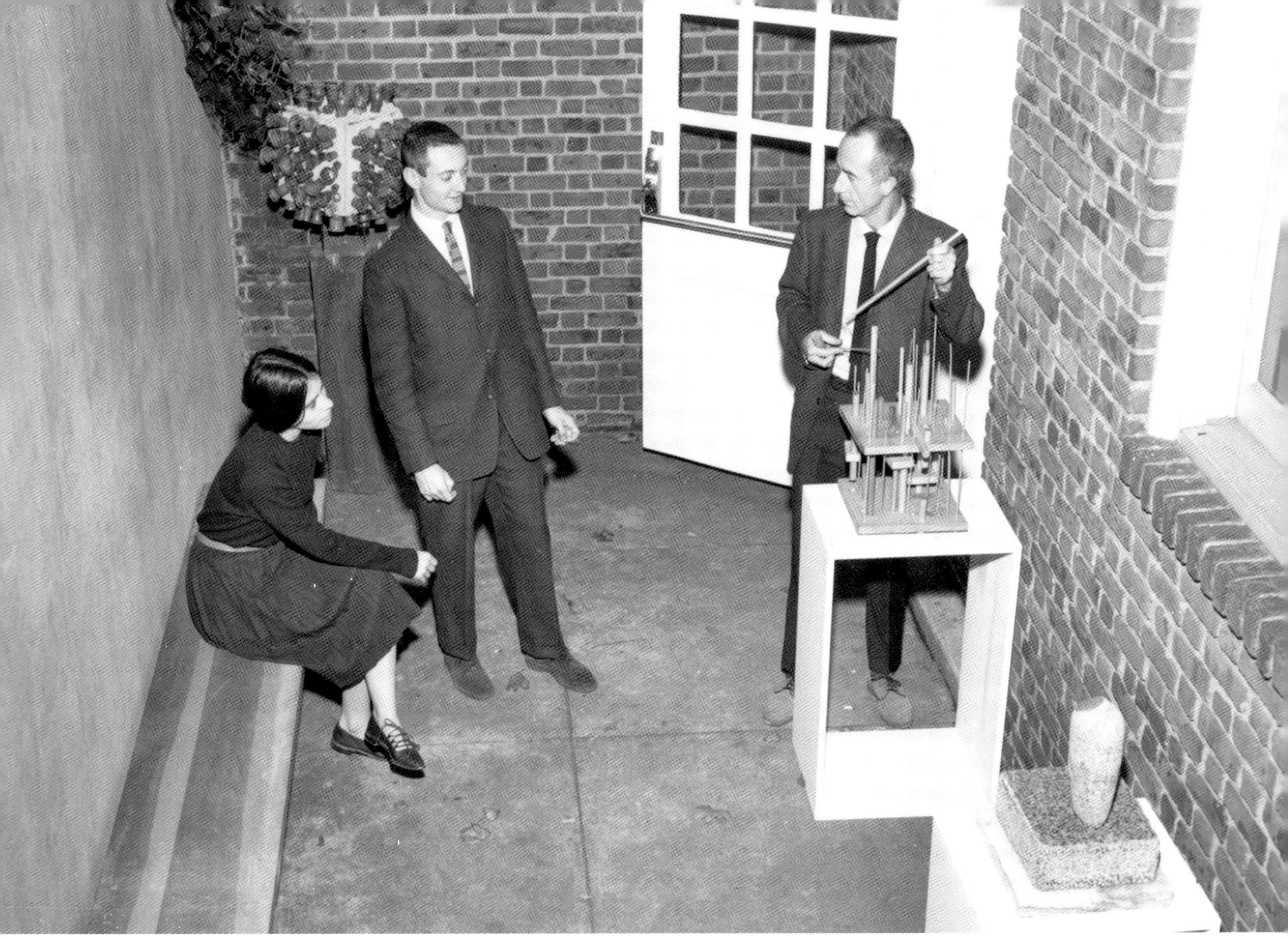

The chair of the Douglass art department was Theodore Brenson, and Robert Watts, Sam Weiner, Mark Berger, and John Goodyear[4] were among those on the faculty. Geoffrey Hendricks, who was to be at the forefront of the Fluxus movement, joined the Douglass faculty in 1956. Initially he taught the introductory studio class and was in charge of gallery exhibitions. He was also the designated adviser to the art club (Pen & Brush). In April 1957 Watts proposed an experimental course to Dean Bunting that would integrate the arts and sciences. He requested new media and the use of audiovisual techniques for teaching. Hendricks recalled, "Polly Bunting, a bacteriologist, was open to these ideas and responsive to our idea of instituting a graduate program."[5] Soon Watts had produced works with electronic components and began making mixed media assemblages in earnest. Ka Kwong Hui, from China, was hired in 1957 to teach ceramics.[6]

Geoff Hendricks recalled:

> Bob [Watts] and I both taught Art Structure I, the introductory studio class. The nature of art and teaching of art were ongoing topics. I remember bringing in recordings of *musique concrete* in relation to work with collage and the *Mustard Seed Manual* in relation to drawing. Before I joined the faculty, Bob had taught

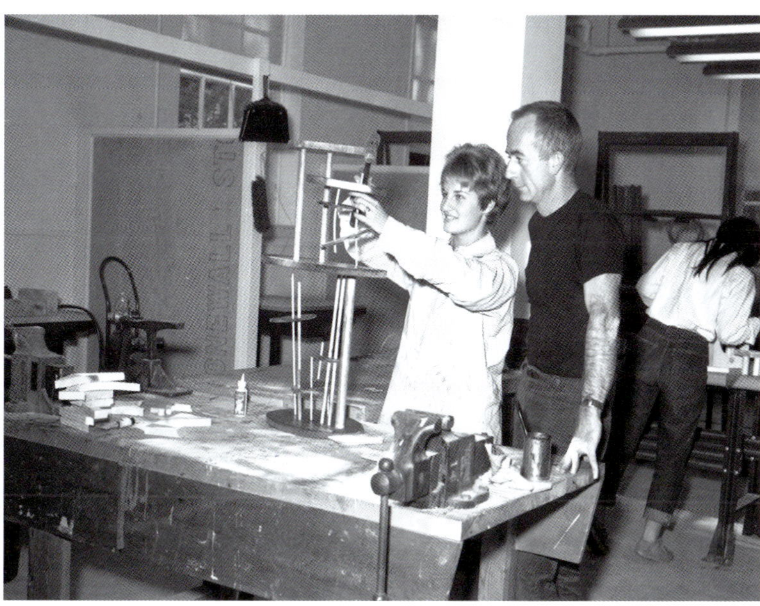

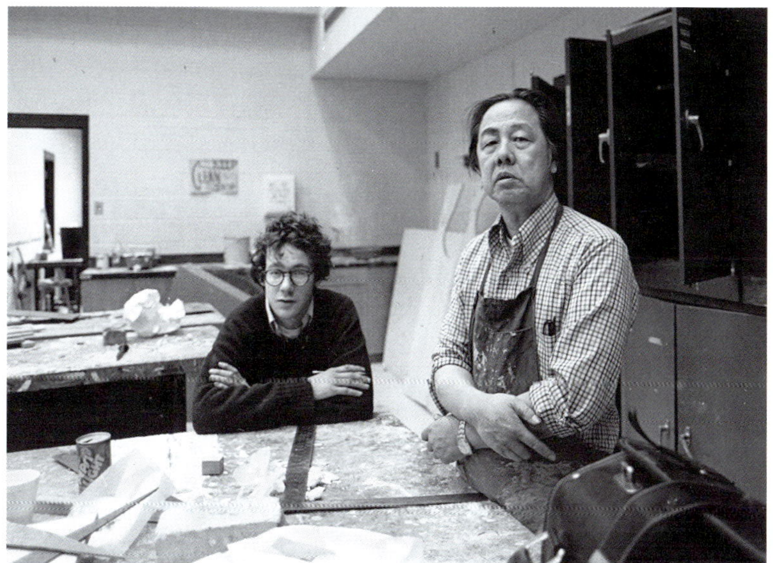

sculpture and ceramics as one course. We split it into two classes that met at the same time. I taught sculpture. Bob taught ceramics. Our dialogue on art and education continued. In May we took the combined group to the Jersey shore to work with sand, plaster, space, and the environment. The next year, after Ka Kwong was hired, Bob returned to sculpture, and I located some presses with the help of Bob Blackburn and introduced printmaking. In addition to developing a more inclusive curriculum, we wanted a serious professional gallery program with an international perspective and exhibitions that would introduce a range of new art to the campus.[7]

Many extraordinary events would soon be staged at Douglass. In the spring of 1958 Watts, Kaprow, and their associate George Brecht created a "proto-Happening" featuring flashing lights and sound, in two rooms of a Douglass classroom building. The previous year Watts, Kaprow, and Brecht had begun work on a grant proposal for "Project in Multiple Dimensions," to be presented to the administration of Rutgers University and the Carnegie Corporation. The artists sought funding for avant-garde projects involving new technology, and submitted their proposal in 1958.

Dean Bunting initiated the Voorhees Assemblies at Douglass. For the 1957–1958 academic year, Bob Watts was on the Voorhees Assembly Board. The theme was "communication," and Watts helped to arrange several related programs. During the spring semester of 1958, a series of vanguard events included a performance by John Cage and David Tudor, and the first Happening by Allan Kaprow in the Voorhees Chapel. On March 11, John Cage read from a text he called "Communication,"[8] which included questions and quotations that were delivered in an order that was determined by chance, while David Tudor sat at a grand piano and played a score that was circular in form and could start or end at any point.

This event was followed on March 18 by a performance of Paul Taylor's *Five Dances*, held in the Little Theater. The program opened with *Resemblance*, danced to a score by John Cage, played by David Tudor. Another of the dances, *Duet*, was performed to Cage's *4'33"* where Tudor did not play the keys, but opened and closed the piano keyboard at set intervals. On April 22, Kaprow presented his first "Happening" involving art works and a range of sounds and events in the Voorhees Chapel. Lucas Samaras and other undergraduate art students participated in the performance.

In an interview Kaprow noted the following:

> It was called Communication, because the whole series of programs was dedicated to mid-twentieth-century communication. I thought that I could set up an event that would be spread around the chapel which could communicate the absurdity of the usual straightforward verbal explication of reality. I tried to design situations that were patently meaningless, including the use of words over a number of loudspeakers. I had quoted from speeches. These quotes were separately recorded on several tapes. They came out one on top of the other until the whole thing became a big mishmash. All of this was taking place while I was delivering the same words in person at the rostrum.[9]

Other performances were held on the Douglass campus in subsequent years. As Douglass became associated with avant-garde art, and Roy Lichtenstein joined the faculty, Hendricks and Watts were associated with the latest developments in art. By 1959 the art department at Douglass had launched the master of fine arts program, which remained at Douglass until the late 1960s. The first MFA degrees were awarded in 1962.

The Douglass undergraduates and new graduate students had many opportunities to participate in exhibitions and events at and around the College. A number of exhibitions including works by faculty members were installed at the Douglass College Art Gallery. In November 1959, Geoff Hendricks and Robert Watts organized "Group 3," which featured works by Rauschenberg (including *Factum I* and *Factum II*), and Kaprow,

1.4
Douglass College Art Gallery ca. 1968.
Left: John Goodyear; right: Geoff
Hendricks. Photo: Linda Lindroth.

1.5
Douglass College Art Gallery ca. 1968.
On floor: Linda Lindroth and Rita My-
ers (standing). Photo: David Lindroth.

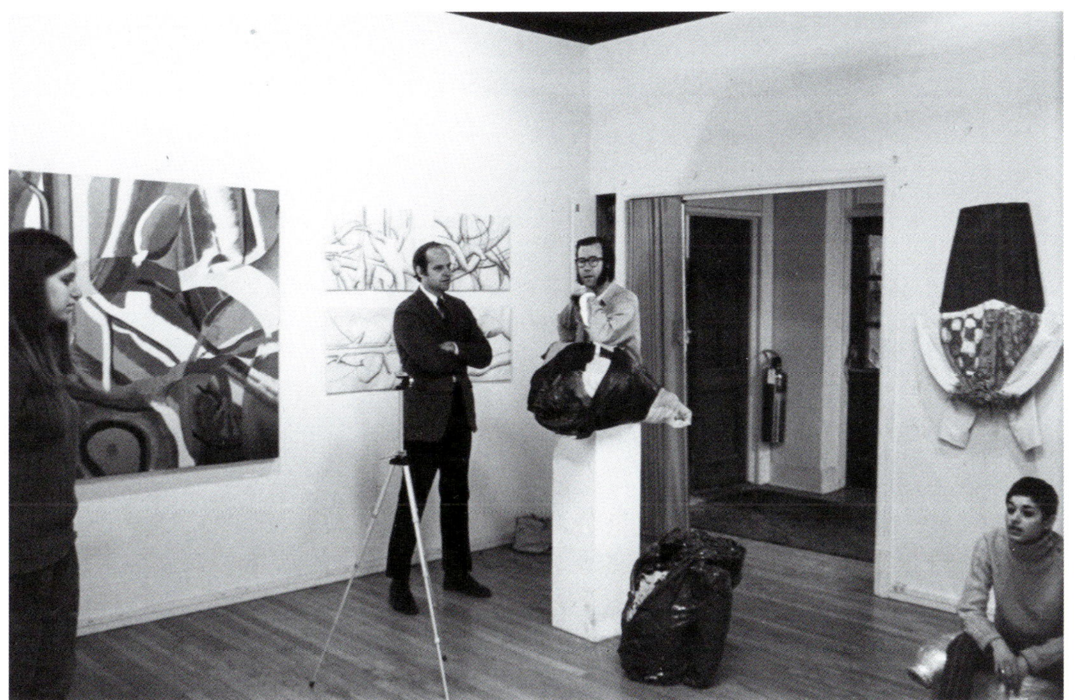

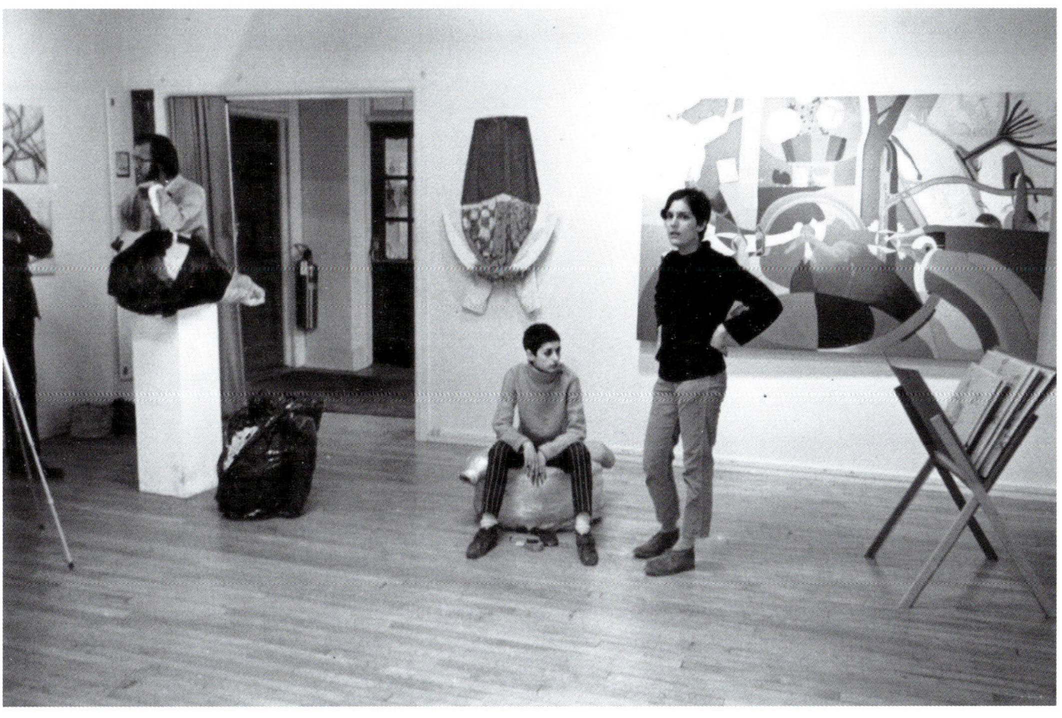

Brecht, Watts, and others. The following June, Watts presented the *Magic Kazoo*, a continuous twenty-four-hour Happening that took place both in New Jersey and in New York City, and Watts also had solo exhibitions in New York of his assemblages and motorized constructions.

In 1960 Roy Lichtenstein was hired at Douglass to teach design courses and a class called Art Structure. In this stimulating environment Lichtenstein created his first Pop painting, *Look Mickey*, which he showed to Kaprow in the summer of 1961. This was his latest effort, but Lichtenstein was also showing earlier that year, in January 1961, a solo exhibition of his Abstract Expressionist paintings at the Douglass College Art Gallery. He was closely involved with Letty Lou Eisenhauer, a 1957 graduate of Douglass, who entered the graduate program in 1961, while also working in the departmental office. Recalling her art classes, Eisenhauer noted: "I would try all kinds of weird things. We were encouraged to experiment. What happened was that people like Bob Watts and Geoff Hendricks opened the door to experimentation. This was a questioning of the formal methods for creating art. Anything you wanted to try you could try. . . . Watts seemed genuinely concerned about his students, their potential and eventual success."[10]

In 1961 Roy Lichtenstein went on to show his first Pop paintings at Leo Castelli Gallery in New York, and the Douglass students gained exposure to the first years of this major new art development. There is no question that both the undergraduates and the graduate students were affected by these new approaches to art. As Mimi Smith has indicated, Bob Watts taught her that "anything could be art."

In April 1962 a weekend dedicated to "An Experiment in the Arts" was held at Douglass College, and included Happenings, experimental music, plays, and various performances. Kaprow was the keynote speaker, and other participants included Lichtenstein, Watts, Dick Higgins, Alison Knowles, and others. Events were staged in various Douglass locations, including Al Hansen's "Parisol 4 Marisol" at the Old Gymnasium, and Hansen's "Carcophany" on the Corwin Campus. The Faculty Art Show in the Douglass Art Gallery that October included stamp machines by Watts, paintings by Lichtenstein and George Segal, and constructions by Hendricks. Segal presented his thesis exhibition at the Douglass Art Gallery in January 1963 and received his MFA degree in June of that year.

The professionalism and active involvement of the Douglass faculty with some of the most avant-garde trends in contemporary art had an important impact on the art students.

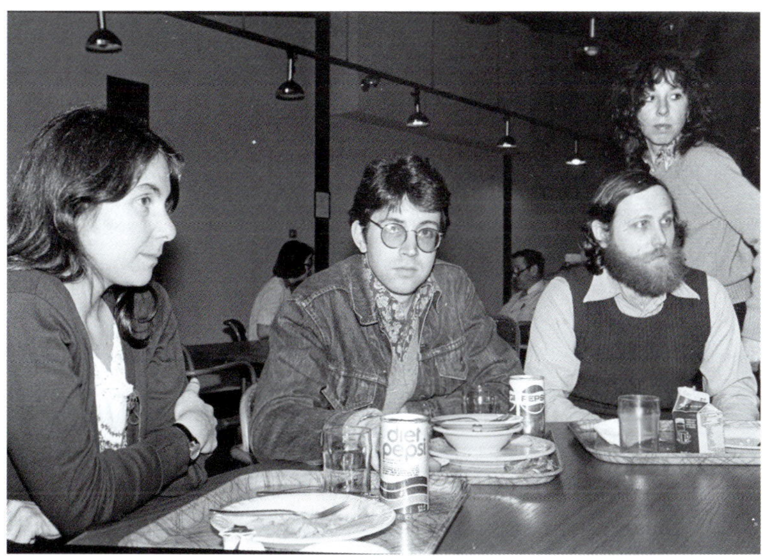

Opportunities to see the experimental works produced by their instructors, and exposure to some of the leading artists of the day, held great interest and excitement for the students. Some, like Alice Aycock, were encouraged to attend graduate school and continue their serious commitment to a career as an artist. Others, such as Letty Lou Eisenhauer, went on to perform in various Happenings staged in New York by Kaprow, Lucas Samaras, Claes Oldenburg, and others. The Fluxus impact continued unabated at Douglass and resulted in the Flux-Mass and other events.

By the early 1970s, noting that no women were available to them on the faculty, certain students wanted a more feminist direction. Joan Snyder satisfied this need and brought a lasting legacy to Douglass as a women's college. Snyder, who would initiate the Women Artists Series in 1971, became politically active with the women's movement in the early 1970s. Born in Highland Park, New Jersey, she attended Douglass College from 1958 to 1962. Although she graduated with a degree in sociology, in a painting course with Billy Pritchard, she was encouraged to study the works of Alexei Jawlensky and other expressionist painters in Russia and Germany. Working on her own to develop her painting style, she enrolled in the graduate program in the visual arts as a nonmatriculated student in 1963 and became a full-fledged MFA student the following year. From the outset Snyder was drawn to painting and sculpture and was attracted to the Combine painting of Rauschenberg. Later, from 1971 to 1974, Snyder was a member of a consciousness-raising group on the Douglass campus. She attempted to define a "female sensibility" in her own work and was part of a movement to determine a feminist aesthetic.

Snyder's Women Artists Series at Douglass was intended to foreground the works of women artists. For the first exhibition Snyder wrote, "In these times when disillusionment with the established order is at an all time high, a new energy begins to be felt. . . . Women are emerging from history because history needs them to show the way to peace and the way to another kind of strength and reflection."[11]

Thanks to Snyder and others, Douglass College was alerted to the need for women to be teaching art and art history. In 1976 Carolee Schneemann was hired to teach film at Douglass from 1976 to 1978, thus becoming, according to Geoff Hendricks, "our first female artist on the faculty."[12] However, Schneemann was not given a tenure-track appointment.

Amy Stromsten, who had been included in the Women Artists Series in 1972, was a photographer who had taught for several years at the School of Visual Arts and the New School. She began teaching part time at Douglass in 1976. She noted that "in 1977 I became the first full-time female member of the Douglass Studio Art faculty."[13] Joan Marter began to teach contemporary and modern art history at Douglass in 1977, and Joan Semmel joined the faculty to teach painting and drawing in 1979.

Joan Semmel taught for twenty-two years at Rutgers and began her teaching at Douglass College by offering a course in painting and drawing. Her gallery at the time was Lerner-Heller, and she was brought up early for tenure. In an interview Semmel recalled that Douglass students demanded a course in painting.[14] Even though many of the faculty and students were involved in new technology and conceptual art, there was a revived interest in the study of painting. She taught the students how to prepare their canvas and work exclusively in oils. Semmel also offered a life drawing class with male and female models. However, Semmel recalled a backlash against women students who were taking painting courses. Painting was considered passé. The belief among male faculty[15] and students was that women should not be working on paintings, but should create performance art projects instead. According to some of the faculty, painting was "dead." But Semmel definitely had new approaches to painting the figure.

As virtually all of the Douglass alumnae noted in their recollections of their years as undergraduates, Joan Semmel also remembered that the art students were "ambitious" and "serious."[16] Students went to New York City to see shows and to learn about the art world. Once women held positions on the art faculty, Douglass women could concentrate on a feminist approach. For example, young women talked to Joan Semmel about their prospects of continuing for the MFA degree, and they sought advice about their career options.

Semmel's recent paintings, such as *On the Grass* (1978) set a new direction for feminism on campus. Semmel's frankly erotic image and provocative use of her own nude body correlate with active discussions of female sexuality. Semmel in her life and in her art made explicit the sexual liberation of the self.

1.7

Joan Semmel. *On the Grass,* 1978. Oil
on canvas, 48" × 74". Courtesy Alexander Gray Gallery, New York.

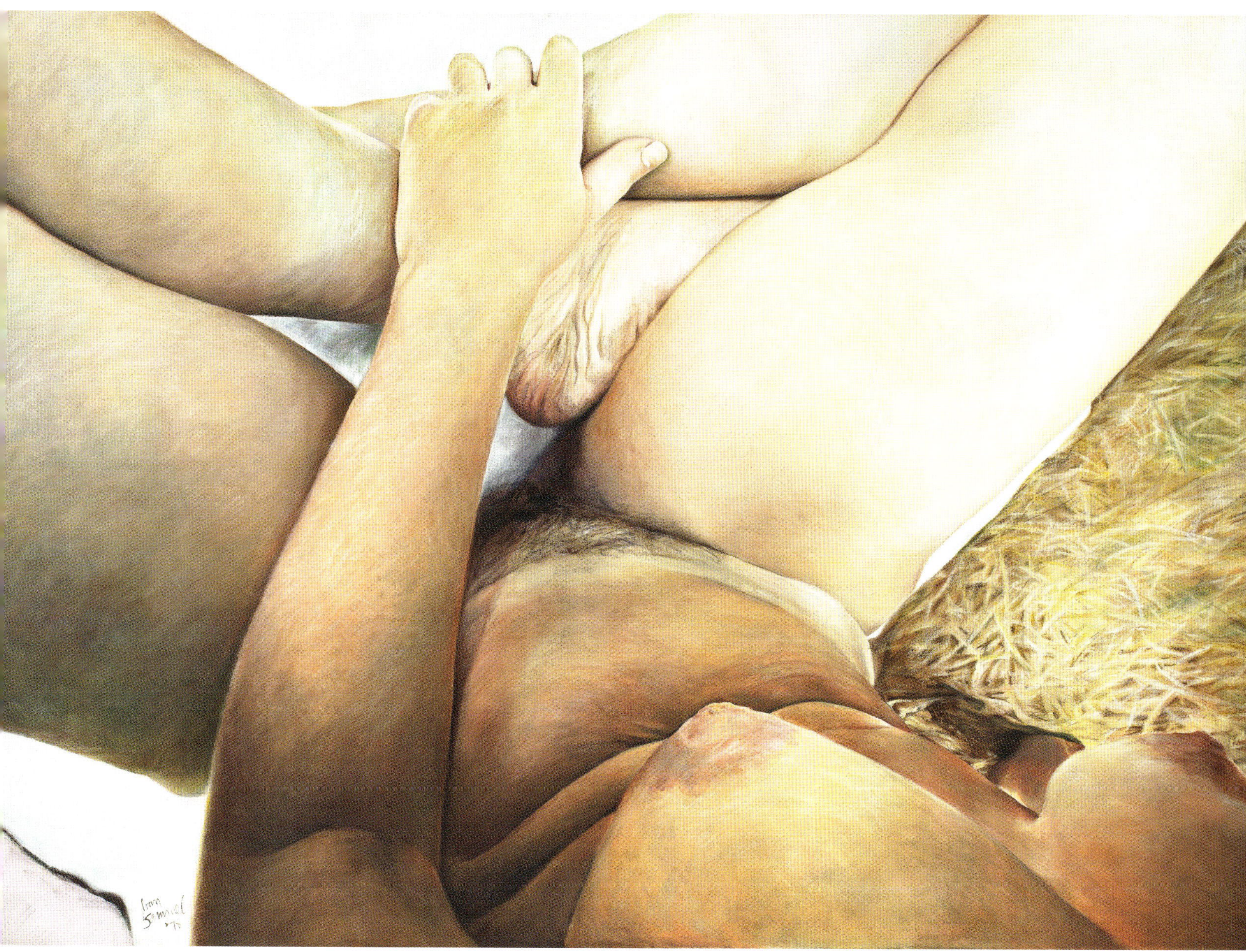

Born in the Bronx, Semmel studied painting at Cooper Union, and later had to unlearn her early instruction in Abstract Expressionist gesturalism. After an early marriage and a child born when she was twenty-three, Semmel returned to her studio, taking classes at the Art Students League. At twenty-nine she enrolled at the Pratt Institute, where she completed a BFA degree. Semmel lived in Spain during the 1960s and began to show her work. When she returned to the United States in 1970, Semmel quickly became involved with the women's movement. After completing her MFA at Pratt in 1972, she began to pose nude male and female models, and her work took an erotic direction. She was teaching at the Brooklyn Museum School before her appointment at Douglass College. Teaching was "productive" for her. Her paintings became a vehicle of communication with other feminists. Co-opting the male "gaze," Joan Semmel continues to explore diverse experiences of the female body. She returns to featuring her own body in recent work, such as *Centered* (2002). Semmel noted: "Now I am more aware of infinite varieties of sexuality in my own art. I moved from sexuality to mortality—aware of body changes—life is more finite."[16]

Joan Semmel, as artist, feminist activist, and educator, was at the forefront of the women's movement when it first developed. As a painter she made an impact on the transformation of the study of the female nude. As a teacher and adviser, she instructed many young women and men. Her use of her own body throughout the decades of her art production stimulated discussion of the role of the female nude in contemporary art. Semmel made a profound contribution to the students of Douglass College and Rutgers University. As she has admitted, it wasn't until other women joined the art faculty that young women could concentrate on a feminist approach.

Mason Gross School of the Visual and Performing Arts was established in 1975, and the MFA program was transferred to downtown New Brunswick and a new administration. Emma Amos, Martha Rosler, and other women joined the Mason Gross faculty in the following years, and there was at least some acknowledgment that women artists were important to art instruction on the Mason Gross campus. In addition, the continuation of the Women Artists Series, and the young women who emerged as professionals after graduating from Douglass College, established a singular precedent for the future of visual arts at Rutgers University.

1.8

Joan Semmel. *Centered*, 2002. Oil on
canvas, 48" × 53". Courtesy Alexander
Gray Gallery, New York.

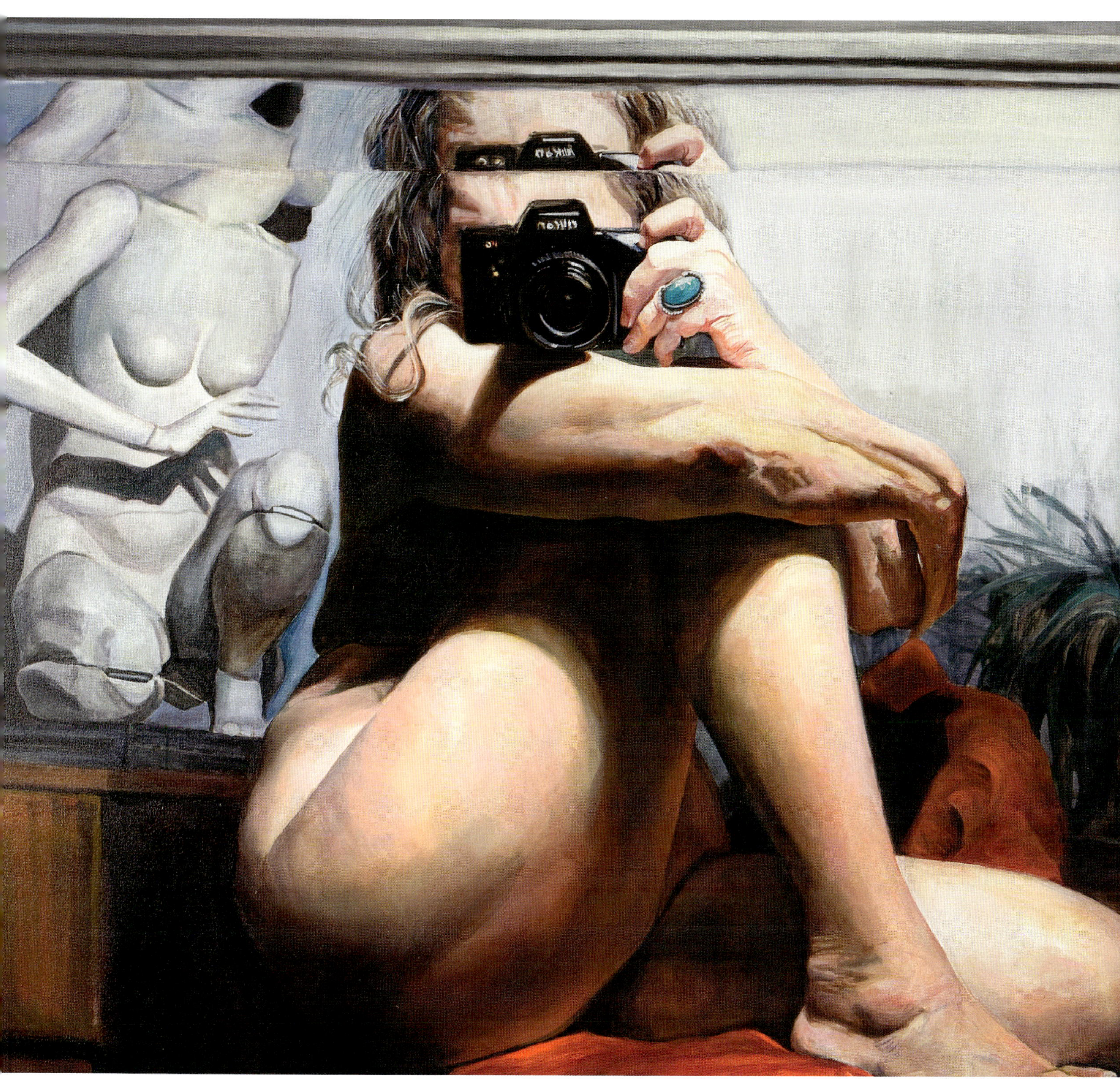

INTERVIEW WITH GEOFFREY HENDRICKS

Geoffrey Hendricks (1931–2018) joined the faculty at Douglass College in 1956. He was a member of the visual arts faculty at the Mason Gross School of the Arts until 2003.

GH   When I arrived Theodore Brenson was the chair. He was a Latvian artist who had been displaced by the Second World War. He'd been in Italy and came to New York with UNESCO, and was hired by Dean Bunting, I think. Then there was Bob Bradshaw, who at that point was a senior professor. Bob painted watercolors. He went to Gloucester in the summer and painted slightly cubistic scenes of the Massachusetts coast and New Jersey, and had a local reputation. Robert Watts was an assistant professor. Evelyn Burdett was assistant professor and didn't get tenure. She painted fine watercolors.

I was hired as an assistant instructor in the spring of 1956. I taught one section of the art history class (seventy-five students or so) and two sections of an introductory studio class called Art Structure. Sculpture and Ceramics was one class taught by Watts, but then the class was divided into two, and I taught Sculpture. After that first year I shifted and started printmaking, which wasn't being offered. So in the summer of 1956 I got a star wheel press from Bob Blackburn and later got an etching press from Charles Brand. I also was in charge of the art gallery, which was a little room beyond the lecture room. It had two windows at the end—it was the width of two windows. The space would have been a fine office. It was 15 by 30 feet or maybe 12 by 24 feet.

In the Recitation Hall building, the library was on the ground floor and basement when I first came to Douglass. The art department had one lecture room that held about seventy-five students, on the floor above the Library. Adjacent to that was an office that held just enough desks for all of the faculty, plus the slide collection, and a small desk for a secretary who came in a few days a week—all in one room. Desks were back to back. On the third floor we had a small room which was our art gallery, with a few windows looking out onto Antilles Field. We put on a lot of interesting shows in there. This was the old art building, now called Ruth Adams [after Dean Adams], located across Antilles Field, near Voorhees Chapel. It was the Recitation Hall building, and then it was the Language Building because Spanish or French was taught there.

In the attic, which was the top floor of Recitation Hall, we had space for the studios. It was unfinished, with steel girders. On one end—the far end toward the Raritan River, we had the foundation courses: Art Structure and drawing. On the other end, toward George Street, Bob had sculpture and ceramics. Then in the middle, painting was taught. When I started the printmaking courses, I had a corner separated off. So that was it. At one end of this big central space was Design and Art Structure II, which was, sort of, advanced artmaking. So half of the big central space was painting, and the other half was design.

JM Where did you have opportunities to perform on campus?

GH There was the Little Theater, which is still standing. It was the theater at the time. The Voorhees Chapel was where Allan Kaprow's Happening took place and John Cage's performance. I did a Happening there in 1969 called Flux-Mass. Chairs were set when we did something together in the downstairs area where the post office is at the Douglass College Center. It was sort of a panel discussion back then, before 1961—probably about 1958.

JM How well do you remember Kaprow's Happening in the Voorhees Chapel, April 22, 1958?

GH When Kaprow did his Happening in 1958 he used the space across the front of the chapel. He had these panels with mirrors, a panel with leaves, and a panel with tar, and one with apples—called *Rearrangeable Panels*. These were panels that he had in the basement of the Judson Gallery when he did *Apple Shrine*. It seems to me there was a student bouncing a ball across the front. The students were sitting, and the performers were moving all around. It wasn't all that radical in certain ways.

JM What about the Cage performance?

GH John Cage was simply in front of the lectern, which as you were facing it, was on the left-hand side, David Tudor was at the piano, which was there in the center of the space and performing this circular score. And Cage read the Questions. That was it.

In the Douglass Art Gallery in Recitation Hall I curated exhibitions called *Group I*, *Group II*, and *Group III* (1957 to 1959); 1957 was painting, 1958 was sculpture (which Bob Watts brought together), and 1959 was New Media that we collectively brought together that had Rauschenberg's *Factum I* and *Factum II*, just hot off the easel.

JM Dean Bunting was important to you in this whole experience.

GH She was great. She came in with a breath of fresh air. She'd been at Bennington, and she had this outlook about experimental education. This was her first serious administrative teaching position. She didn't know how to do things. So, she just said, "Do it. Try." She loved the arts and was a real supporter of the department.

JM She really encouraged progressive, avant-garde activities?

GH Sure. Plus serious scholarship. She wanted to have the best research investigation. She thought the sciences should be built up, because she thought it was foolish that the sciences were for men. Women should be scientists, as she was. It should be possible for older women who had raised a family to come back. She started the Bunting Center.

JM At some point the faculty decided it should start a graduate program.

GH We started our program about 1958. The first degrees were given in 1962. The program started in the fall of 1959, the year we hired Reginald Neal. We had a lot of ambition. There was plenty of talk about Black Mountain College, and what was going on there, and about the Bauhaus. How could we get a similar program going— similar but of its own nature? But we didn't want to do just anything. Three of us [Watts, Brenson, Hendricks] met with the people over at Rutgers College. In 1957 we hired Ka Kwong Hui, a ceramicist, and there was a wonderful spirit in the graduate program. He was the teacher for Betsy Wittenborn, Marion Munk, Marianne Easton. Hui worked with Roy Lichtenstein to make his Pop Art ceramic plates and tiles.

JM You had to devise a curriculum?

GH That was very simple. I guess there was a little dialogue with the graduate school

that we would be doing this. The first year there were two students. Marion Levinston
Monk, who's on the faculty at Middlesex Community College, and Ronald Stein, who was
the nephew of Lee Krasner. The next year we had a few more students, including George
Segal, Robert Miller, and Bill Barren. But it was small. I guess we got some teaching assistants, and they were able to do some teaching. Early on Bob Watts got a grant from the
Carnegie Foundation to get some media equipment and set up an experimental workshop,
which included performance, intermedia, and sound.

JM   Did you have a philosophy for this program? For example, did the faculty announce, when
forming the curriculum, that they wanted to be experimental?

GH   It was small, and we were there in the midst of new media and new thinking. John Cage
was certainly a guiding spirit. Allan Kaprow was spiritually there. Bob Watts and I did
plenty of talking about how to get the students to be more open and free in expressing
their ideas. Bob and I were into a discussion with them about Zen and reading sources outside of art; reading Joseph Campbell's *Hero with a Thousand Faces*. This was our approach
to a foundation course. Right from the beginning there was this feeling that teaching
wasn't confined to the classroom. We had been involved ourselves in this searching and
opening up to change. Then, as faculty began to do things in the city after Roy Lichtenstein
came, and Kaprow was involved with Happenings and Events in New York, the faculty and
students were in New York City as much as they were in New Brunswick. It was back and
forth. The whole place was a classroom.

Now I know when Roy was there in 1960, we were involved in a serious discussion
about curriculum and course description. This is when I started the artist-book class. I
had been teaching printmaking, and then Reggie Neal came along. He was a printmaker,
and he was basically taking over the printmaking area. I was interested in artists' books,
and Fluxus was coming about at that time. I had money for Black Mountain Press. A class
on artists' books was a natural sort of thing. This was like a foundation course. We were
restructuring the introductory program, getting the idea of process and transformation,
media, more into it. There was another course that was called Image and Idea (or something like that), where it was about perceptual issues. We put through a curriculum that
had a lot of new titles that reflected the spirit of what we were doing.

In the early 1960s, with space available, it was about the time that Reggie came as

                    WOMEN ARTISTS ON THE LEADING EDGE

chair, and Roy was there. The library moved over into the building where it is now, and the downstairs two floors became available. So we had the whole basement for art. We designed it so that offices went down there, and the ceramics studios were at one end, sculpture at the other. A big art foundation room was there. And on the top floor, printmaking, painting, and sculpture remained with some of the foundation courses. The space that had been for artmaking became graduate studios.

Before we moved downstairs, we got another room adjacent to the room that had been our office. A classroom was given over to us. That became our office, and cubicles were divided up there. Bob Watts and I shared a cubicle. Letty Eisenhauer was secretary at that point. Ted Brenson was still chair. When we moved downstairs, the old art gallery became a slide room. We hired Roy Lichtenstein because we were looking for a person in design. He had come from Ohio, and worked in Cleveland in furniture design, and was teaching in upstate New York at the State University of New York at Oswego. In his slides he was showing us his cut-out assemblages of *Washington Crossing the Delaware, Custer's Last Stand*, playing with American history in a playful way with the figures sort of stylized out of Picasso. There was a wonderful sense of humor about them. There was a playful quality about the way he thought anyway. And there was an openness to him. We were immediately drawn to him— Watts and me especially. He came to develop the foundation drawing program, and to teach design. I guess Roy and Allan Kaprow visited each other, had kids, and did things together. Kaprow was very supportive of Roy when he was starting to express these ideas to Allan: that he wanted to paint big comic strips—blowups. He did some Mickey Mouse images. They may even have been done after he came to Rutgers, done simultaneously with his striped paintings. Kaprow was saying, "Roy, go ahead and do them. See where it takes you. You can go back to striped paintings if it doesn't seem to make sense. But it obviously did. There is a little Cal Arts publication of an interview with Kaprow and Lichtenstein where Roy is speaking directly about the impact of his association with Rutgers, with the whole program and with Kaprow, that was a catalyst for him to get into Pop imagery. Kaprow was the one who said take your work to Castelli Gallery. Castelli had Rauschenberg and Jasper Johns, and because of that it was the gallery that was very exciting for looking at new work. There was this great energy that shot up.

JM   When did Mail Art start at Douglass?

GH   Mail Art grew out of my artists' book class at Douglass. Probably the late '60s is when I started the Mail Art shows.

In 1963, Al Hansen came out and in the old Gymnasium at Douglass did an Event called "Parasol 4 Marisol." There were performances by Dick Higgins, Alison Knowles, Joe Jones. Al Hansen did an elaborate performance. Al just loved Marisol's name. Gracie Mansion, when she was getting Al's show together, called Marisol, who said she doesn't keep anything over three years. If she had anything, it would have been thrown out. There was a range of other events that took place at Douglass or some other campus location, with people coming to visit.

Bob Watts did an installation in the building that is now the Speech Building on George Street, opposite the Women's Center. I took over the Experimental Workshop when Watts was out at Santa Cruz in the late '60s. Besides taking a class to the beach or out into the woods to do things, or out into the fields, Happenings, Fluxus, and Pop Art were already coming in solidly. Roy Lichtenstein was involved in terms of the curriculum. Roy was putting the studio together in terms of the ideas he had learned at Ohio State University. We were having a lot of discussion of curriculum, and setting up classes that were intermedia in nature, dealing more with concepts and trying to break down the compartmentalization of the media.

JM   How would you characterize the philosophy? What were some of the issues that arose?

GH   We were talking about how to get students to open up their thinking, to deal with contemporary issues, and move into new ideas in art, and go on from there.

JM   What new was there drawing from the live model?

GH   Sure there was. There was oil painting, printmaking, a wide range of things. With the experimental workshop there was new media, and bringing technology into a relationship with art. We were certainly very conscious of Black Mountain College and the Bauhaus, and we were doing a lot of talking about their art programs, and what they were doing. We didn't want to model our program on the Bauhaus too closely, because there was already involvement at other art institutions with the Bauhaus approach. Josef Albers was up at Yale, and doing solid work with color theory. We were searching elsewhere, and Black Mountain was certainly a model for a major portion of our approach to experimental education.

JM What about the influence of John Cage?

GH John Cage had a very strong contribution to the thinking here. Both Allan Kaprow and George Brecht went to his class at the New School for Social Research in New York City.

1.9
Roy Lichtenstein, Douglass College yearbook photo,
Quair, 1962. Courtesy: Special Collections and
University Archives, Rutgers University Libraries.

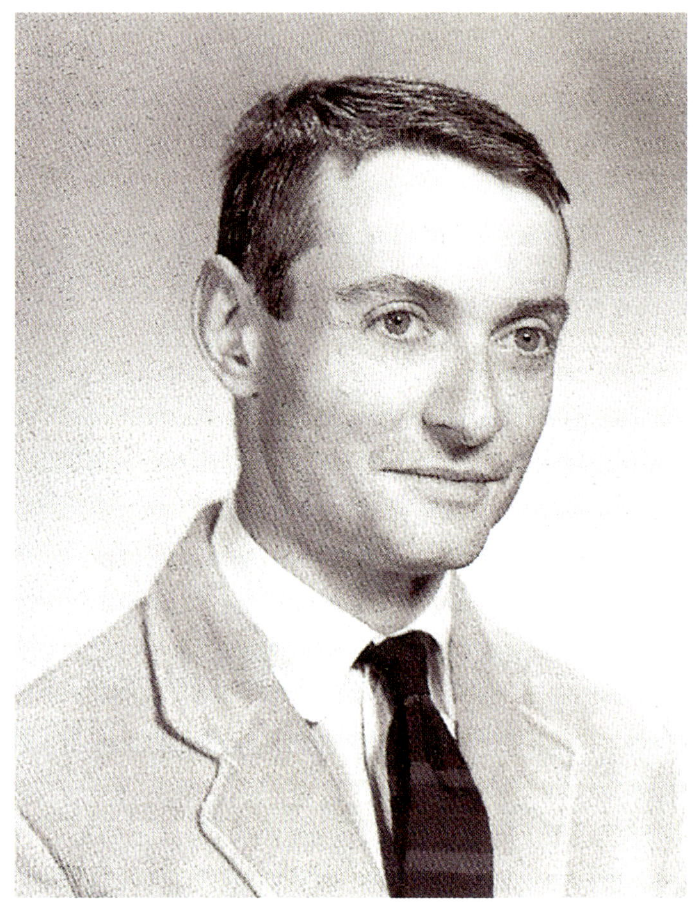

INTERVIEW WITH ROY LICHTENSTEIN

Roy Lichtenstein (1923–1997) was hired to teach at Douglass College in 1960. In 1964 he resigned to continue his career as a Pop artist.

RL I think the thing I got from him [Allan Kaprow] most was this kind of statement about it doesn't have to look like art, or how much of what you do is there only because it looks like art. You always thought artists should be original, whatever it was. But there was a little bit of feeling during Abstract Expressionism, this is really what I was doing very late, until 1961, how much of that was because it looked like art to me.

JM You came to Douglass to be interviewed for a job. Do you recall the people you met?

RL I met Reggie Neal, who was the head of the department up at SUNY, Oswego, where I was teaching. He really came because of a friend of his, who was up there teaching, and invited us both to come down. Probably to counteract what he saw as this kind of nutty stuff that was going on.

JM What was the "nutty stuff"?

RL Fluxus and all of this. Because I was painting in an acceptable way, I think. Yes, I was doing my Abstract Expressionist paintings. I'm sure that's why we were invited. . . . I knew Bob Watts very well. We have several of his pieces.

JM Did you respond to what Watts was doing?

RL Yes. My wife was running the Bianchini Gallery. She gave Bob Watts a show. He's the only one of the group who actually had a show at the gallery. I was very interested in his work. We have a slice of bread of his, which is a sort of blue Plexiglas thing on a bright ground, and it's supposed to be plugged in a box and they're all gray—gradated from fairly light to fairly dark.

JM	They asked you to restructure the Art 101 course. So you came with this idea from Hoyt Leon Sherman.[1] About the "flash lab"—I wonder how you implemented this at Douglass?

RL	I couldn't really get the flash lab, because it's very hard to make a totally dark room, because if you let any light in you get light adapted, and it had to be totally dark. I didn't do that. I did other things. Like showing slides of rather Baroque things upside down and out of focus, and had them [students at Douglass] draw what they saw. Like these Rubens drawings that are somewhat amorphous. And slowly bring it into focus. And it was funny because as soon as they realized the horses are people, the whole drawing fell apart. They would get very specific and start to draw. The other way they would be drawing the modulation all over because they didn't know what it was. I think they got an idea of how abstract this thing was supposed to be.

That was one thing I did. The other thing I did was to have them draw without looking—or underneath the first sheet of paper—setups: things and people as models— and drawn without looking. I would do things like put an *x* on a piece of paper on either side of whatever the model or construction—which could be lots of things, and have them keep those *x*'s in their focus while they were looking up there. In other words, don't focus on anything, but keep your periphery open. The same thing when they drew. Say, keep two marks on either side of their paper in view the whole time they're drawing. These are things that are derived from Sherman, but it wasn't the flash because it's very hard. You have to be able to project slides at a tenth of a second. But what would have been hard was to make the whole room totally dark.

JM	Did you talk about this with Watts, or the other faculty?

RL	I must have. I don't remember specifically.

JM	You had a show at Douglass. Here's the little brochure from it.

RL	I haven't seen this in years. This must have been a sort of abstract show.

JM	That was in 1961. The little blurb says "Roy Lichtenstein who joined the Douglass faculty department last fall" So I presume this is 1961. I was curious about the show because it says it's a show of recent paintings.

RL	In fact, just after that, I possibly did the other. It may have overlapped. I'm not sure.

JM	Do you remember if Bob Watts was using any commercial imagery at this time?

RL I'm not sure of the dates of his things. One thing he had was a table that was formica or something, with knife, fork and spoon. And that sort of thing, in the formica of the tabletop. There may have been collage under glass, but I think it was all one surface. This was a table setting I think for four. That's one thing I do remember. I remember the signatures in neon of Picasso and Braque. I thought it was a terrific idea.

JM Did Watts have any impact on you?

RL Because I think there was a very big Duchampian influence on Watts maybe, or maybe I'm just projecting this, which I felt I had more of a Picasso [influence]. Things that were conceptual weren't as interesting to me. I was just painting. Although I don't think I'm seen that way. But I think my work is influenced by that whole business. But I don't think the fundamental impetus was the same. I think Letty Eisenhauer had been in Paris, and she came back and she was the secretary at Douglass, and I went out with her. She was very nice. She was in a lot of Happenings. She was very involved with that whole genre.

I am sure that if I had stayed in Oswego, New York, nothing would have happened. It just wouldn't have, I don't know what I would have gotten. It's amazing how much luck plays in this thing. Being there at the right time.

JM In another interview you talk about the industrial landscape or the "wasteland." You said that you lived in Oswego and Ohio and that your background was in those areas. "It was almost entirely of industrial sludge, or advertising, or builders' houses, or the prosaic, the banal." Do you think as you came to Rutgers that you saw that New Jersey was more of the same?

RL Yes, I would say so at the time. I think the whole of America is really that way, but that's what's different from Europe. There's a little more aesthetic input or something. But I think what was new about American was the kind of commercial architecture and visual things.

JM Allan Kaprow talks about this in the Bianchini catalog [*Ten from Rutgers University*, 1965], the industrial landscape of New Jersey, and how these artists all seem to come out of that environment.

RL I think it did. There are many parts of New Jersey. They're just completely advertising signs, junk, things, that you think of as blight, but all of it has a certain energy.

PART TWO

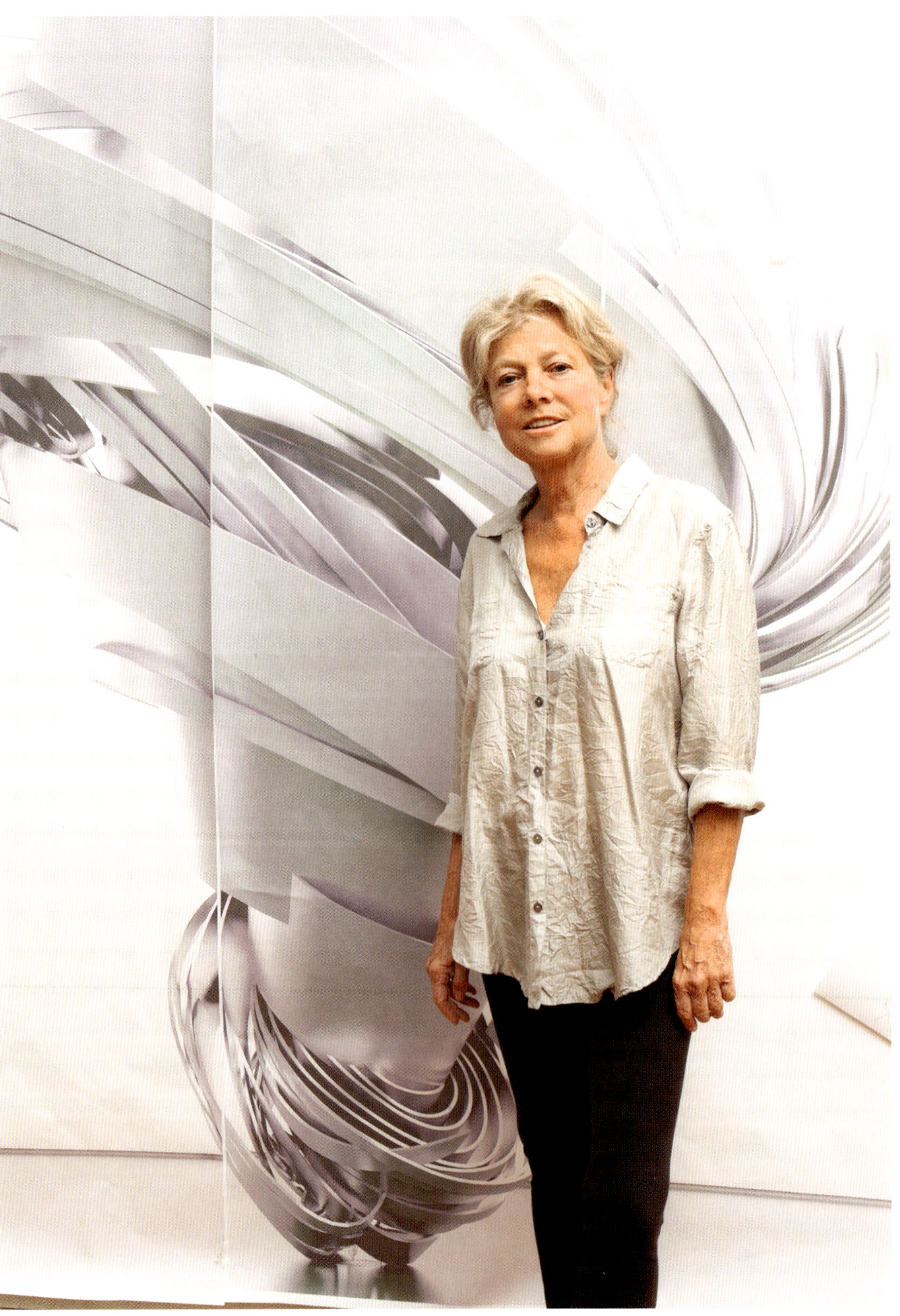

2.1
Alice Aycock in her studio, 2017.
Photo: Kristine Larsen.

ALICE AYCOCK

Alice Aycock is a celebrated sculptor who has created installations and environmental projects in many American cities. Born in Harrisburg, Pennsylvania, in 1946, Aycock enrolled at Douglass College in 1964. Her impression was that Douglass was a liberal arts college with the same rigorous program found at the Seven Sisters colleges, and she was determined to succeed in this competitive environment. Students at Douglass seemed determined to become professionals in various fields, and they were very serious about their educational opportunities at the college.[1] Although she experienced a great interest in the visual arts since childhood, Aycock decided to major in creative writing with a minor in sociology. She wrote for the campus publication, *The Caellian*,[2] and completed several poems, but her writing instructor was not impressed by her written work.[3]

A studio art course taught by Sam Weiner introduced her to an intellectual and literary approach to art. Aycock learned the writings of John Cage, read art historians Irwin Panofsky and Meyer Schapiro, and studied connections between psychology and art. She took art history courses with Mark Berger, but she credits Sam Weiner with her decision to change her major to studio art. Subsequently she took painting courses with John Goodyear and a sculpture course with Bob Watts.

Aycock found herself meeting with the MFA students who had studios and instruction on the Douglass campus. Jackie Winsor became particularly important to Aycock, and she often joined the graduate students on trips to New York City. Both the advanced undergraduates and the MFA students were encouraged to see exhibitions in New York galleries and museums. Faculty gave the students details about lectures and performances in New York. As an example, Aycock mentioned the first festival of art and technology, at the Sixty-Ninth Regiment Armory, held in the fall of 1966. She attended "Nine Evenings," organized by

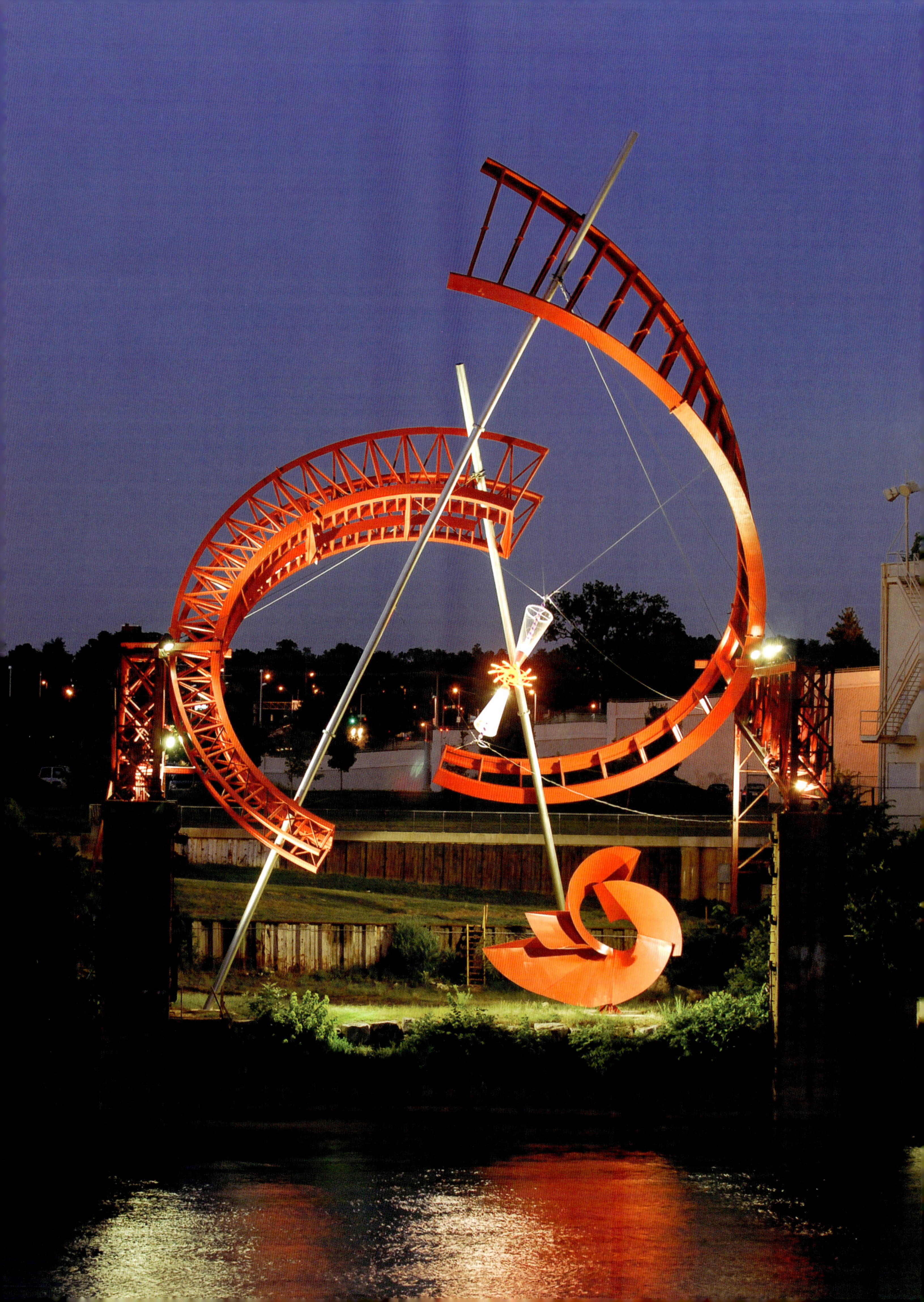

Billy Kluver, a physicist from Bell Labs in New Jersey.[4] At Douglass she often watched the critiques of the MFA students' work. In her sophomore year she registered for a summer course in drawing at New York University with the intention of learning about various drawing techniques. During the summer of her junior year, she was an intern at the Guggenheim Museum in New York. Aycock made shaped paintings and various sculpture projects as an undergraduate, and found a direction that led her to minimalism and conceptual art in subsequent years.[5]

Aycock was determined to go to graduate school and was accepted into the program at Hunter College, where she studied with Robert Morris. Her master's thesis summed up the basic tenets of systems theory. From the 1960s Aycock developed site-oriented sculptural projects. Her interests included metaphor and simile. As Robert Hobbs noted, "In creating these works she used minimalism to make viewers aware of their own bodies, and conceptual art to help them think epistemologically about their experiences while trying to reconcile the often contradictory clues her art provides."[6] Her early interest in writing comes to fruition in the many statements that elaborate her drawings and sculpture. References to machinery, construction, and archaeological sites appeared in her complex projects. Works are often a synthesis of a diversity of elements, including references to the natural world as well as the spiritual realm. Later she dwells on the information age that has opened up new ways of looking.

Art historian Christine Filippone notes, "Aycock's works place the towering miracles of science and technology on shifting sand. Drawing from contemporary sources of energy and power, including nuclear plants and nuclear accelerators, she juxtaposed these contemporary wonders with those of the past. Her impotent machines highlight the transience of scientific beliefs, and the dangers of uncritically accepting the scientific worldview."[7]

In the early 1980s, Aycock constructed *The Miraculating Machine in the Garden (Tower of the Winds)* on the Douglass College campus, adjacent to the Mabel Douglass Library. One of her "machine works" that follows *How to Catch and Manufacture Ghosts* (1979), the *Miraculating Machine* is constructed of steel, Plexiglas, neon, and piping. The subtitle alludes to the potency of ether winds and nuclear power as a new form of energy. This fantastical machine has no practical function. If there is a reference to nuclear power plants here, it can be credited to Aycock's awareness of the 1979 partial meltdown of Three Mile Island, located near Harrisburg, where she spent her childhood.

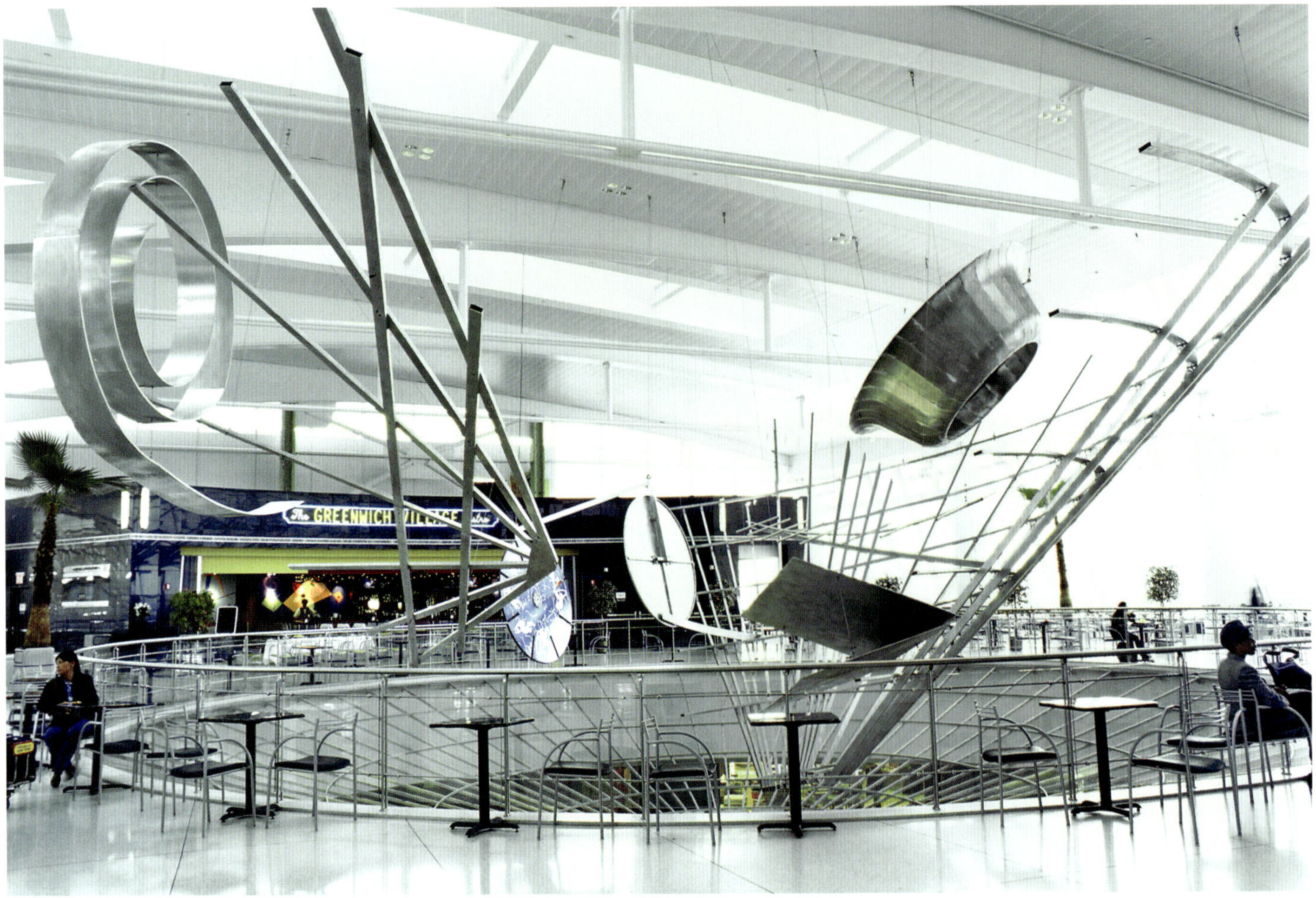

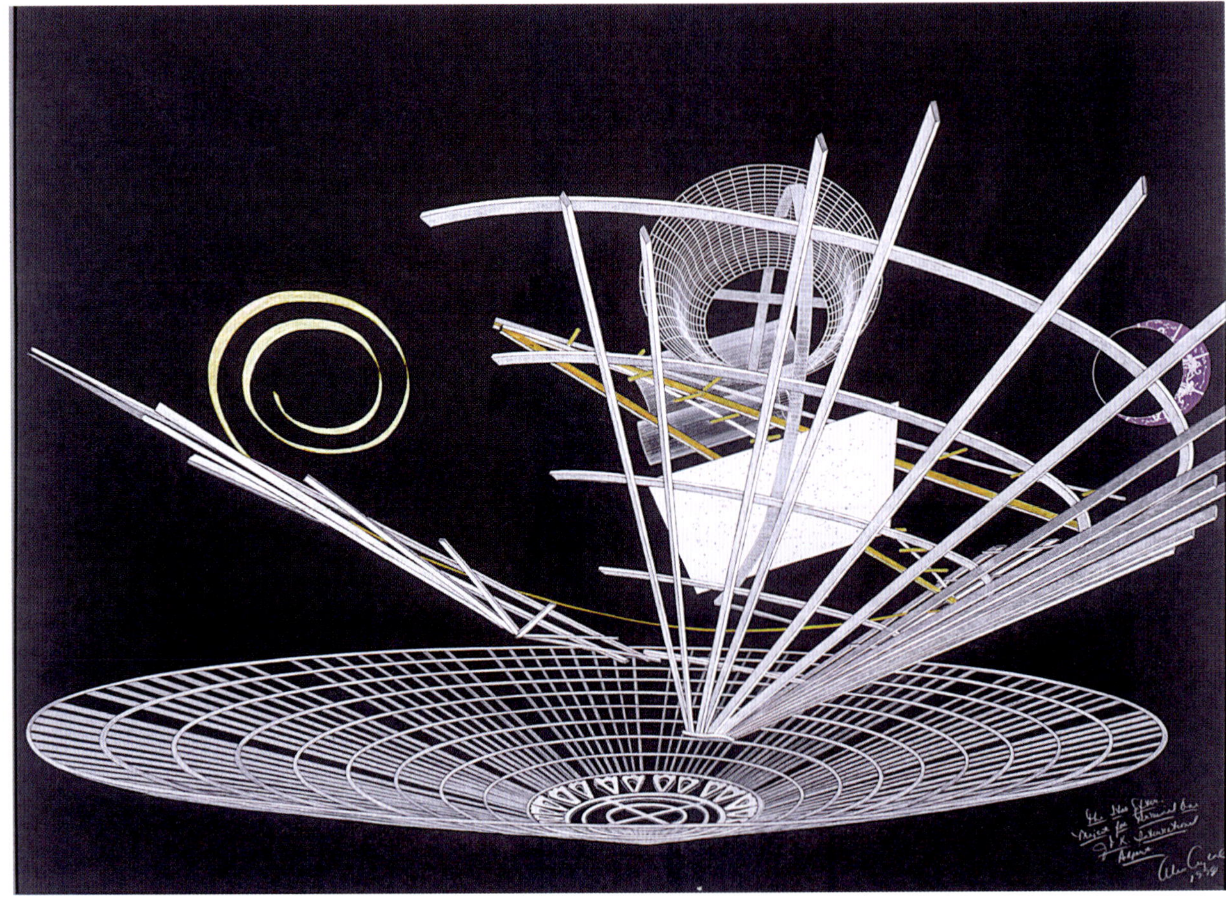

As Christine Filippone has noted,

> The artist further emphasized the destructive capability of industrial technologies
> and the energy they produce by situating *Miraculating Machine in the Garden* in a
> low-wall sculpture garden, as the title notes. Sculpture gardens gained popularity
> in the nineteenth century as a means of escape from the tensions of industrializa-
> tion. Aycock alluded to this period in her primary medium, steel, a material that
> revolutionized the development of technology and the industrial production of the
> nineteenth century. . . . The unlikely juxtaposition of a nonfunctioning machine
> within a bucolic environment posed questions about the hopes engendered by
> technological discovery and common belief in progress arising in the nineteenth
> century. By situating a machine-like form within a space of repose and contempla-
> tion, Aycock disrupted the notion of the garden as haven.[8]

In the 1990s and later, Aycock created complex gallery installations, and numerous
projects on public sites. For example, *Star Sifter* (1998) is an ambitious transformation of
space at Terminal One, Kennedy International Airport in New York City. Joining the essence
of flight with physics, astronomy, and celestial discovery, Aycock created a site-specific project of great interest. *Star Sifter* is a giant steel sieve that "captures and attempts to siphon
everything in its stratosphere."[9]

Art historian Mary Tinti wrote, "*Star Sifter* is a seductive work by a calculating artist and
intellect, an exceptionally inquisitive scholar on a never-ending quest to discover new ways
to stimulate herself and her audience. . . . *Star Sifter*, which may be Aycock's safety net,
wormhole, tear in the universe, and optimistic receptacle of inquiry, is a call for viewers to
value asking intelligent probing questions."[10]

With monumental works installed permanently on public sites in Nashville, Tennessee,
Kansas City, and New York City, Alice Aycock continues to populate the country with her
unique vision. *Ghost Ballet for the East Bank Machineworks* is located on the eastern edge
of the Cumberland River. With it dramatic steel forms that spin and curve like dancers, the
sculpture appears to respond to the skyline of downtown Nashville, and recalls the industrial past of its environs. Aycock has been recognized for her sensitivity to historical factors
and the dynamic future of a site in creating her public art. Alice Aycock was honored for
Lifetime Achievement in Sculpture by the International Sculpture Center in March 2018.

2.5
Loretta Dunkelman, 2017, pointing to
A. I. R. Gallery Artists by Sylvia Sleigh,
1977–1978. Dunkelman in back row in
black flowered dress. Photo: Courtesy
of the artist.

2.6
Loretta Dunkelman. Untitled, 1957–
58. Oil and enamel paint on linen, 34"
× 42". Photo: Courtesy of the artist.

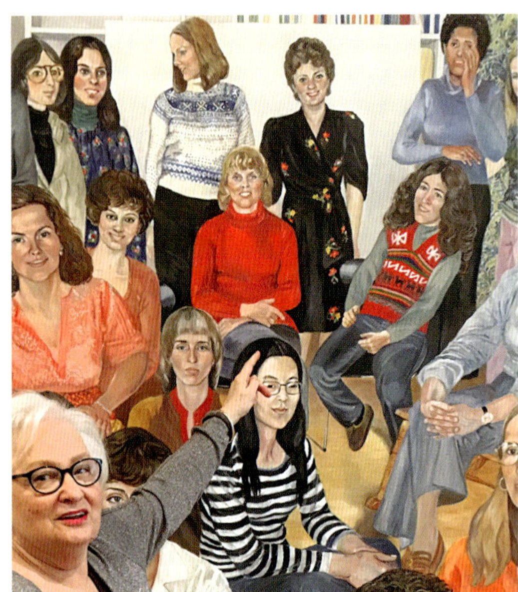

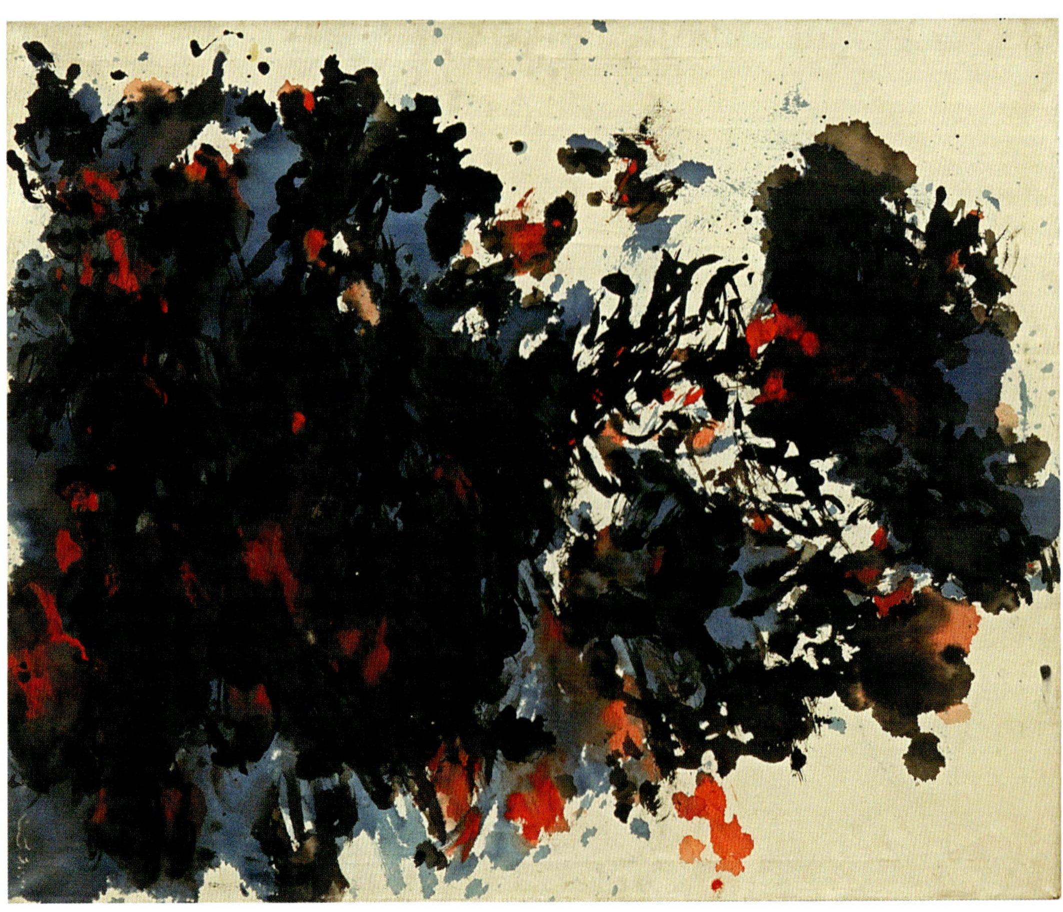

LORETTA DUNKELMAN

Loretta Dunkelman was among the earliest Douglass students to benefit from changes in the visual arts curriculum in the 1950s. Later she became a leader of the women's art movement in New York City. Dunkelman was born in Paterson, New Jersey, in 1937, and came to Rutgers just at the time of transition from the designation "New Jersey College for Women" to "Douglass College." Dunkelman noted about her time on campus, "I was there when it all started."[1] By the time she graduated in 1958, Dean Mary Bunting had supported many avant-garde programs in the arts. For example, during the 1957–58 academic year, the Voorhees Assemblies sponsored Allan Kaprow's first Happening in the Voorhees Chapel. Other events included a lecture by John Cage, and a performance by the Paul Taylor dance company, David Tudor, and other luminaries in music, dance, and the visual arts.

Having enrolled at Douglass with the intention of becoming an English major, Dunkelman was soon attracted to the art program. She took art history courses, and her first studio class—Art Structure, taught by Bob Watts. Dunkelman went on to change her major to studio art. She was adventurous in her course selection and traveled to the Rutgers College campus, where she took a painting class with Allan Kaprow. Other art courses included a painting class with Theodore Brenson and sculpture with Geoffrey Hendricks. An untitled painting that dates from her senior year at Douglass combines oil paint and enamel on linen and suggests that the gestural effects and bold compositions of the Abstract Expressionists were of primary interest to her.

Dunkelman recalled trips taken with her art classes to museums and galleries in New York City. Theodore Brenson told students about The Club, where discussions and programs attended by Abstract Expressionist artists were held in New York City. Douglass students visited the Hansa Gallery, where Kaprow and others were showing their work. At the Museum of Modern Art she recalls seeing paintings of targets by Jasper Johns. Robert Rauschen-

berg was frequently mentioned by Douglass faculty members. Dunkelman also remembers going to the Jersey shore with Bob Watts and Geoff Hendricks. While on the beach, the students made sand sculptures by pouring plaster of Paris onto the sand and incorporating shells and other found objects into the surface. She recalls that Marion Engelman Munk was an undergraduate at the same time. Dunkelman noted "we were encouraged to express ourselves."[2] The open-ended approach to artmaking suited Dunkelman. She flourished under the nontraditional teaching and unstructured assignments. But Dunkelman observed that Douglass classes were tough, "You couldn't stay there unless you worked."[3]

Loretta Dunkelman's recollections of her years at Douglass elicit an evaluation of the quality of the education she received there. She commented on the overall excellence of her courses. Instructors were outstanding, and her fellow students were eager to learn.[4] The environment was competitive because Douglass accepted only very bright young women. Her courses in philosophy and literature were satisfying. But the studio program was particularly exciting. She recalls attending the first Happening by Allan Kaprow in the Voorhees Chapel in 1958.

In the same year there was another project of note: Douglass students were asked to participate in an "Environment" in the basement of the Admissions Building. Dunkelman recalls that Watts created a "sound piece" in a black box. Many of the materials were provided by George Brecht, who worked at nearby Johnson & Johnson, and was an associate of Watts and Kaprow. Dunkelman painted muslin using a poured and staining technique, working on the floor with black enamel paint, and then the painted muslin panels were installed on the windows. She admits that the materials and style were probably inspired by Jackson Pollock. There was still some interest in Abstract Expressionism on campus, particularly among students of Brenson. Dunkelman recalled: "Kaprow criticized the group effort as a whole, as he didn't think we understood the concept. But I think it was a great experience to have done it, and opened us up to new possibilities. As for my own contribution, in thinking back upon it, had I installed the panels directly on the walls and left the windows uncovered, it would have been much more effective. So I am still learning from that experience in a way."[5] But Dunkelman felt that her contribution to the Environment was not what the faculty had envisioned.[6] She worked hard to fit within their expectations of an avant-garde approach.

After she graduated from Douglass in 1958, Dunkelman taught art in a junior high school. Then she left to see the art and architecture of Italy. She had a studio across the street from the Pitti Palace in Florence, and continued to make paintings. Unfortunately, when she returned to the United States these works were "left behind and then later lost in the flood of the Arno River."[7] Dunkelman enrolled in the MFA program at Hunter College in the early 1960s. By that time she had some distance from the faculty at Douglass, and she began working first with Tony Smith and Ralph Humpfrey in painting. She took Ad Reinhardt's course in Islamic Art.[8] Her paintings at Hunter College took a minimalist direction, with hard-edge compositions in acrylic paint—different from the Abstract Expressionist influences she experienced in classes with Theodore Brenson.

In 1970 Loretta Dunkelman spent the summer in Greece and had a strong reaction to the beauty of the sky, natural forms, and classical sites. Large-scale works on paper commenced after this experience. For example, *Ice-Sky*, 1971–72, combines oil-wax, chalk, and pencil on paper and relates to Dunkelman's impressions of the sky on a visit to the island of Ios. Here the artist had taken up another minimalist approach: the use of seriality. Dunkelman also developed new ideas about surface layering and process. This large wall piece is composed of fifteen segments with variants from dark to light. Assembled here by the artist into one work, they seem to respond to a range of perceptions of the sky over a period of time. She described her process: "[This is] a painstaking process of applying in rows one layer of colored wax over another until it is built up to a hard, smooth surface. The surface appears fragile and vulnerable, like a patina of soft rain or lines from the clouds, but at the same time is tough and hard. The grid interacts with the surface as the modulated and veiled colors act upon it. The grid dissolves and reappears encrusted with the layered wax."[9]

By the late 1960s Dunkelman became actively involved in the women's art movement. She was a member of the Art Workers Coalition. In 1969 she joined W.A.R. (Women Artists

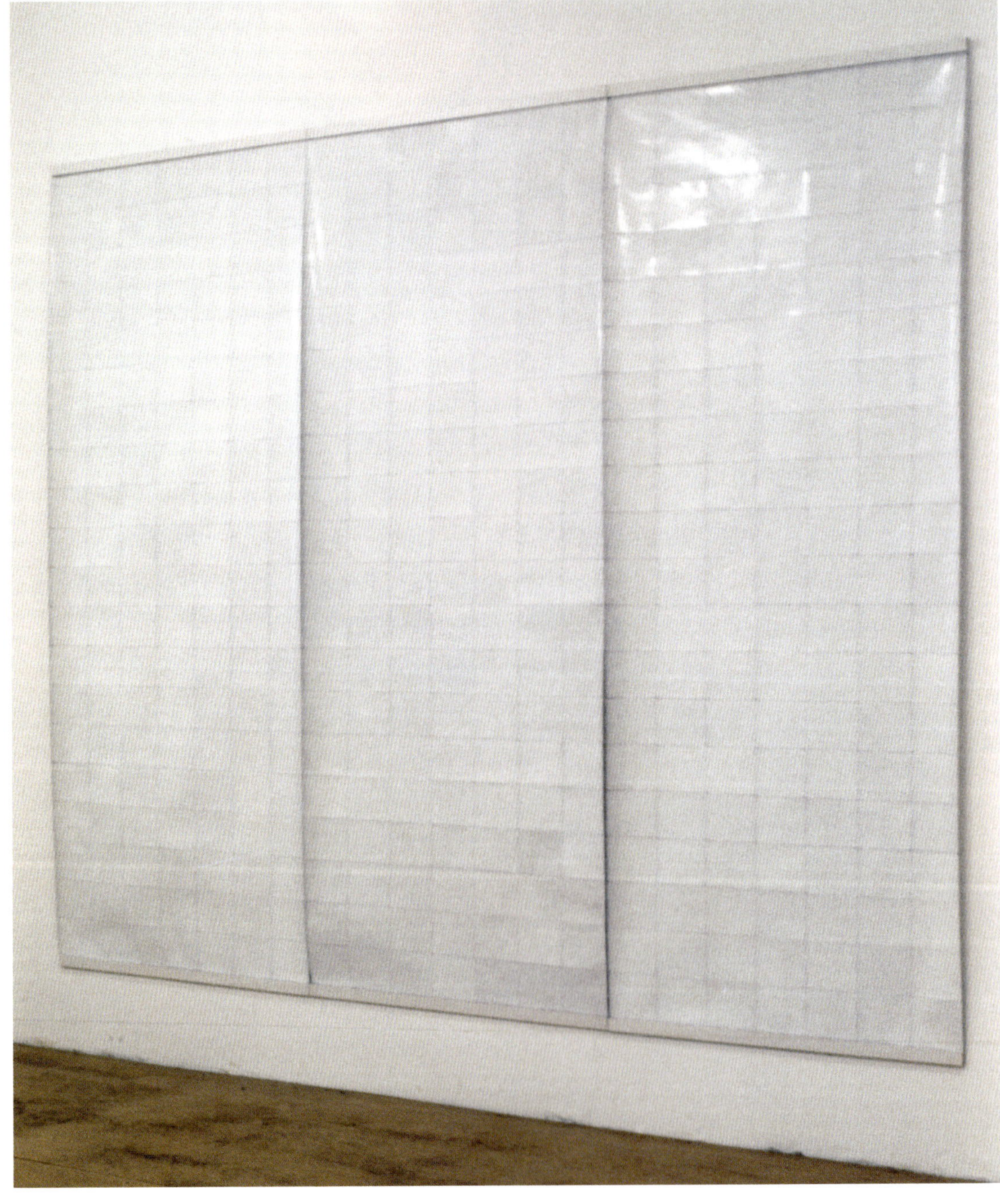

   WOMEN ARTISTS ON THE LEADING EDGE

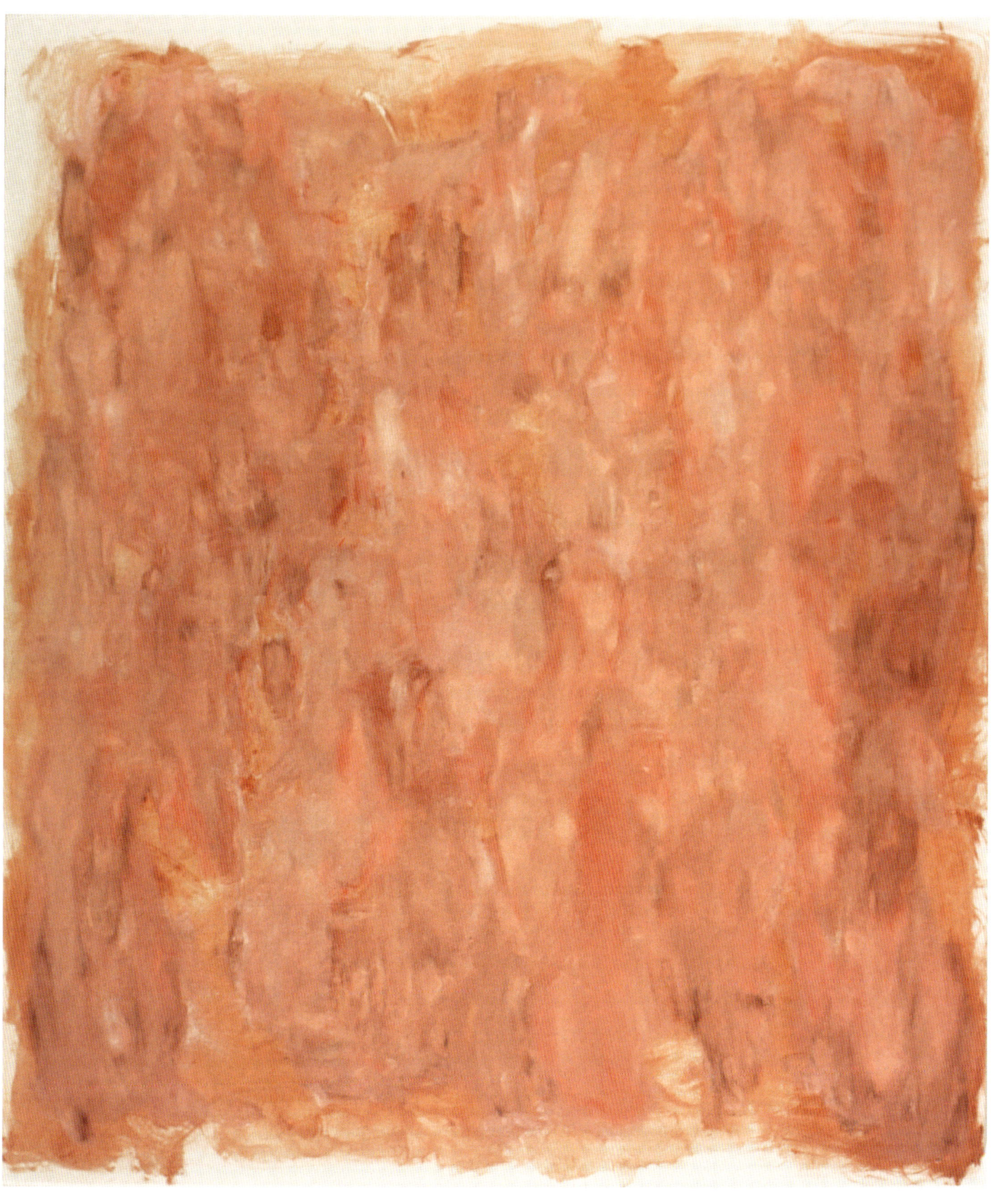

in Revolution). Lucy Lippard formed the Ad Hoc Committee of Women Artists and the Women's Art Registry, and Dunkelman joined this group. She realized that women artists needed more opportunities to exhibit their work. In 1972 she co-organized *Thirteen Women Artists*, an early example of a show organized by women artists in New York City. *Ice-Sky* was included in the *Thirteen Women Artists* show, and then was selected for the Whitney Biennial in 1973. She also participated in *Women Choose Women*, an exhibition in 1973, organized by Women in the Arts, and installed at the New York Cultural Center.

Dunkelman was a founding member of A.I.R. Gallery, the first women's co-op gallery in the United States. Dunkelman appears in a painting of members of A.I.R. Gallery by Sylvia Sleigh. Between 1972 and 1987, Dunkelman had six solo exhibitions at A.I. R. Gallery. Her paintings and works on paper join minimalist seriality with surface layering and rich effects. For *Ice-Wall*, 1972, Dunkelman employs oil-wax, chalk, and pencil on paper to construct a large-scale installation of three panels that assume an architectural presence. She combined the memory of Greece with her study of architecture, particularly Frank Lloyd Wright and his interest in the concept of the void. Also important to her study of form was the philosophy of Lao-tzu, which was presented to her in a book, *The Existence of Intangible Content in Architectonic Form, Based on the Philosophy of Lao-tzu.*[10] Dunkelman considered the effects produced by symmetrical shapes as contrasted with asymmetry. Her works on paper and her paintings are formal, and classical. Geometry is fulfilled by a rich surface layered by Caran d'Ache, oil-wax, and chalk on paper. Dunkelman's large-scale works on paper were made from 1971 to 1979. She returned to painting in oil on linen beginning in 1980.

With her "Flesh Series" of the 1990s, Dunkelman returns to the use of oil paint on linen. Her large paintings in flesh tones allude to personal vulnerabilities, and the memories and wounds of human existence, which can be both beautiful and difficult.

Loretta Dunkelman's paintings have been exhibited at the Phoenix Art Museum, Whitney Museum, Virginia Commonwealth University, P.S.1, and Kulturhuset Stadtsteatern in Stockholm, Sweden, as well as in many university galleries. Her works can be found in many public and private collections, such as the Smithsonian Institution, the Spencer Museum of Art, and The Graduate Center, City University of New York.

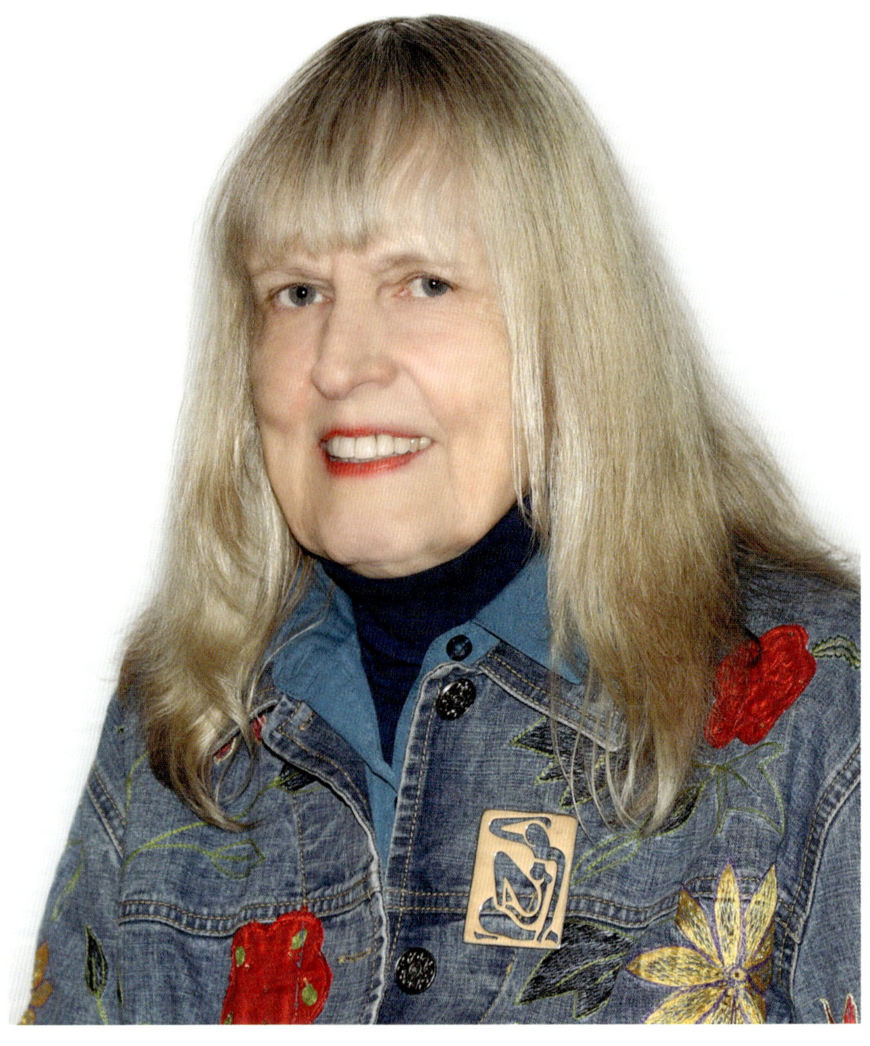

2.10
Kirsten Kraa, photo, 2019.
Photo: Jody Oliveri.

KIRSTEN KRAA

Kirsten Kraa had a childhood in Germany before coming to Douglass College in 1959. She was born in Munich in 1941 to a Danish actor who appeared in films and worked as a cabaret star.[1] Kraa's parents brought her to Fort Lee, New Jersey, in 1956. Kraa attended high school in Butler, New Jersey, before coming to Douglass College. Because she grew up in Munich and was fluent in German, she was happily assigned to the German House, where she found a congenial group of students. From the beginning Kraa was interested in studying art. She took an art history survey course with Geoff Hendricks and was pleased to begin painting instruction with Ulfert Wilke and Roy Lichtenstein. Kraa deeply admired Wilke and viewed him as a lyrical Abstract Expressionist who knew many artists. She claimed he was a "wonderful teacher who was passionate about art."[2] Among Wilke's friends, whose work he collected, were Marc Rothko, Lyonel Feininger, and George Segal. Wilke lived in a New York apartment with the set designer Eugene Berman.

Kraa spoke glowingly of her instruction with Roy Lichtenstein, who came to the Douglass campus in 1960. She recalled that Lichtenstein introduced "tricks" in teaching his students about perception. For example, he showed slide images that were out of focus, and asked students to draw what they saw. Gradually he would bring the images into focus so that the identity of the object was recognizable.[3] Kraa was fascinated by his evolution from the creator of Abstract Expressionist canvases to cartoon imagery.

After graduating from Douglass in 1963, Kraa enrolled in the MFA program, which she completed in 1965. Her adviser was Geoff Hendricks. Although she took courses with other faculty members, she had already launched NeoImages, which has become a signature for her art.

Kraa made her personal breakthrough by introducing a wide-eyed character in her paintings. Through Ulfert Wilke she was introduced to Richard Feigen, a successful art dealer,

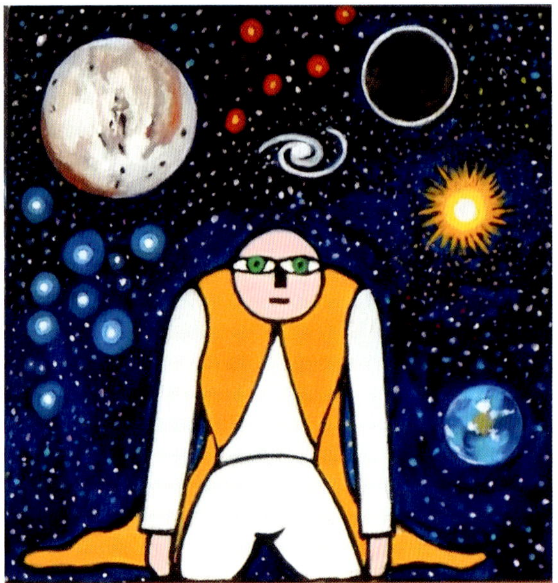 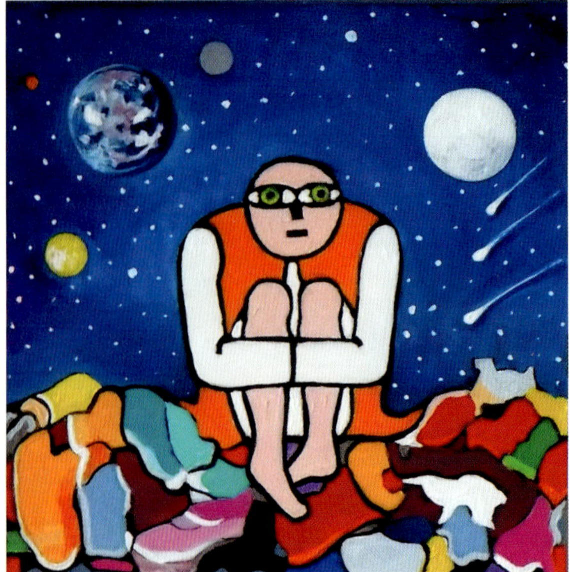

who agreed to represent her work. One of her paintings (untitled, 1964) was purchased by the collector Larry Aldrich and given to the Museum of Modern Art in 1965. Although executed with a thick impasto, the image is heavily outlined in black and includes a stylized body. A circular face features prominent green eyes that stare at the viewer. A circular bowl of peas appears on a raised purple surface below.

In addition to album covers Kraa has designed for various singers, such as Janis Joplin, Kraa continues to create variations on the character that first appeared in the early 1960s. The wide-eyed circular face appears in a cosmic setting in *Sitting on the Edge* (2014) and *Waiting* (2015). As in the earlier paintings, the character is outlined in black and appears in a frontal position while cosmic bodies traverse the sky beyond the figure. A different work is *Tom Mix* (2017), which features a trompe l'oeil effect: a comic book *Tom Mix Western*, shares the composition with collage-like fragments that appear to be attached to a whiteboard. The cowboy image certainly is reminiscent of Lichtenstein's use of imagery from historic comic books in his works. Undoubtedly Kirsten Kraa has created a unique series of images that show some indebtedness to Pop Art of the 1960s.

Kirsten Kraa's paintings have been exhibited at the Museum of Modern Art, at the Kyoto City Museum, Montclair Art Museum, The Morris Museum, Indianapolis Museum, Newark Museum, and the Larry Aldrich Museum in Litchfield, Connecticut.

2.11

Kirsten Kraa. *Sitting on the Edge*, 2014.
Acrylic on gessoboard, 5˝x 5˝.
Photo: Courtesy of the artist.

2.12

Kirsten Kraa. *Waiting*, 2015.
Acrylic on gessoboard, 5˝ x 5˝.
Photo: Courtesy of the artist.

2.13

Kirsten Kraa. Tom Mix, 2017.
Acrylic on gessoboard, 16˝ x 12˝.
Photo: Courtesy of the artist.

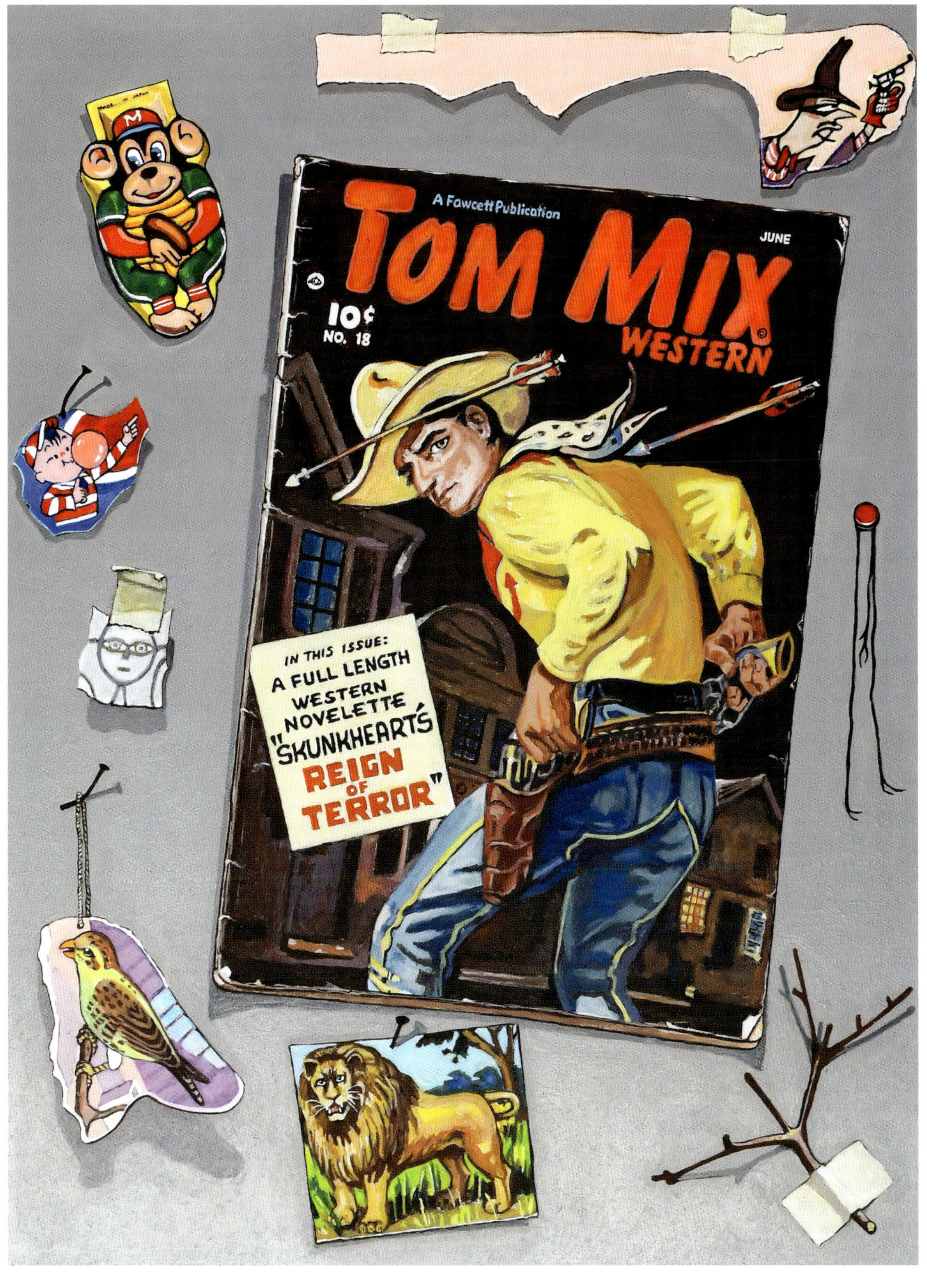

A Fawcett Publication
JUNE
TOM MIX
WESTERN
10¢
NO. 18
IN THIS ISSUE:
A FULL LENGTH
WESTERN
NOVELETTE
"SKUNKHEART'S
REIGN
OF
TERROR"

2.14

Frances Kuehn in her studio, 2014.

Photo: Ray Hoobler.

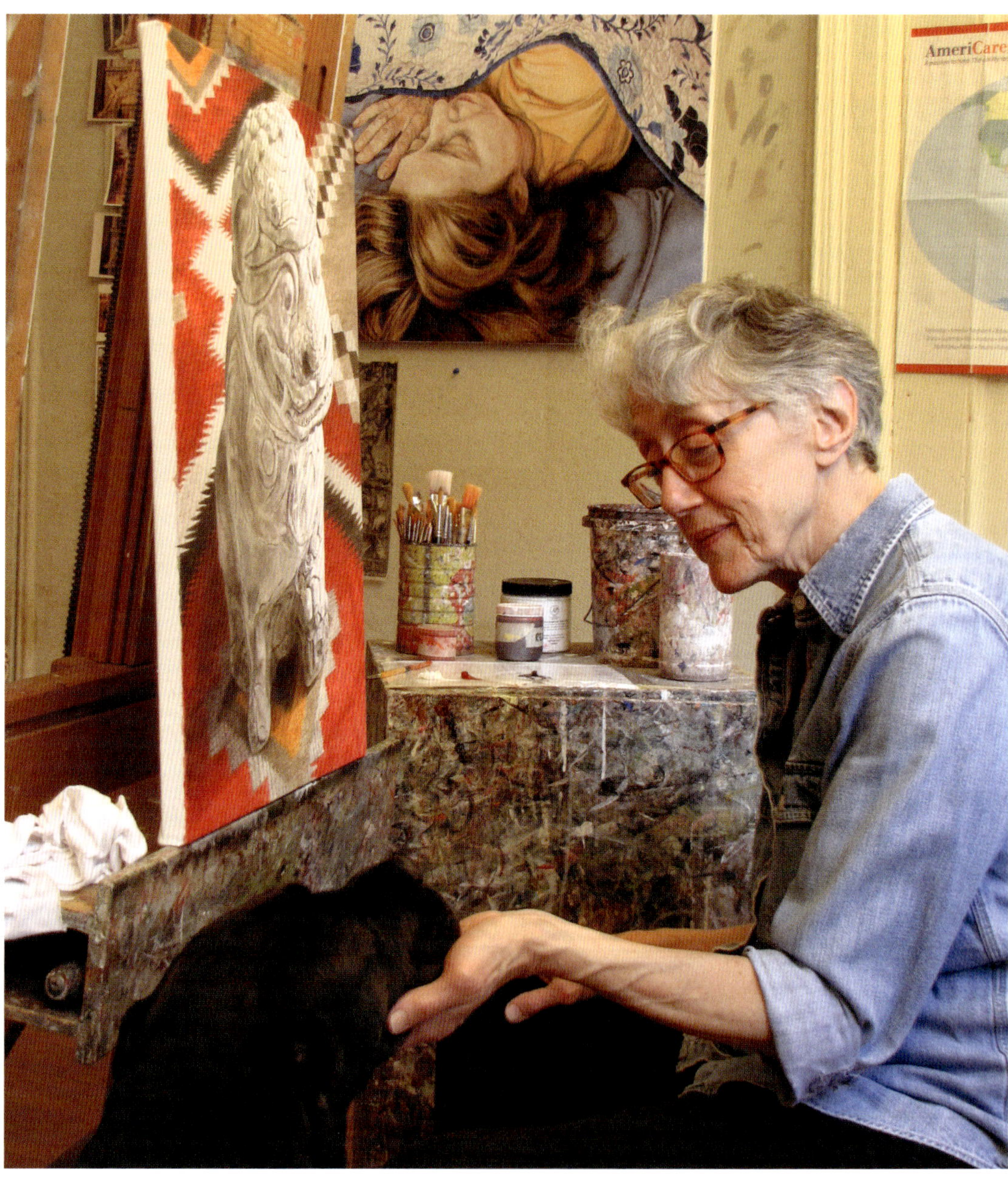

FRANCES TANNENBAUM KUEHN

Frances Tannenbaum spent her childhood in Cranford, New Jersey. She received a state scholarship to Douglass College, and enrolled there in September 1960. Although she had studied art in high school, it was mostly commercial art, and not rigorous like the curriculum at Douglass. Kuehn found the students at Douglass very smart, and serious about their studies. Initially Kuehn was impressed with the art of Roy Lichtenstein that she saw displayed in the Douglass Art Gallery in Recitation Hall. She took Art Structure, an introductory course, with Lichtenstein in 1961. Kuehn remembers that Lichtenstein talked about kinesthesia and had other ideas about perception that she did not really understand, given her limited background in art and science.[1] When she saw Roy Lichtenstein's early cartoon paintings she was "dumbfounded."[2] She continued to take painting courses with Lichtenstein and was encouraged by his critiques of her work. Her instructor, who became one of the earliest creators of Pop Art, supported the direction of her paintings and drawings, which remained committed to realism and the study of the human figure.

George Segal was another important influence during her undergraduate years at Douglass. Segal, who was a graduate student at the time, had taught in the New Jersey public school system, and he eventually helped her new husband, George Kuehn, find a teaching job. George and Frances Kuehn also appeared as an embracing couple in one of Segal's sculptures. Probably Segal's interest in contemporary subjects, and his attempt to combine classical nudes with everyday objects, had an impact on Frances Kuehn. Her early paintings of the figure combined ordinary objects and interiors with the realistic depictions of the human body. Kuehn recalled that Segal arranged a life-drawing group and hired a model.[3] She studied and drew nude figures in these extracurricular classes.

After graduating from Douglass in 1964, Frances Kuehn immediately began her study in

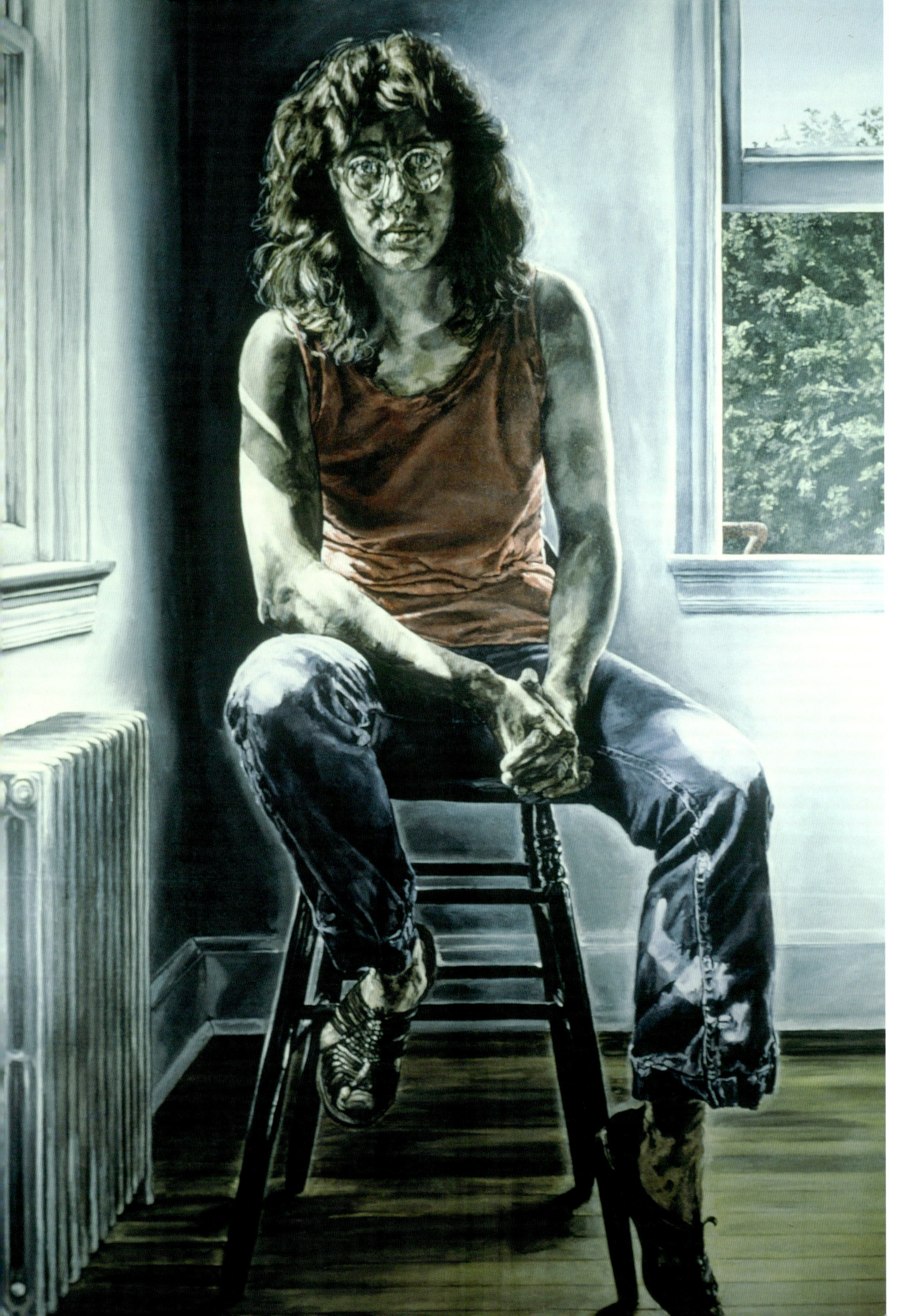

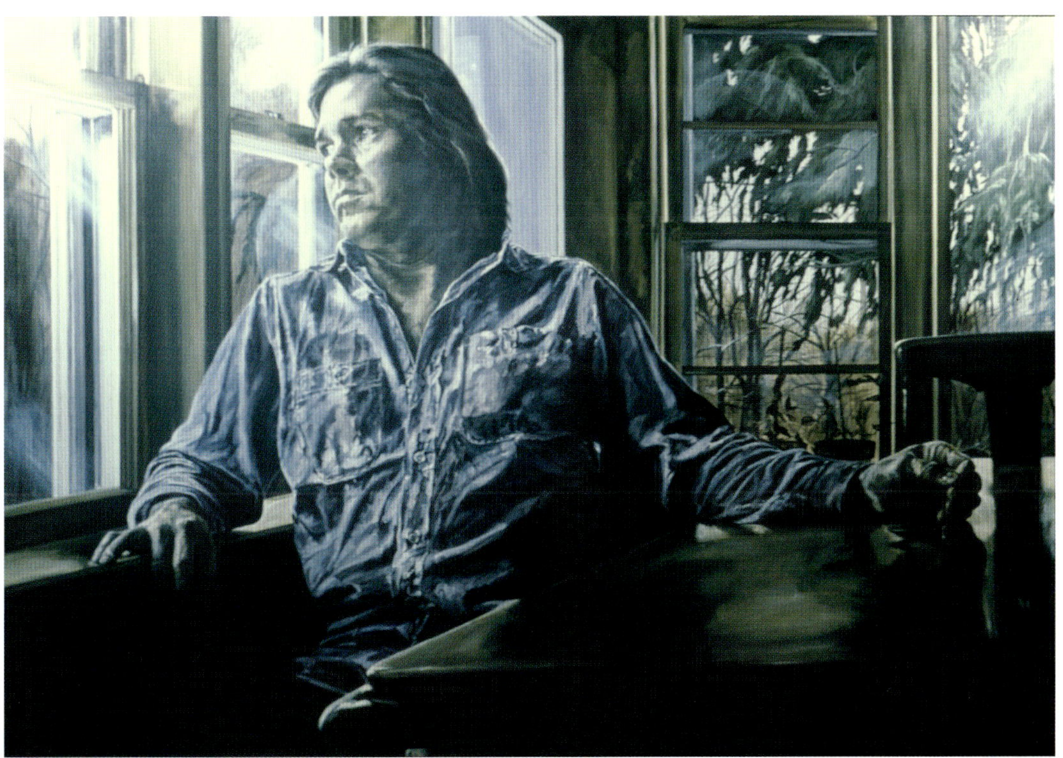

the MFA program. However, she was newly married and soon pregnant with her first child. She decided to suspend her MFA studies after the first year and returned in 1969—when her daughter was five years old and starting school. While she was at home with her child, she continued her study of the nude through magazine images, which became preliminary studies for her drawings. Then she began to make her own photographs. Kuehn's acrylic paintings of the 1970s show an admiration for Philip Pearlstein and Alfred Leslie. Her compositions are broadly brushed, but more painterly than they appear in reproductions. Kuehn uses a range of subjects and approaches to the figure. Her compositions have addressed the figure in motion and at rest. Often her works still rely on photographs as "sketches" for the final composition. Although in reproduction her paintings seem to have the slick surface and sharp focus of the Photorealists, her works remain more closely related to the realist tradition.

Hineni, a Self-Portrait (1972) is among a number of self-images. This one has a more casual stance and an inquiring attentiveness. The artist confronts the viewer, and seems to

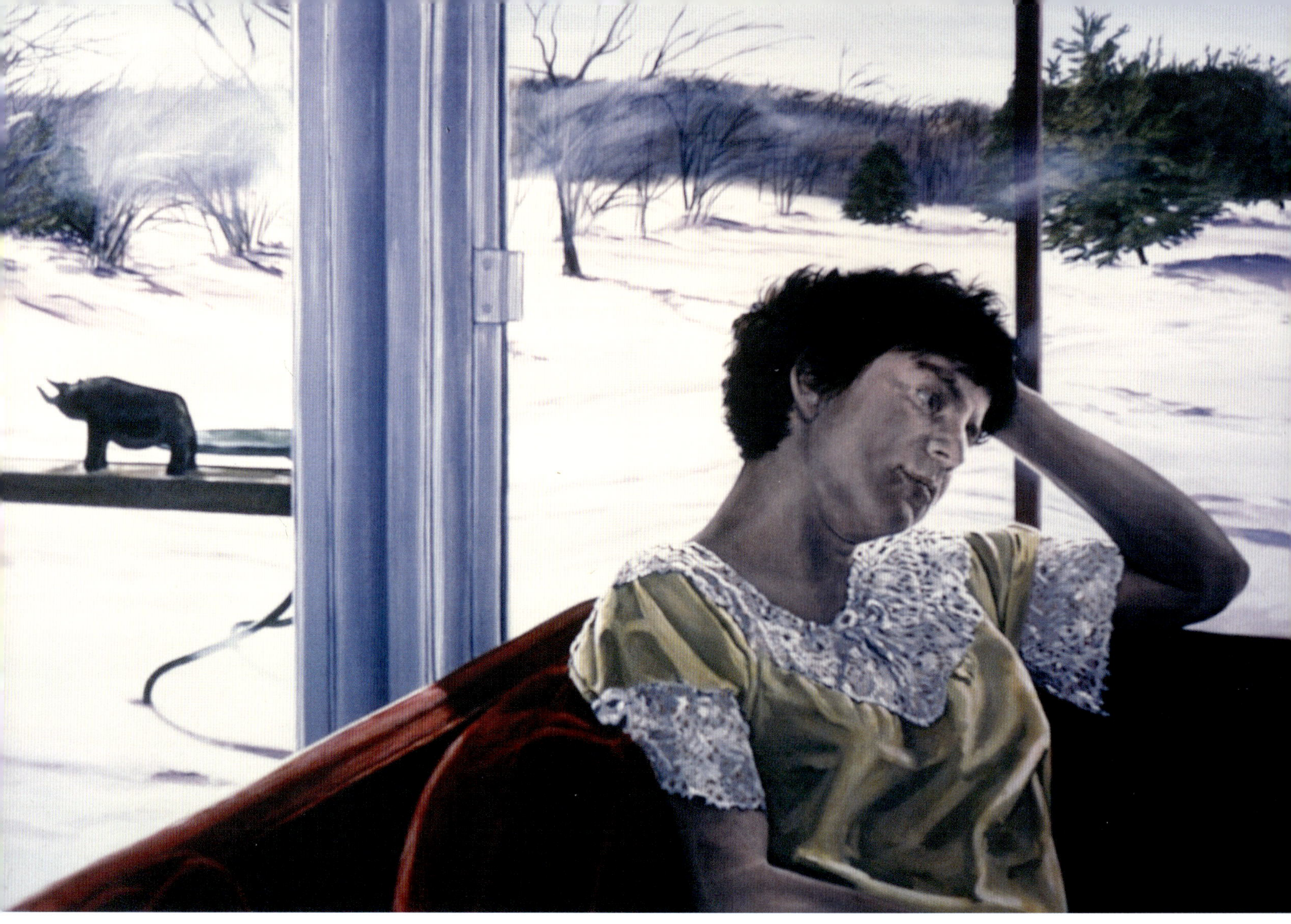

offer herself for a response from her audience. The clothing suggests an artist at work, who pauses to contemplate her situation in a sunlit interior. Completed in the year following the completion of her MFA degree at Rutgers, this painting includes no indication of her work as an artist, but it shows Kuehn's awareness of the viewer's gaze. The title comes in part from a word in Hebrew that is a statement "here I am."[4]

Frances Kuehn was married to George Kuehn, whom she met while she was an undergraduate at Rutgers.[5] Gary Kuehn, George's brother, was a sculptor in the graduate program and then joined the Rutgers faculty. Gary became a subject for one of her oversized painterly compositions, *Gary Seventy-Three*. Not shown as an artist, Gary Kuehn gazes thoughtfully out of a sun-filled window. His position seems to combine motion and rest, and the left arm stretches across a table, while his body twists toward the light. According to the artist, "seventy-three" actually refers to a sonnet by Shakespeare, which makes reference to nature.[6]

In *The Student's Vacation* (1977), a young woman rests indoors, with a wintry landscape behind her. She is contemplative with a raised arm resting on her head, in a pose that has a long history in other works of art over the centuries. The artist has noted that on

    WOMEN ARTISTS ON THE LEADING EDGE

a cold day, with snow in the landscape beyond, the woman wears a short-sleeved blouse, suggesting a determination to stay indoors.

In her later work Kuehn reflects on many subjects, and explores illusionistic effects. Kuehn considers *Vertical Composition with Chair* (2004) among her "geometric" works.[7] Folded pieces of linoleum with a brick pattern rest on a table covered with a geometric cloth. A fragment of a chair seems to anchor the composition, which has become a still-life of competing lines and shapes.

Sleeping Woman (2013) suggests that Kuehn has studied colors, patterns, shapes, and textures to form a composition of visual certainty.

Although Kuehn has been called a realist and a photorealist, she considers herself an expressionist. Kuehn's painting *George, Portrait Near Window*, was included in the annual exhibition at the Whitney Museum of American Art in 1972. She joined the Max Hutchinson Gallery in SoHo, New York, and had her first solo exhibition there in 1973. In 1980 she was offered an artist's residency at Rice University in Houston, Texas. In 2002, Frances Kuehn was included in a group exhibition at the Mitchell Algus Gallery in New York City, which featured "Ten Realists." She had a solo exhibition at the Ben Shahn Galleries, William Paterson University in Wayne, New Jersey. Her paintings have been featured in several group exhibitions at Douglass College and Mason Gross School of the Arts.

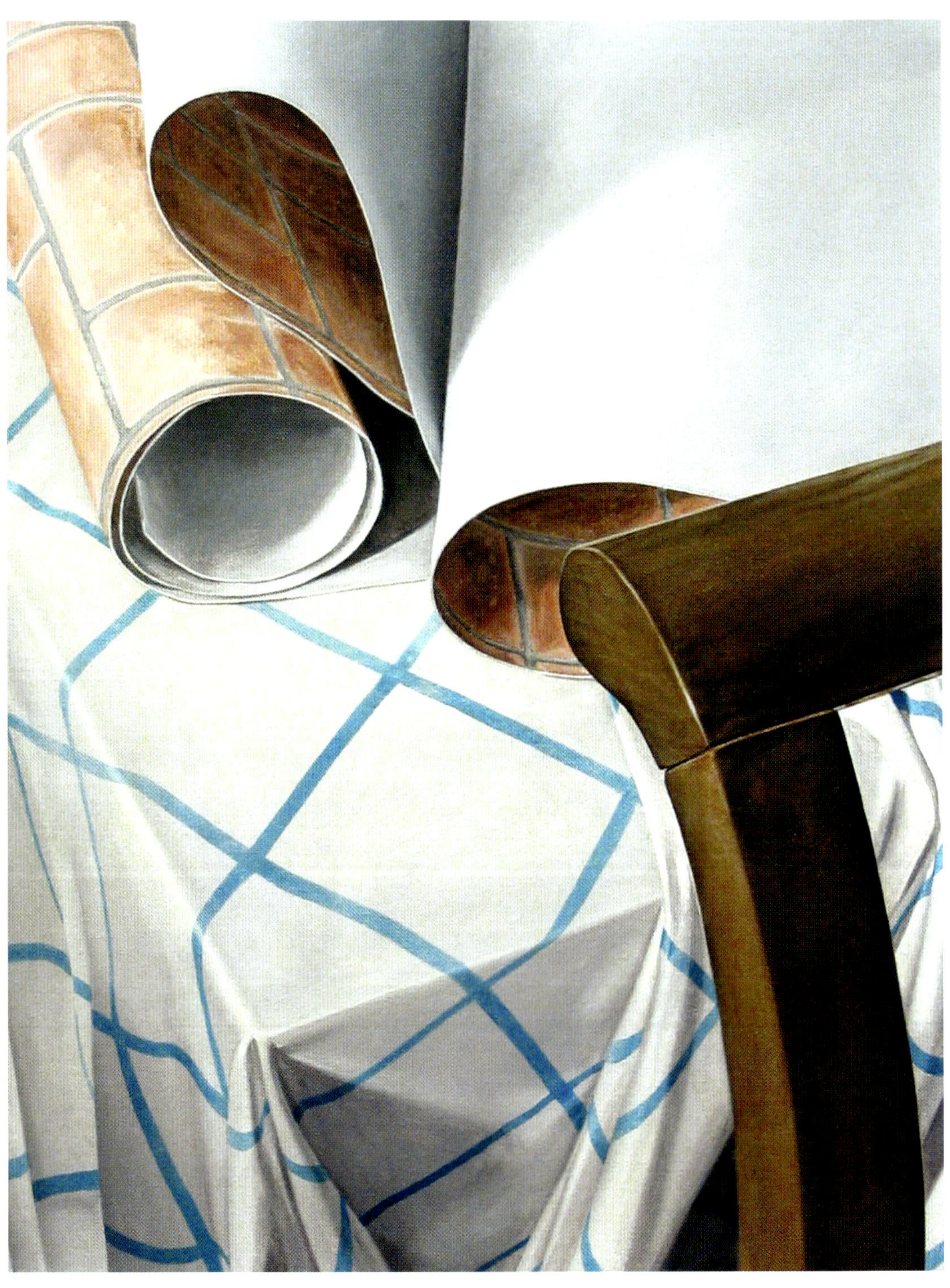

   WOMEN ARTISTS ON THE LEADING EDGE

2.19

Frances Kuehn. *Sleeping Woman*, 2013.
Acrylic on canvas, 24" × 30". Collection of
the artist. Photo: Courtesy of the artist.

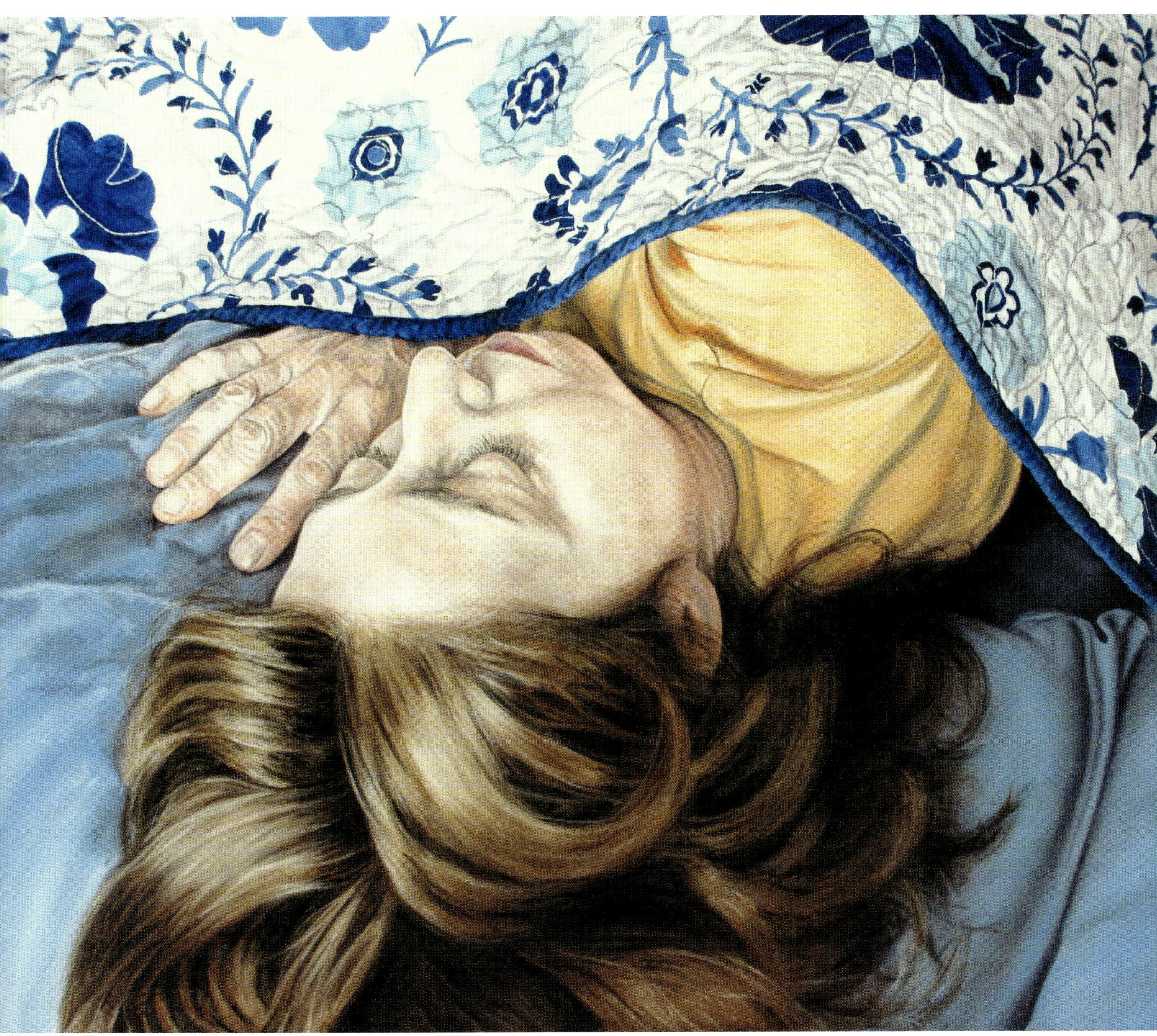

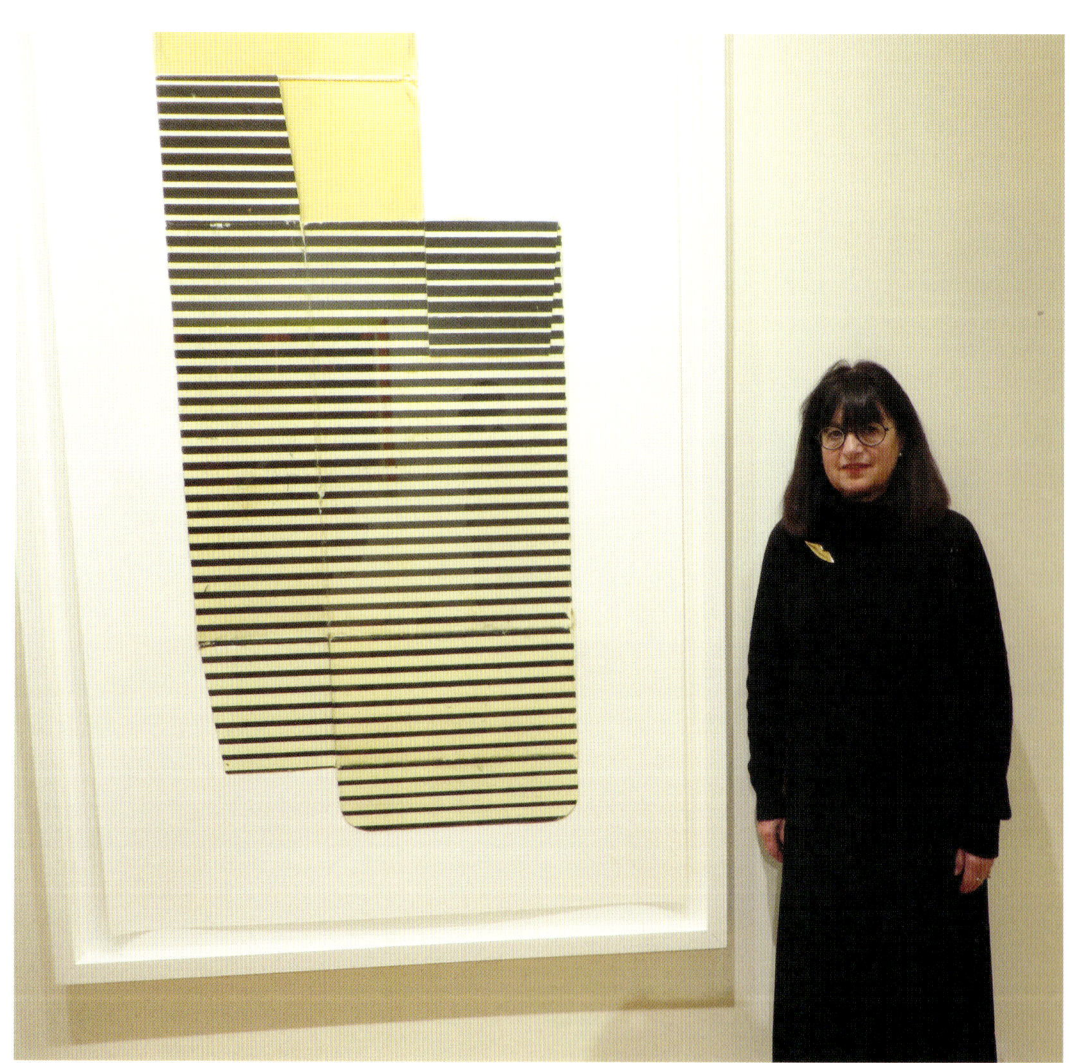

2.20

Linda Lindroth with *Loos*, 2013. Exhibition
at Garvey/Simon Gallery, New York, 2018.
Photo: Joan Marter.

LINDA LINDROTH

Linda Lee Hammer was born in Miami Beach in September 1946. When she was seven, her father moved the family to Coral Gables, Florida. Lindroth began her lifelong interest in photography by making images of popular tourist locations with her Brownie camera. When she was thirteen, the family moved to Springfield, New Jersey.

In 1964, she came to Douglass College and took up residence on the campus. Initially she majored in modern languages, but several art courses gave her the incentive to change her major to art. While at Douglass she worked as the photography editor of the yearbook *Quair*, and wrote a column for *The Caellian*, the student newspaper. She also worked part time for the Division of Instructional Television at Rutgers. There was no faculty member teaching photography at the time; she took classes with Geoffrey Hendricks and John Goodyear. From her sophomore year on, she acknowledged the importance of the MFA students as mentors and friends to the undergraduate art majors. One student, John Wilkes, who was knowledgeable about various techniques in photography, gave her some assistance in processing film and making her own prints in the college darkroom.[1] Her friends at Douglass included Rita Myers, Alice Aycock, and graduate students Mac Adams and Ed Hee. While she was an undergraduate, Linda Hammer focused on printmaking. She recalls that Geoff Hendricks took his students to New York City to galleries and to various Fluxus performances. While she was at Douglass, she met David George Lindroth, an MFA student, whom she married a few days before her graduation in 1968. The wedding took place in Voorhees Chapel on campus. She recalled that there were male faculty members who warned that her career would suffer if she married.[2]

After her graduation Linda Lindroth took many jobs. She worked as a copywriter for radio station WCTC in New Brunswick, New Jersey. By 1969 she was an art editor at Harcourt Brace Jovanovich and worked as a freelance photographer.

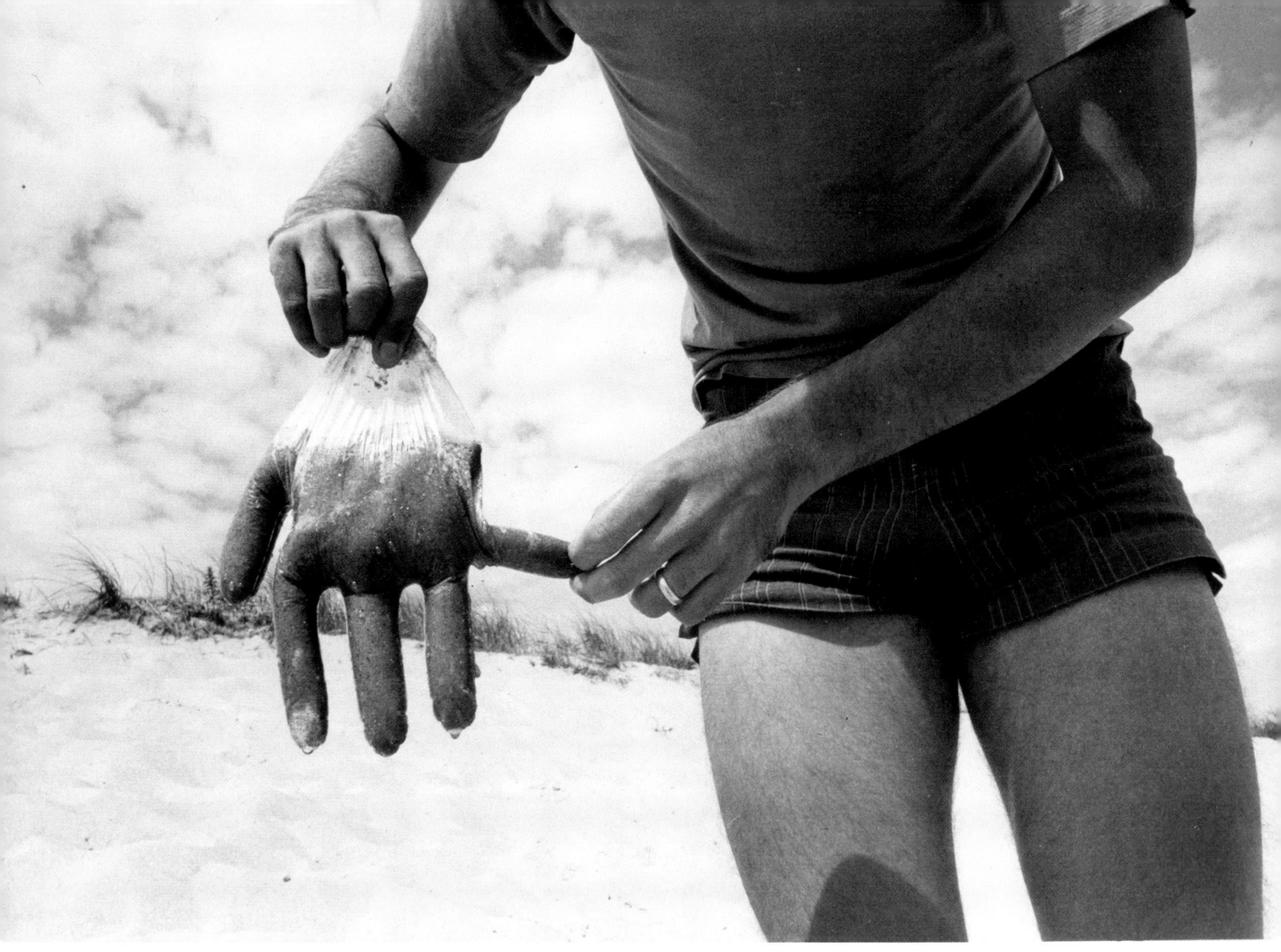

Her photographs and mixed media art appeared on record album covers and book jackets. After leaving the campus, she studied photography with George Tice at the New School. At the School of Visual Arts, she took a course in photoetching with Gordon Matta Clark and also enrolled in classes in graphic design. In 1975 a mixed-media artist's book in a limited edition, entitled *BOOK*, was produced in a class with Gordon Matta Clark and purchased for various collections, including the Metropolitan Museum of Art and Franklin Furnace Archive. In 1976, she was able to take a "master class" with Garry Winogrand at St. John's/Germain School of Photography, and then she received a grant from the New Jersey State Council on the Arts. Peter Bunnell, who had left his position as curator of photography at the Museum of Modern Art for Princeton University, chose her photograph as the cover image of a publication.

In 1977 Lindroth returned to Rutgers to teach photography. At this time she was making large-scale photographic portraits. She received the MFA degree in 1979. Her MFA thesis show included nine photographic enlargements, 65 by 50 inches, which were accompanied by text. Titled *American Portraits,* these images were part of an ongoing project to include a photographic likeness with a text that revealed personal details about the subject.

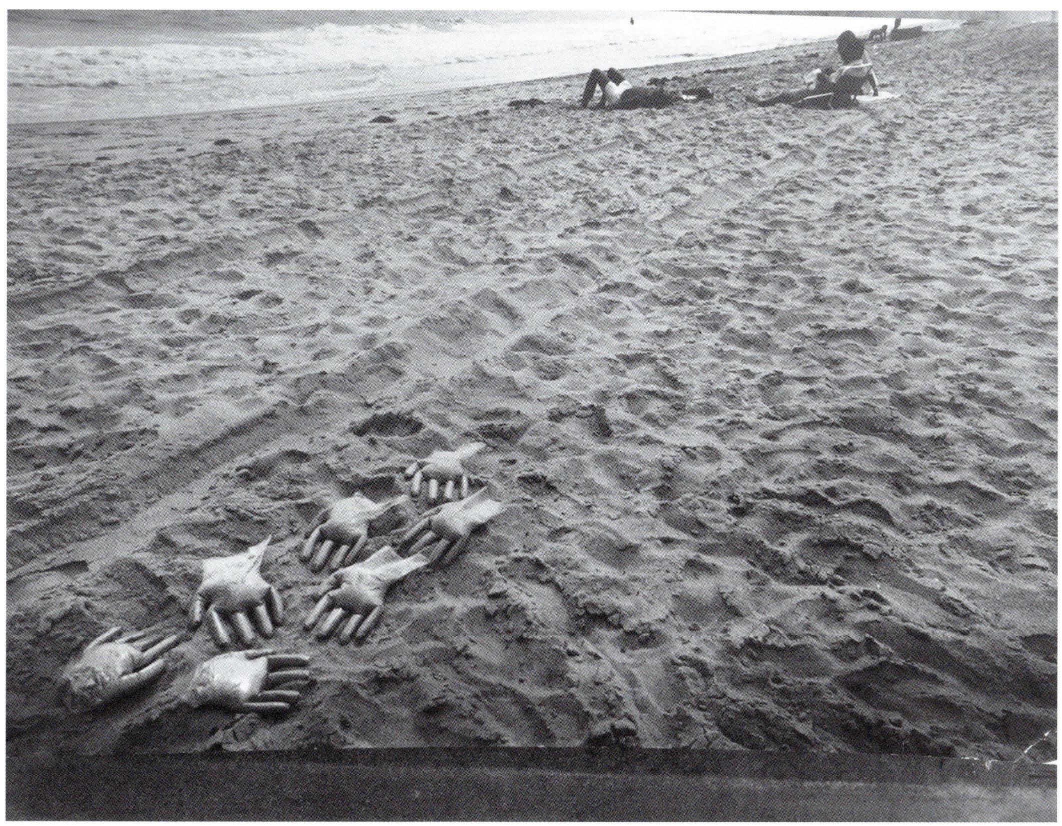

In some cases Lindroth's images are combined with a text alluding to a painful or revealing experience. But Lindroth's sitters are often seen as survivors of childhood trauma. Therefore the stories are uplifting and transcendent.[3]

At Random House she worked as a picture editor for Joe Fox until the mid-1980s. For three years, beginning in 1984, Lindroth owned an art gallery in New Haven, Connecticut, called Gallery Jazz, where she exhibited the work of photographers and architects. In 1985 the Lindroths were divorced. Two years later she married Craig David Newick, an architect with whom she would do a series of mixed-media installations from 1990 through early 2005. Together Lindroth and Newick would win over a dozen grants and prizes, including those from the Foundation for Contemporary Performance Art and the Architecture League of New York.

Lindroth's early photographs included self-portraits, street photography, and mixed-

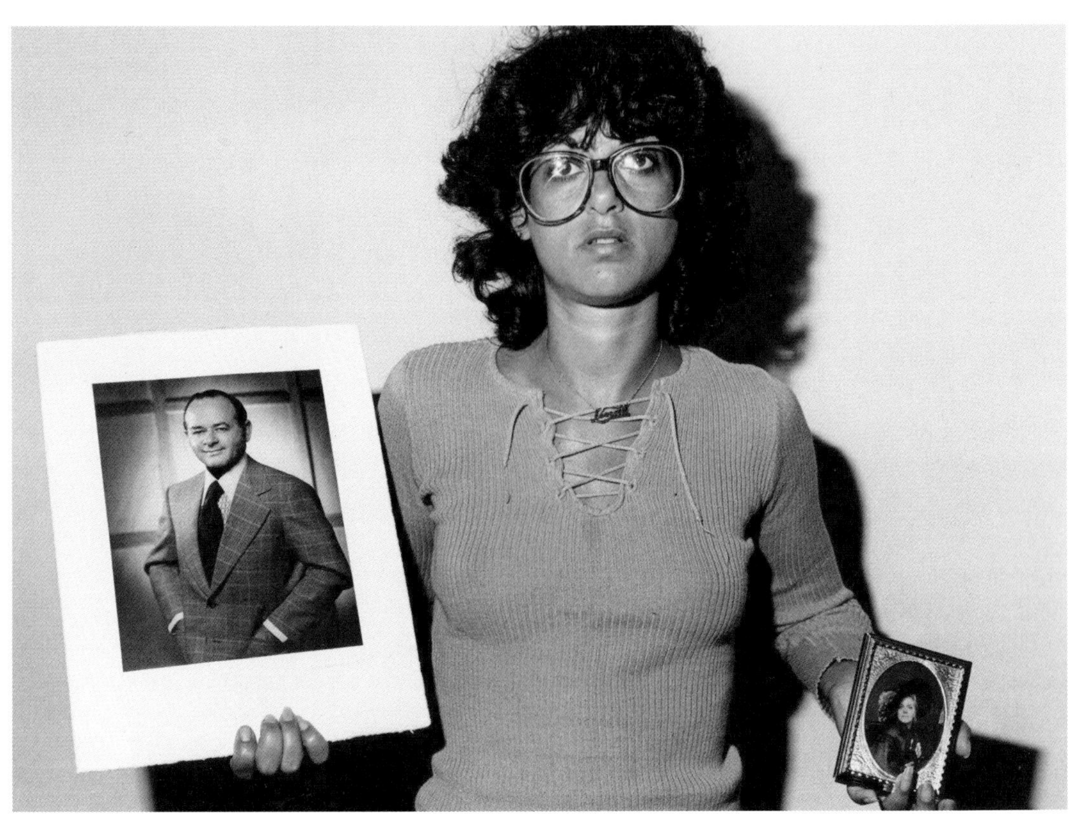

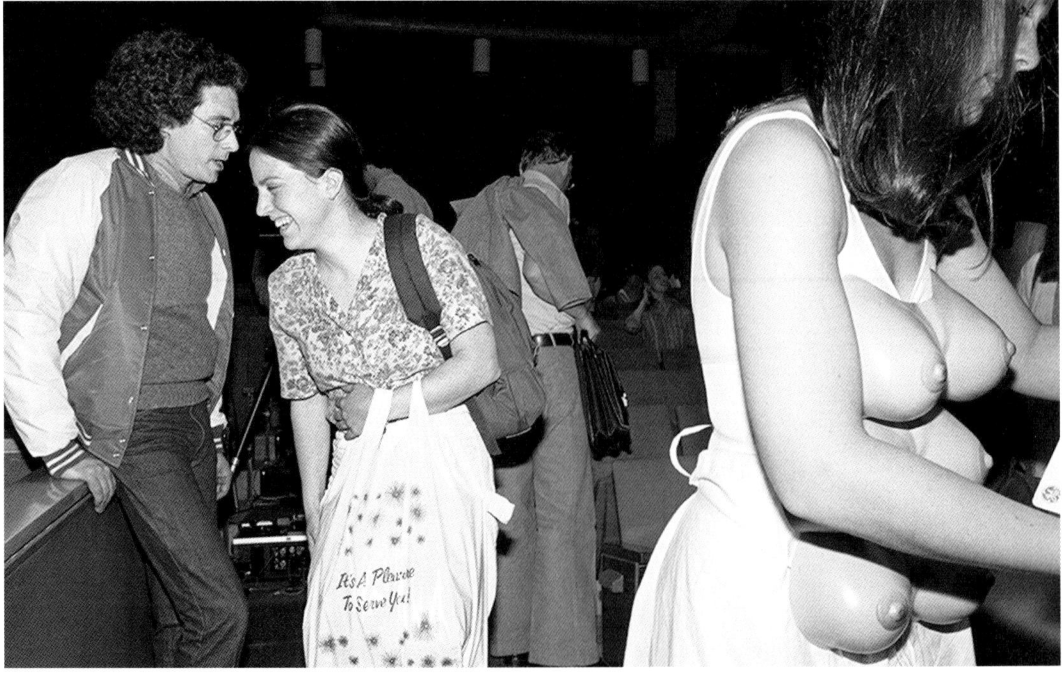
It's A Pleasure
To Serve You

media works. In 1973, she produced *Plastic Glove, Amagansett, New York.* In this image a young man holds a plastic glove filled with sand. Lindroth has mentioned that the "plastic glove" series references a photographic series by Eleanor Antin entitled *100 Boots*.[4] In another image by Lindroth, plastic gloves appear in a cluster on the beach.

Family Portrait on My 32nd Birthday (1978) alludes to the estrangement she felt from her immediate family. She acknowledged that her mother was hospitalized with bipolar disorder and depression. During manic episodes, her mother destroyed her daughter's photographs and early journals.

Lindroth explained in a wall text accompanying the photograph, which was one of nine works exhibited during her MFA thesis exhibition in the Walters Hall Gallery at Douglass:

> Sometimes the most difficult obstacle in one's life can be their family. It is not uncommon to share stories with others and discover that they too have survived some difficulty which began in the home. Many artists experience some early pain—"hurt into art" is an expression used to illustrate this.
>
> I call this "Family Portrait on my 32nd birthday." The photos I am holding were given to me by my parents several years ago. My father's is a formal publicity shot for his job: corporate executive. My mother's was taken in a shopping mall by a photographer who specialized in "Daguerreotype-style Polaroids." My parents—now divorced—and I have not been a happy family. We rarely speak to each other—in fact when this photo was made we had not communicated with each other for over a year.

For *Les Krims* (1979), Lindroth noted: "The photograph was taken at a lecture series I started in grad school. The speaker was Les Krims (left) who was known for taking nude pictures in strange settings—for example, his nude mother making chicken soup. The undergraduate student on the right was making a statement about the exploitative nature of his photos. She was radical for 1979. This photograph was exhibited in 2017 at a "Nasty Woman" exhibition in New Haven."[5]

Beginning in the 1970s and continuing for the next decade, Lindroth worked with the Polaroid Artists Program. She used the Polaroid SX-70 camera, and later the Polaroid 20 by 24, which was featured in her first solo exhibition at the Newark Museum in 1986. *Diptych*

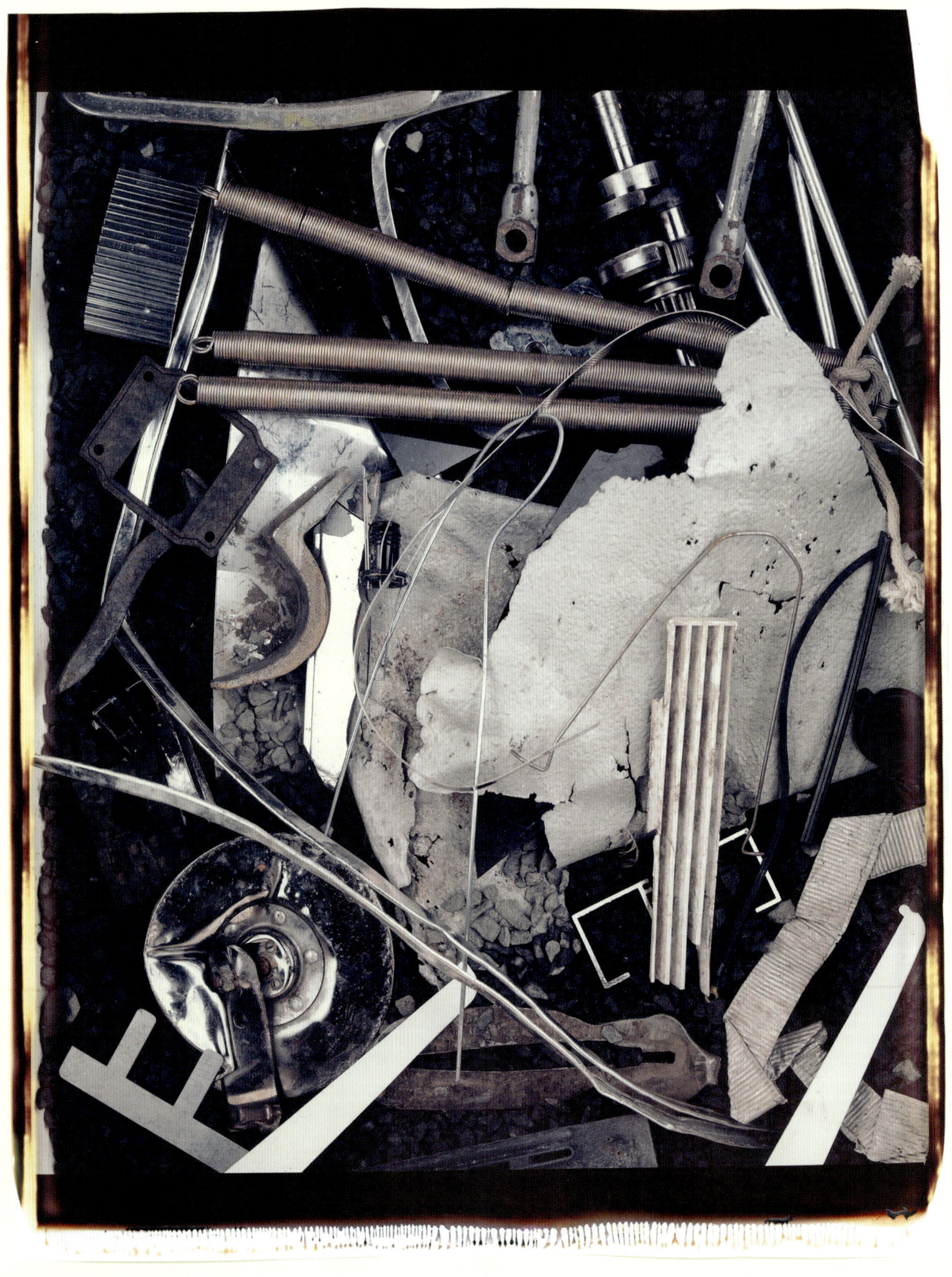

Linda Lindroth. *Diptych with Springs*,
1985 (left). Polaroid Polacolor ER Land Film,
20" × 24". Courtesy of the artist.

Diptych with Springs, 1985 (right).
Polaroid Polacolor ER Land Film,
20" × 24". Courtesy of the artist.

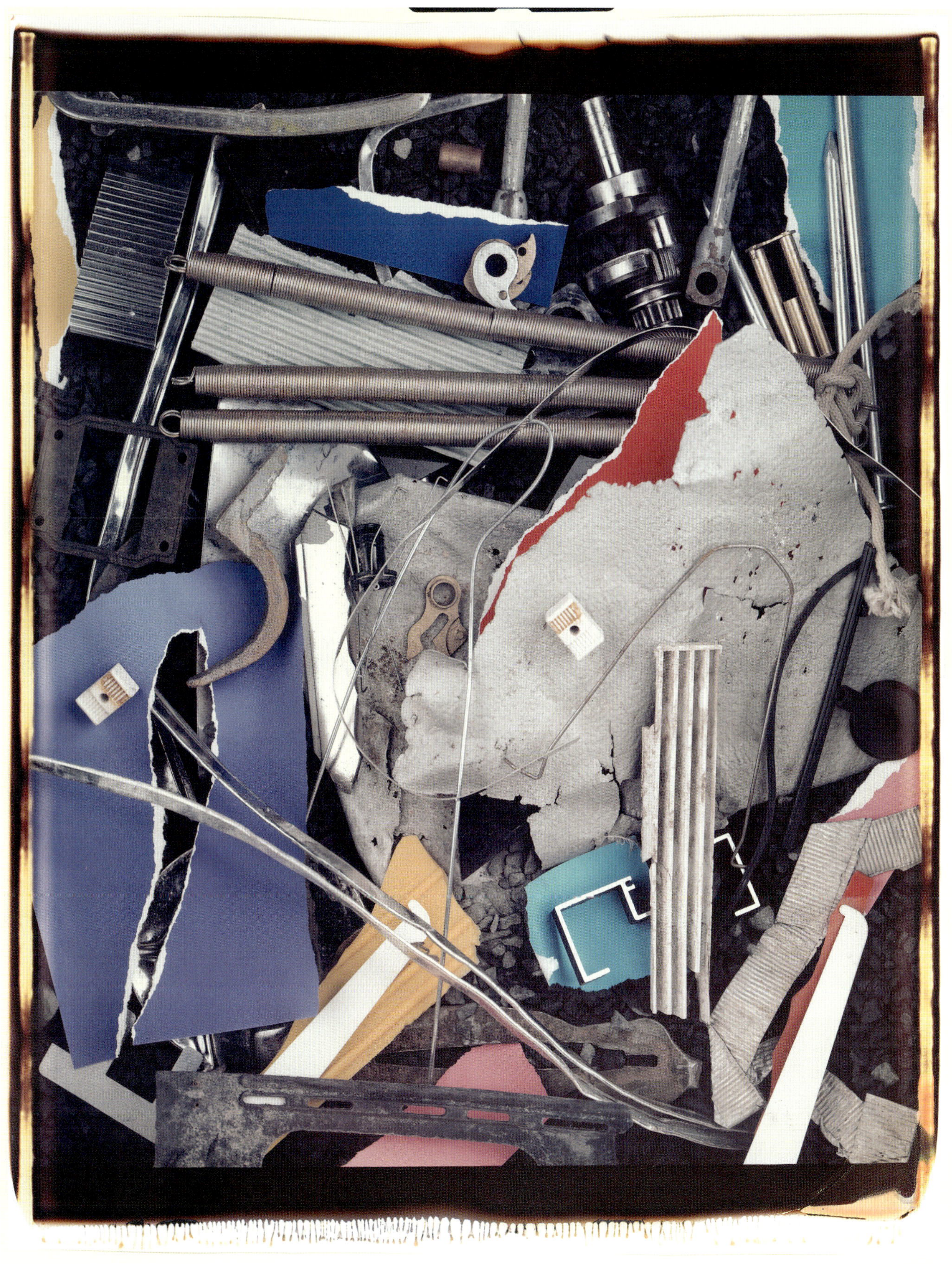

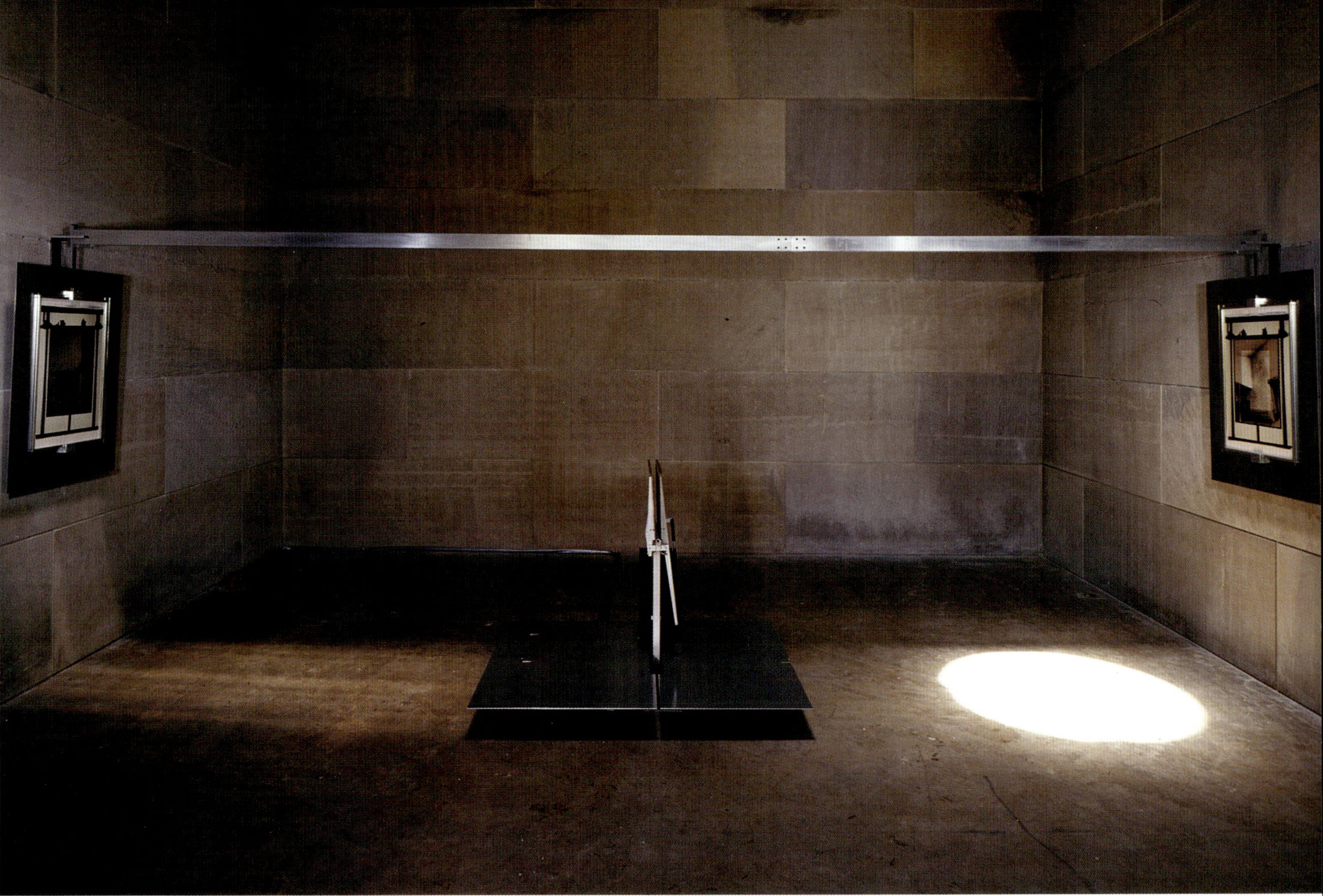

with Springs (1985) is among her Polaroid images. In this work she contrasts what appears as an image with limited color, with the other half of the Diptych, featuring springs, mechanical parts, and fragments of paper in various colors.

A celebrated example of a site-specific installation is *Simultaneous Space*, a project that is credited to Linda Lindroth and Craig Newick. The project was installed at the Zilkha Gallery of Wesleyan University in 1990. Construction included an aluminum beam stretched between limestone walls with joinery that held a pair of Polaroid photographs, measuring 20 by 24 inches, and framed in aluminum. A mechanical book at the center of this installation opened and closed, due to a motorized system. This project was funded by the Foundation for Contemporary Performance Arts in New York, and the New England Foundation for the Arts.[6]

In 2011, Lindroth began her "Trickster in Flatland" series. In these photographic images she explored American commerce through small boxes that once contained products manufactured in the early twentieth century. Her archival pigment prints feature the superior design elements in the original packages. Amazing trompe l'oeil effects are achieved by

     WOMEN ARTISTS ON THE LEADING EDGE

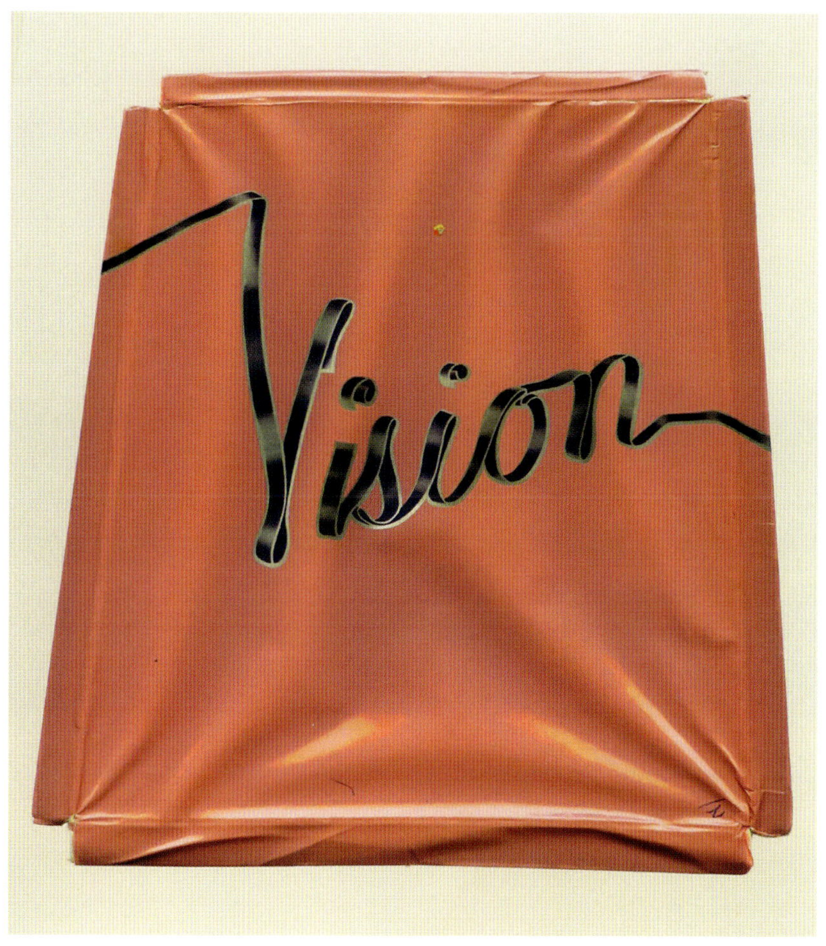

Lindroth's photography that employs these flattened-out boxes. The artist wrote in her book introduction: "I am beguiled by the super-sized, abstracted and flattened objects you see before you. The details and colors invigorate my senses and I am dizzy viewing them on the screen before me. The objects I have collected, hoarded because they had a strange visual hold on me, resided in so many corners of my life before they came out, encountered Trickster—and now take the stage."[7]

Loos (2013), for example, is an archival pigment print that resembles a constructivist painting from the 1960s. The "throwaway" item has been transformed into an abstract composition of great visual interest.

Vision (2015), an archival pigment print, is based on a box for nylon stockings. The exuberance of this design is enhanced by the lyrical use of ribbon folded to form the product's name. Allusions are here to the costly, desirable nylon stockings that once were stored in a pink box labeled "Vision." The sides of this small box are now flattened out but are still distinct from the surrounding white background.

Linda Lindroth was inducted into the Douglass Society in 1986 for her achievements in the arts. She has been an adjunct professor at Quinnipiac University in Hamden, Connecticut, since 1998. Her works are in numerous public collections, including the Museum of Modern Art, The Metropolitan Museum of Art, the Bibliothèque Nationale in Paris, and the High Museum of Art, Atlanta.

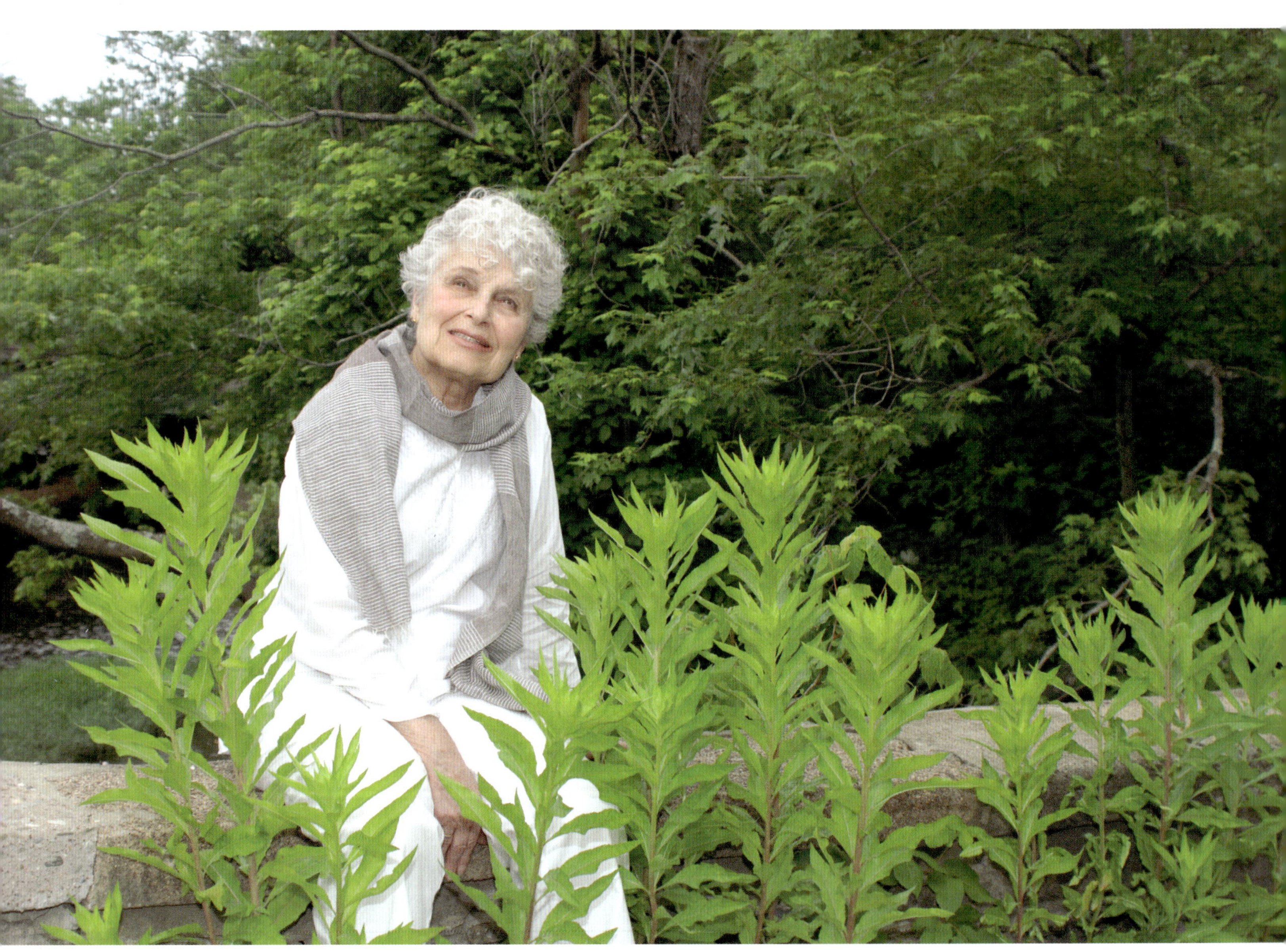

2.29

Marion Munk, 2017.

Photo: Sue Stember.

MARION ENGELMAN MUNK

In 1937 Marion Munk was born in New York City, and she grew up on the family's farm in Toms River, New Jersey. She recalled that the farming community was primarily composed of Eastern European immigrants, many of whom were politically radical and saw themselves as a minority—threatened by the outside world.[1] She had hoped to attend Bennington College or Smith, but was awarded a state scholarship to Douglass College, where she found the programs and faculty challenging and exciting. She intended to become a painter. Marion Engelman (her name while an undergraduate at Douglass from 1955 to 1959), came to the college at an extraordinary period in its history. The college had changed its name from the New Jersey College for Women to Douglass College. Dean Mary Bunting, the administrator, initiated a series of events, generally called the Voorhees Assemblies.

Marion Engelman Munk found the other students very serious and the classes competitive. In her sophomore year, she had a first interaction with Bob Watts: "A man of few words, he approached me, and asked me if I had studied Mayan art. Bob had a really profound effect on my work—particularly his interest in primitive art. I worked with him on sculpture and painting. He was a remarkable teacher with an engineering background and an interest in tools."[2]

She did not feel that the women students were "held back" because of their gender. In fact, they were "pushed" to develop their skills. The young women were urged to go to New York City galleries to see contemporary shows. She observed, "I always felt the need to meet the expectations of the faculty."[3] Munk was able to attend many of the contemporary dance events and lectures, including John Cage and Merce Cunningham, who performed on campus. She took a course with Allan Kaprow at Rutgers College who was very active in creating performance art. At Douglass she enrolled in a painting class with Theodore Brenson, who was a great favorite among the students, and chaired the art department. She studied sculpture and pre-Columbian art with Bob Watts, and she took courses with Geoff Hendricks when he had first arrived on campus. "I felt that a lot was expected of me."[4]

A great revelation to her was the work of Ka Kwong Hui, who joined the art faculty in 1957.[5] Munk noted that Hui was also teaching at the Brooklyn Museum School of Art. She saw an exhibition of Hui's work in the Douglass Art Gallery in Recitation Hall and bought her first piece of his art. Munk noted, "He was a magnificent artist in his own right. It was because of that exhibition I decided to focus on ceramics."[6] She was intrigued with Hui's ceramics, which were created in the Oriental tradition of using organic forms and earthen tones. After taking a course with him, she decided to continue her study of ceramics. The faculty did make references to Black Mountain College, and she learned more about the curriculum at Black Mountain, which included ceramics and avant-garde interests. She recalled bringing a series of old doors to the Rutgers campus so that she could collaborate with another student on an installation for Allan Kaprow's class.[7]

Marion Engelman Munk graduated from Douglass in 1959 and was the first to enroll in the newly established MFA program. Other MFA students included Loretta Dunkelman and Jackie Winsor. As Marion Levinston, she developed a lifelong relationship with Hui as a mentor and adopted his concentration on the traditionalism of Oriental ceramics, but with unpredictable contemporary twists. For her master's thesis Munk worked with ash-glazed pieces, which originated in China in approximately 1500 BC.[8]

In the early 1960s, she became the "curator" of the Douglass College Art Gallery. In January 1961 she assisted Roy Lichtenstein as he installed a first exhibition of his abstract expressionist paintings in the Art Gallery. Later Munk was intrigued by the collaboration of Ka Kwong Hui and Lichtenstein in the creation of a series of ceramic works featuring primary colors and Ben Day dots.

After graduating from the MFA program, Marion Munk taught at Douglass College in 1962–63. She developed the art department at Middlesex County College in 1968. Her ceramics began to change, especially when she started working with white clay after developing a skin allergy to iron found in the darker clay. The use of white clay made it possible to introduce brightly colored overglazes.

In 1981 Marion Levinston Munk wrote:

> Initially my attraction to clay as a medium of expression was not only to the physical involvement with the material and its almost magical transformation through

2.30
Marion Munk. *Vessel #4*, 1995. Porcelain,
13" × 11" × 8.5". Photo: Brian Weitz.

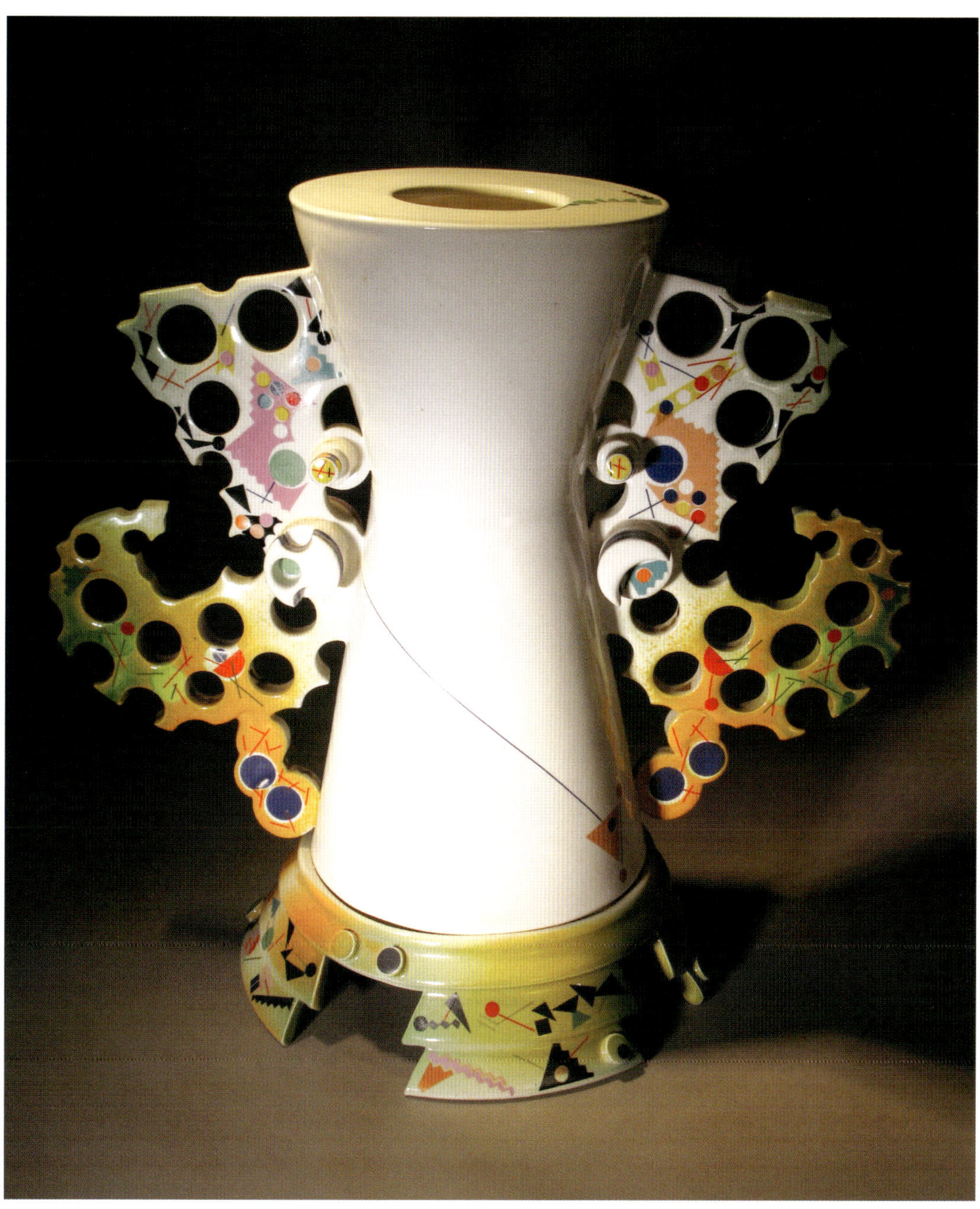

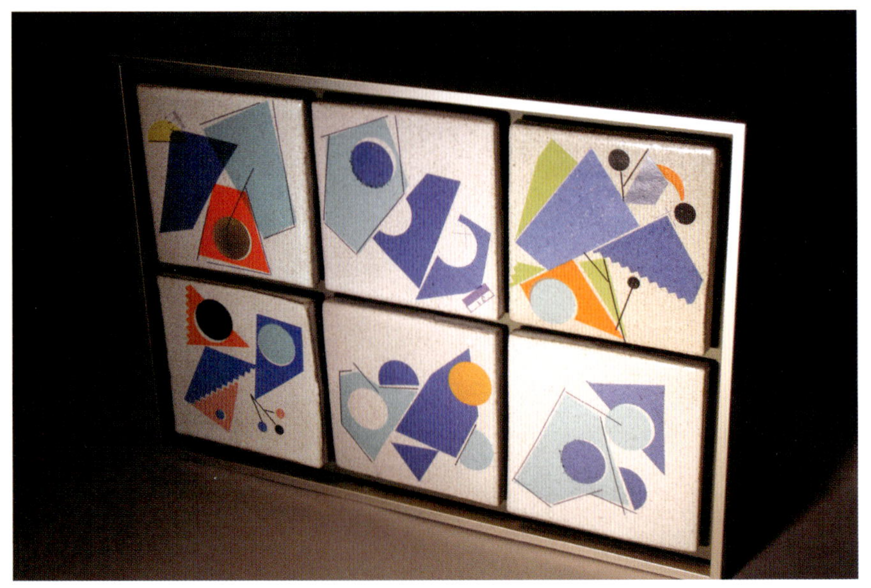

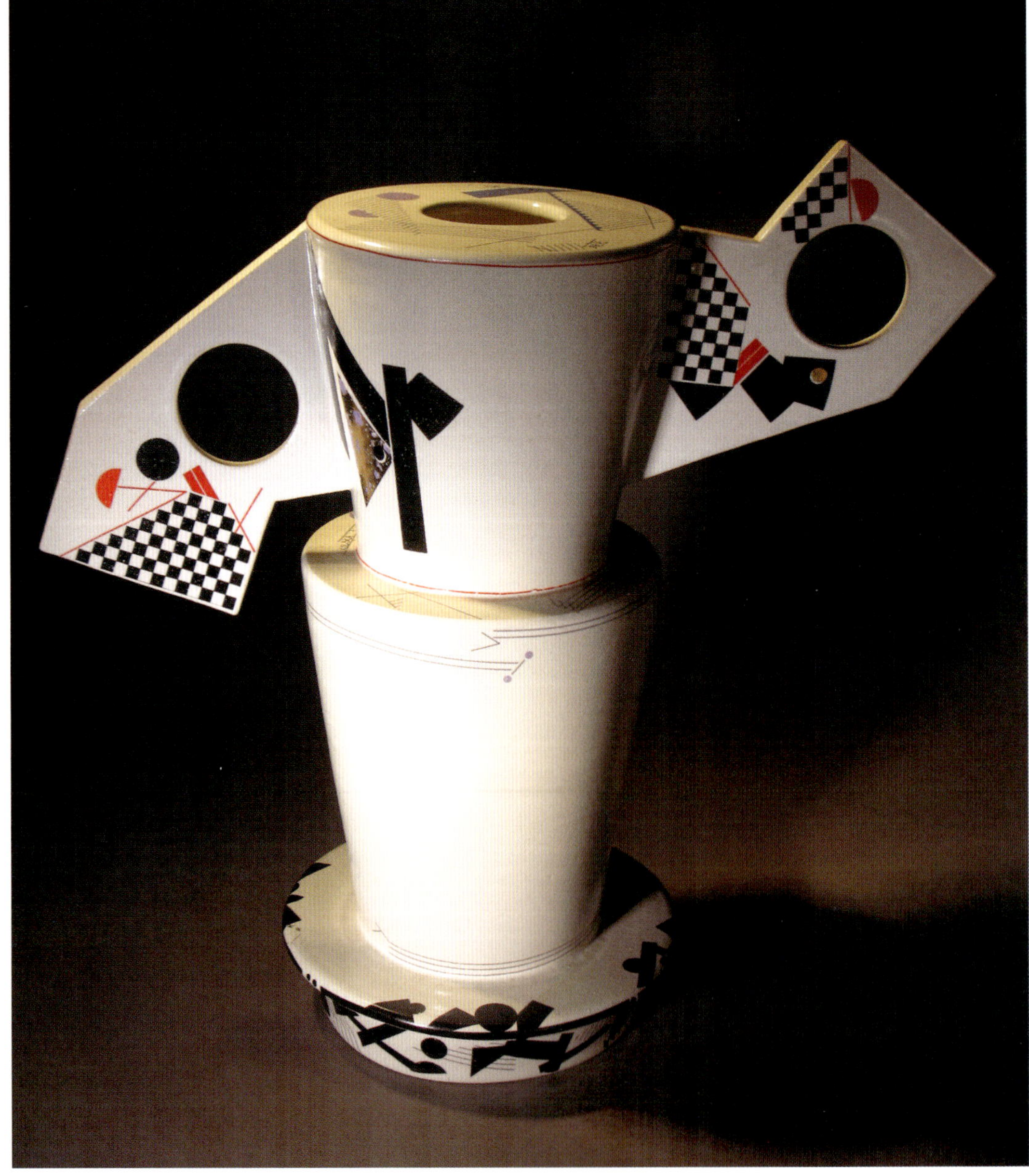

fire, but the appeal of a tradition of useful objects. While function seems to be a somewhat secondary issue at the moment, it still is an important element in my work and a point of departure. Recently my work has become more complicated in both form and painted surface. The tension between these two elements is a preoccupation. I work on a relatively small scale. Ideas emerge from the manipulation of a supply of raw shapes which are finally organized into a formal whole.[9]

Beginning in 1986 she traveled repeatedly to design symposia organized at porcelain factories in Czechoslovakia, now the Czech Republic. At these annual events ceramic artists from various countries developed designs for production. Munk lectured on Czech art at the Maryland Institute of Art in Baltimore, and wrote articles about Czech artists.[10]

Munk was also attracted to the colors and geometric designs favored by Soviet artists at the beginning of the October Revolution (1917–25). There is a progression in Munk's work from organic, functional objects to more abstracted, sculptural forms. Early on she had created tea sets and vases, but her ceramics became more experimental. *Vessel #4* (1995) is an ornate work featuring a solid core of white porcelain combined with an intricate pattern of open circles and small geometric embellishments.

In an untitled work (Semaphore Series) of 2003 Munk makes reference to a system of signals.[11] The use of prominent diagonals extending out from a core could be viewed as a torso with arms raised. With this work and others, Munk combines slab construction with thrown clay and silk-screened decals. Using stoneware tiles, Munk designed a wall piece of geometric forms. Russian Constructivist Liubov Popova comes to mind at the suggestion of Munk's intersecting geometric forms that are silk-screened decals.[12]

Marion Munk has been given solo and two-person exhibitions at Douglass College in 1972; at the New Jersey State Museum, Trenton, and the American Craftsman's Gallery in 1974; and at Middlesex County College in 1987. In 1994, her work was featured at the New Jersey Designer Craftsmen Gallery in New Brunswick, and in 1995 at the International Gallery of Ceramics in Cesky Krumlov, Czech Republic.

She has been included in many group exhibitions in the Czech Republic and the United States. Her work is found in many public and private collections, including the Museum of Applied Art, Prague, Czech Republic; the Newark Museum; and the International Ceramics Museum, Santiago de Cuba.

2.33
Rita Myers, 2017. Photo: Courtesy of
the artist.

2.34
Rita Myers. Untitled photograph from
John Goodyear's class, 1968. Courtesy
of the artist.

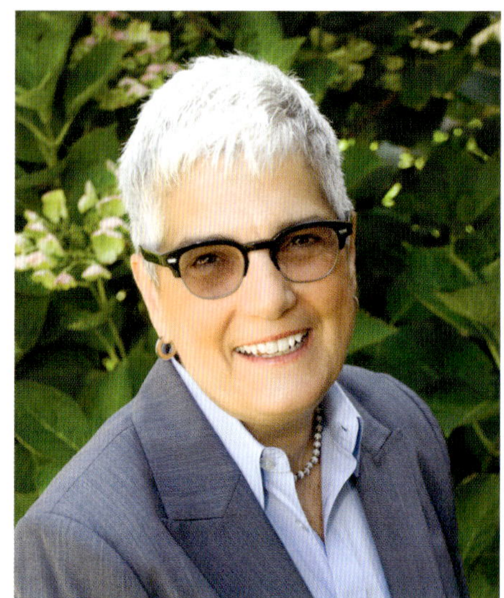

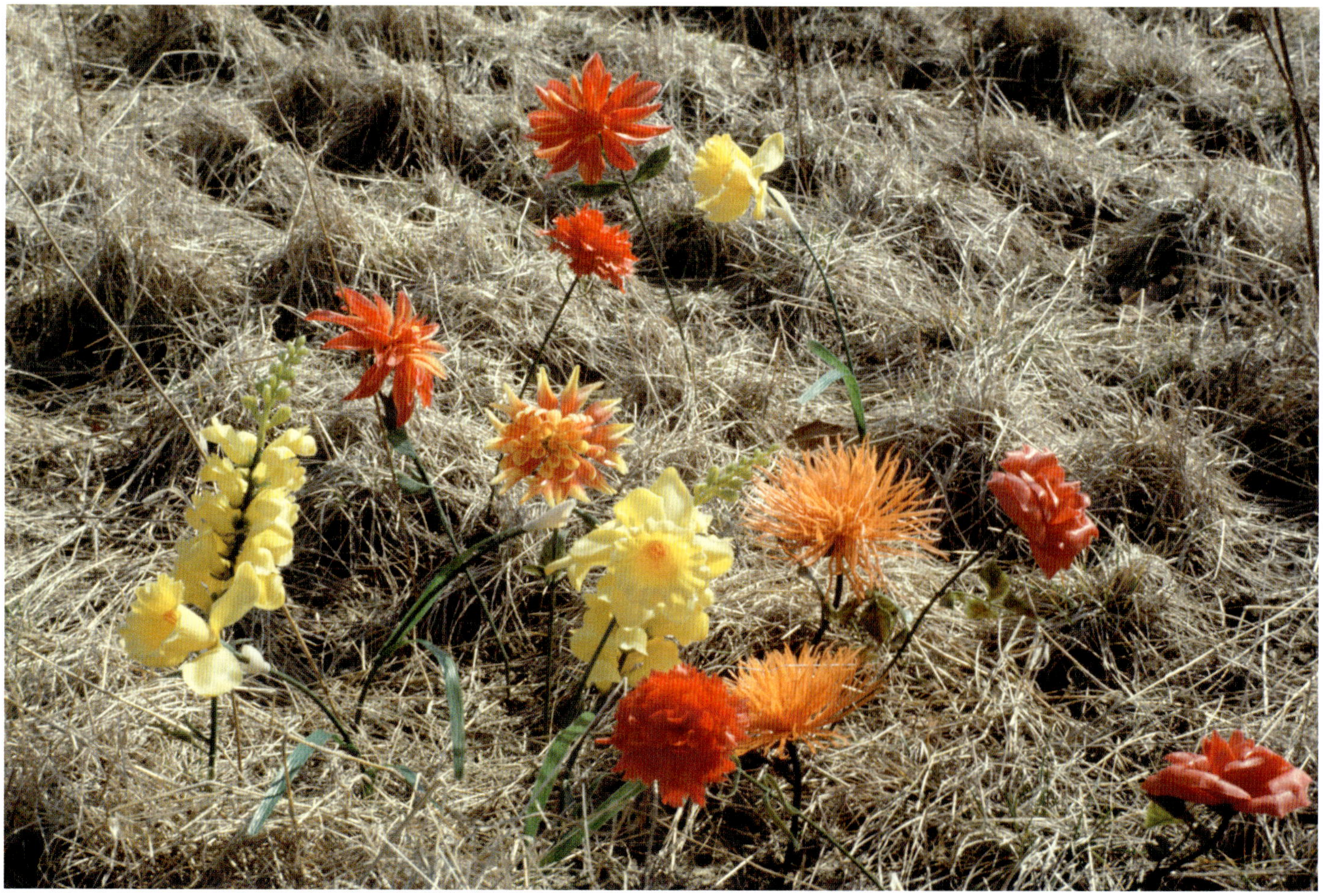

RITA MYERS

Rita Myers attended Douglass College on a state scholarship, and her experiences there were life changing. Born in 1947, she grew up in the small rural community of Hammonton, New Jersey. At Douglass she could not decide on a major initially, but in her sophomore year she enrolled in an introductory-level art course. The choice of a major in studio art was determined by that class, and the art students that she met. She noted, "I decided to be an art major because it would help me find the solutions to the questions that I needed to ask."[1] Among her most valued instructors was John Goodyear, who later became her honors thesis adviser. "He was a guiding light in nurturing the sense of inquiry."[2] A "defining moment" in the direction her work would take was seeing a 6-foot-sided cube by Robert Morris in a New York gallery. She recalled "I had no idea what it was, and that was most intriguing because there was no preestablished category for what I was looking at."[3] Commenting on the direction of her work as a Douglass art student, after seeing the cube, Myers noted "I didn't know where this belonged in the universe of things or objects or experiences. It so challenged everything I knew about everything else. That was what I decided I wanted to do."[4] Douglass provided many answers to the questions she had about materials, methods, scale, and form. Graduate students worked as teaching assistants for the Douglass undergraduates, and were generally available for advice and sometimes technical help. Myers remembers an occasion when Jackie Winsor, a graduate student, participating in undergraduate critiques, said of her work "This one is definitely art."[5]

At Douglass, the studio art faculty promoted the idea of free expression. Her instructors included Goodyear, Geoff Hendricks, Peter Stroud, and Mark Berger for art history. Berger combined the "understanding of art history in relation to the culture of the world."[6] Although she focused on sculpture, Myers recalls that she used photography as part of an

2.35 and 2.36

Rita Myers. *Phantom Cities*, 1990. Installation,
University Museum of Contemporary Art.
University of Massachusetts, Amherst.

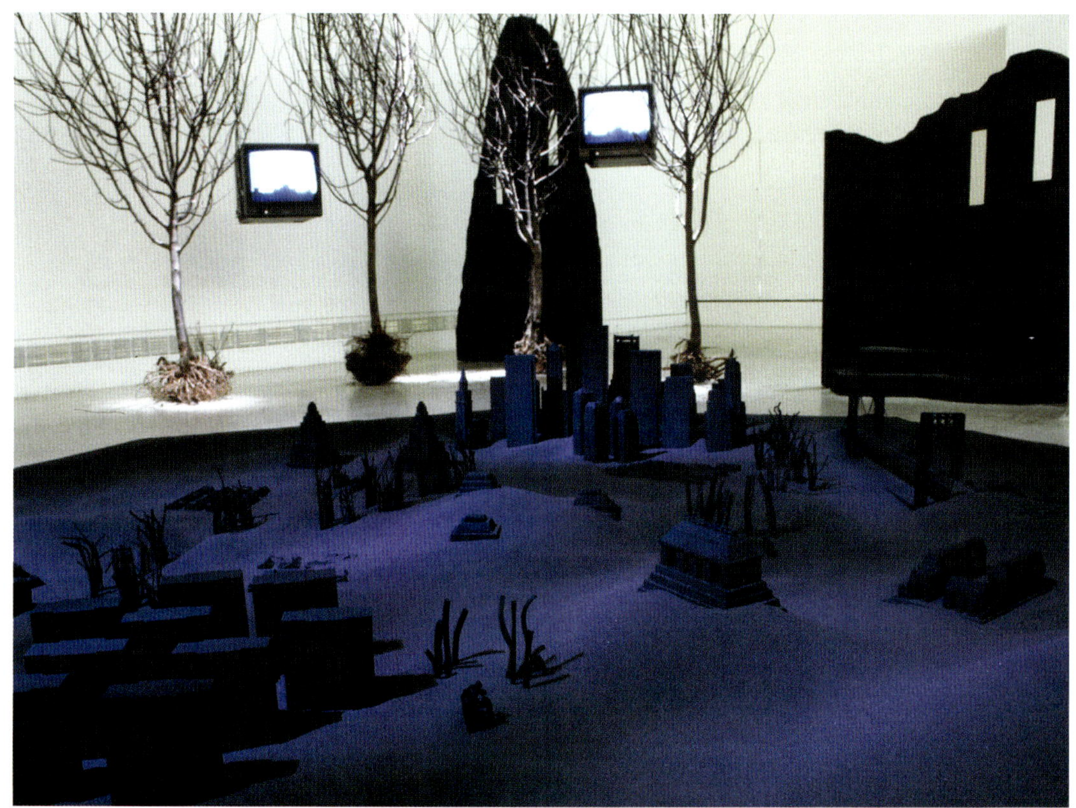

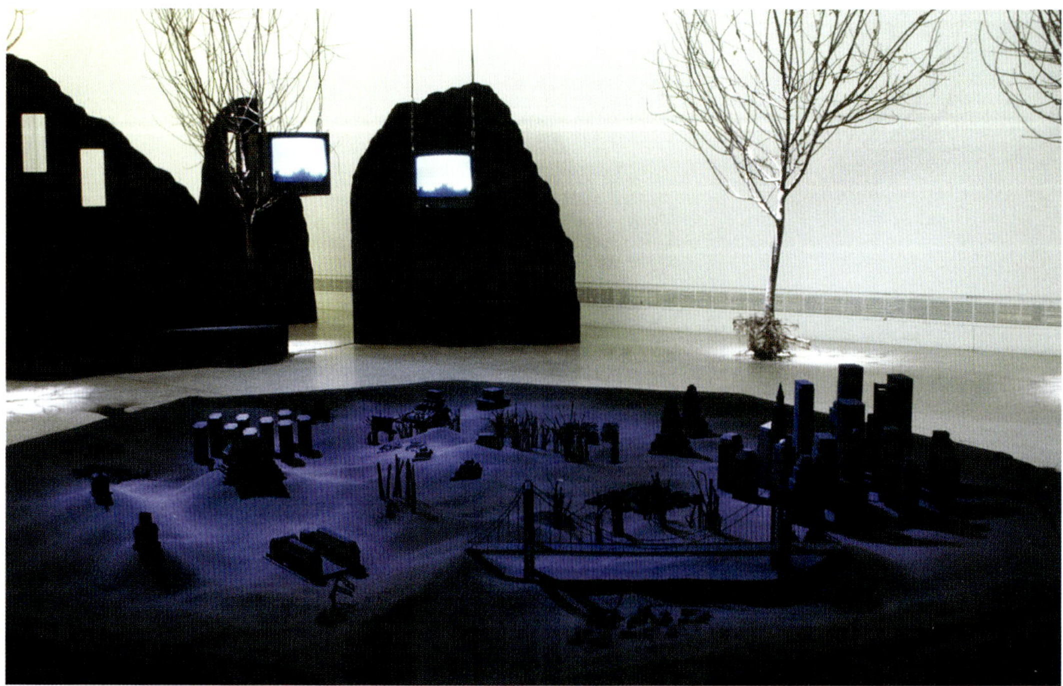

assignment for a design course with Goodyear. In a rural New Jersey landscape, she introduced plastic flowers to a barren setting. Myers explained: "A series of slides had an accompanying soundtrack, probably on a tape recorder. The soundtrack was of wind—rumbling noises, and ended with the sound of jet planes overhead, synced with the final images. I have no idea how I synced it. Anyway, it's interesting when I look back on this piece as it presages interests in moving images and nature/artifice tensions."[7]

For her sculpture she combined soft materials with hard materials. Myers remembers that her honors thesis was fashioned out of five or six wooden pieces compressing fake fur. And Myers notes that she was aggressive in finding faculty members to critique her work, and was already determined to pursue an artistic career. She graduated from Douglass in 1969, and worked for several years before continuing her studies.

In 1972 Myers enrolled at Hunter College for the MFA degree. Her instructors there included Robert Morris; Vincent Longo, with whom she had already studied at the Yale Summer School of Music and Art; and Linda Nochlin, for art history. In 1973–74 Myers was included in an exhibition organized by Lucy Lippard at the California Institute of Arts, Valencia. In her work *Body Halves*, Myers used photographs of her nude body, front and back, to demonstrate "bifurcation and re-alignment of bilateral asymmetry."[8]

Myers's exposure to new media resulted in a different direction: she began experimenting with video. At first video was used to document her performances, but it was soon incorporated as an integral part of the performance itself. In 1973 she performed "Slow Squeeze," "Tilt 1," and "Jumps" using her image on the video monitor as immediate feedback to guide her movements. In "Slow Squeeze" for example, the artist attempts to remain within the camera's visual field as it slowly zooms in, and diminishes that field until there is only a cramped space in which she can barely fit. Eventually Myers recognized that video could offer other possibilities as an emerging art form. She completed the master's degree in 1974 and began to make multimedia installations that create theatrical effects by combining video, sound, text, and sculptural elements. These large-scale works also explore the dichotomy between the tangible world and the illusionistic world through the use of words and images. In 1975 Myers presented *Investigation/Observation* at the Walters Hall Gallery, Douglass College. This work concerned the gap that alienates humans from the environment they inhabit.

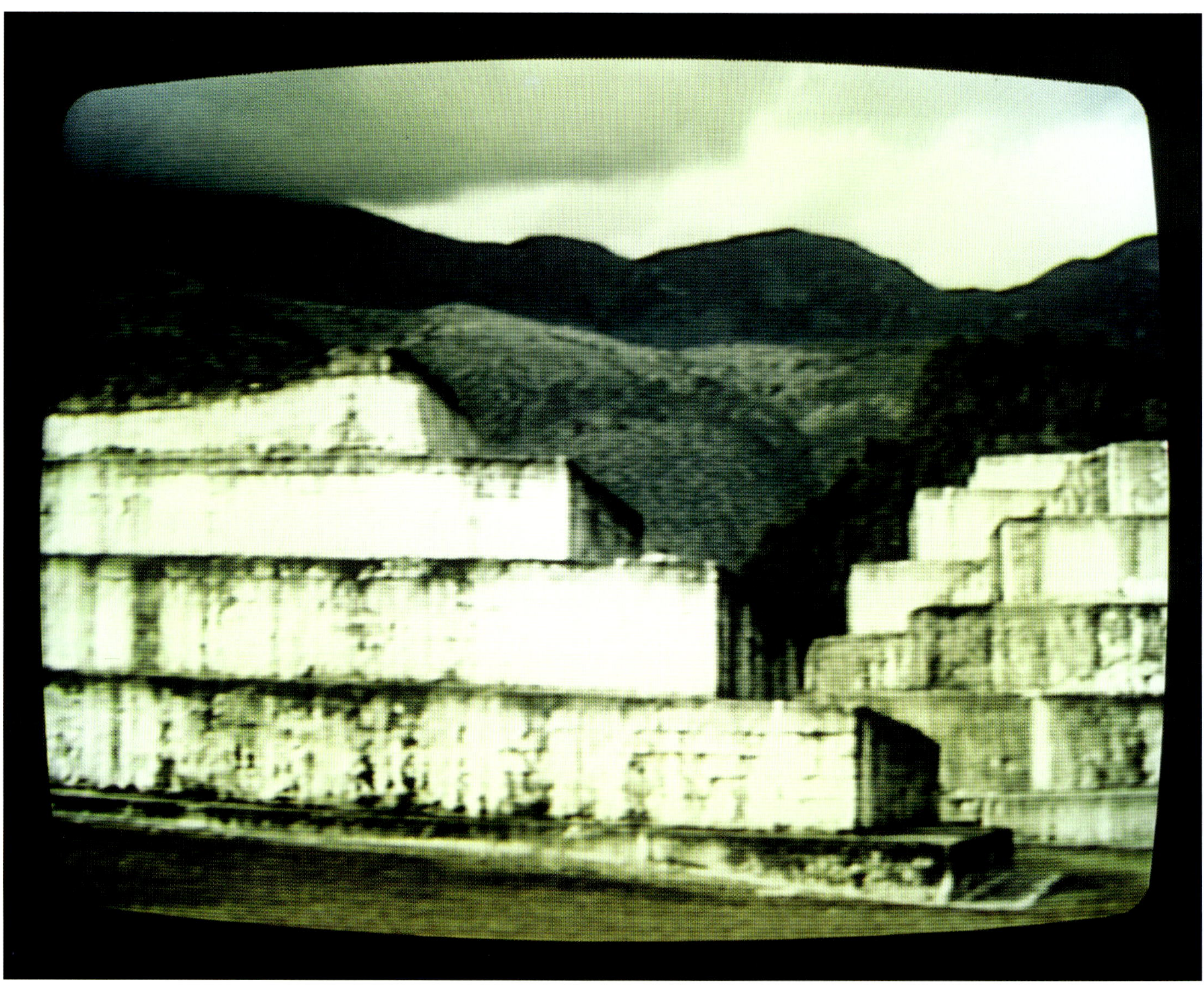

Critic Shelley Rice noted in *Afterimage*: "Since 1975 Rita Myers has been creating installations which explore the intangible aspects of tangible reality. The duality of mind and matter, the physical and the spiritual, is Myers's central concern and is reflected in her use of materials. All of her works incorporate sculptural forms, videotapes, and audio-taped narrative texts in self-contained spatial environments. All confront the viewer with the dichotomy between "real" space containing "real" objects and the metaphoric illusions of video and sound."[9]

Phantom Cities, 1987–1990

This remarkable project includes a three-channel video, sound, and sculptural installation. Myers explores both historical time and mythological time. New York City (including the World Trade Towers) is juxtaposed with Mayan ruins in Mexico and Guatemala. Video monitors suspended amid burned walls and skeletal trees surround a miniature city whose components are drawn from the architecture of these two civilizations, all partially buried in black sand. On the video monitors, images of people, the built environment, and the landscape are aligned. Myers prophetically evokes the life cycle of civilizations by showing the ruins of some modern cities and grave sites, littered with skeletons. Myers notes, "It was certainly a wonderful experience making this piece, contemplating the juxtaposition of NYC's potential for ruin with that of the Mayans, a people of immense knowledge and sophistication. There have recently been discoveries of literally thousands more structures in the area surrounding Tikal."[10] The sound for this installation includes claps of thunder and a steady heartbeat.[11] This installation was commissioned by the University Gallery at the University of Massachusetts, Amherst, and shown there from February to April 1990.[12] Then it traveled to the Madison Art Center, and the Carnegie Museum of Art.

Resurrection Body, 1993

This installation has personal associations for the artist. It was created in October 1993, just a few months after the death of her father. Personal elements with strong emotional valence included photographs mostly of deceased family members. This installation included a nude male performer, who was prone on a bed, with a tree suspended above his body. Sensors are attached to the performer, providing an ambient heartbeat. Nearby miniature monitors, suspended over a miniature bed in the shape of a tree, registered the image of an echocardiogram. Variations in the heartbeat of the performer changed the image to photographs of Myers's family members, which were stored on a laser disc. When the heart rate was elevated, the images of family members appeared.

Video historian John Hanhardt wrote,

> In *Resurrection Body* Myers brings the human body, a central referent to all of her art, into the center of the installation. . . . Myers has created a powerful and

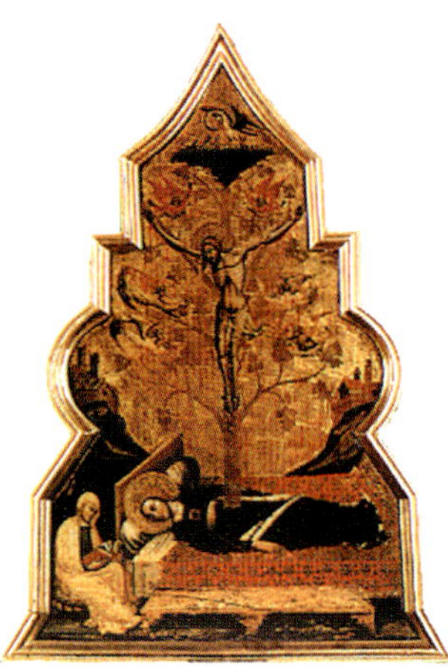

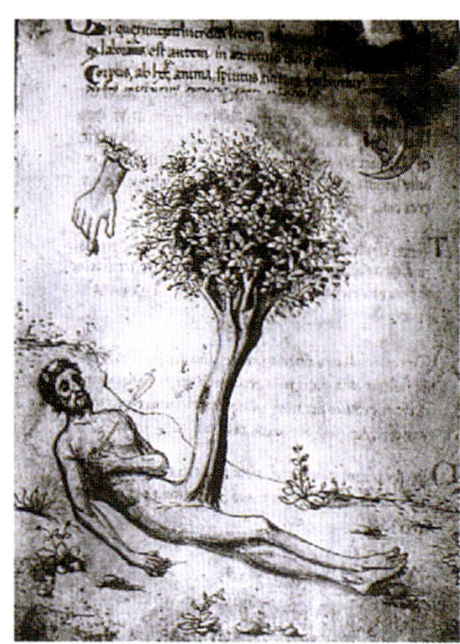

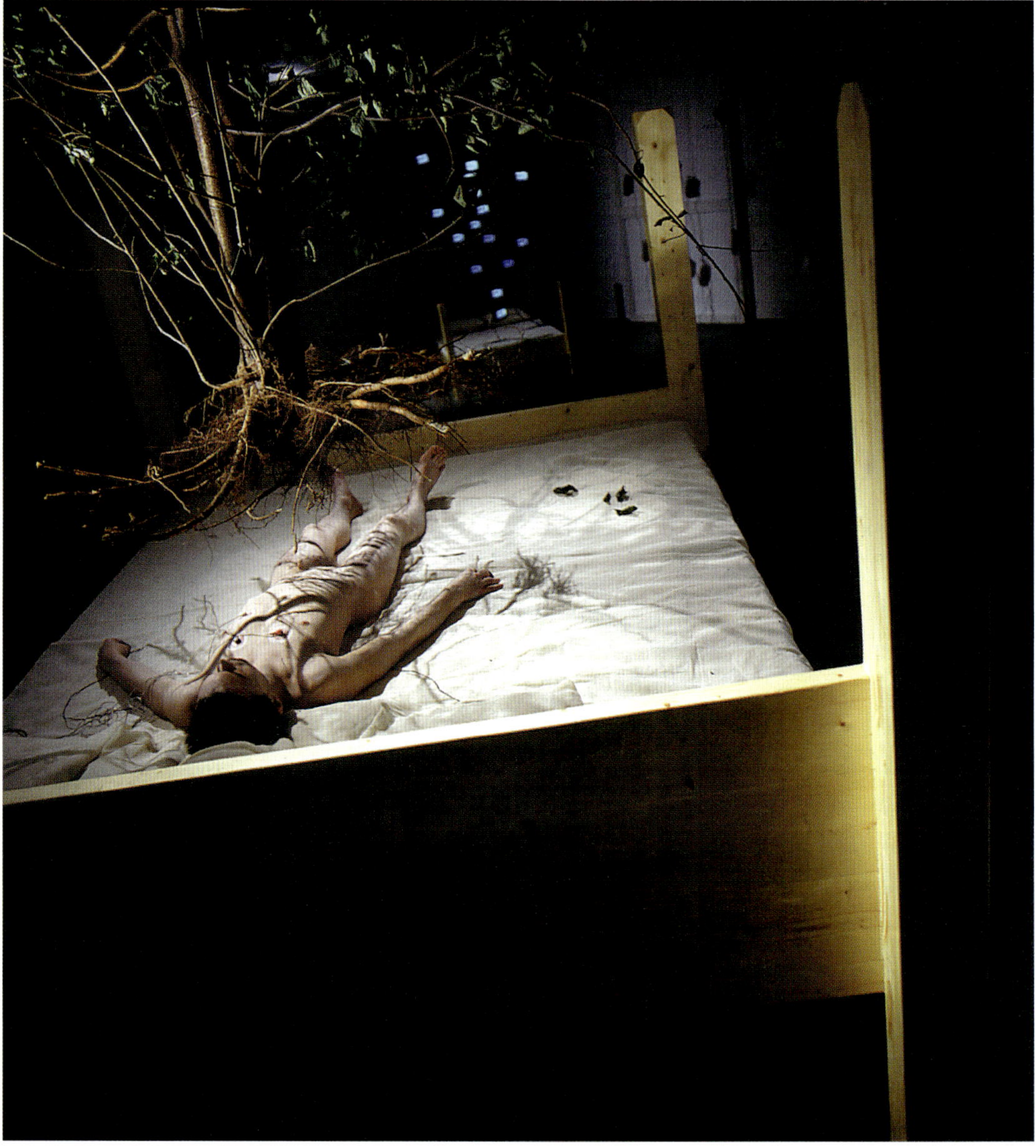

 WOMEN ARTISTS ON THE LEADING EDGE

compelling installation that extends performance and installation art into a complex web of biological and personal meanings. . . . The grounding of the installation is Myers' fascination with nature and the cultural strategies for representing the natural within the human was developed with uncanny insight in this installation.[13]

Resurrection Body (1993) was awarded first prize at the Tenth World-Wide Video Festival in The Hague, the Netherlands. The work was shown in Brazil the following year at the VIDEOBRASIL International Festival. In the catalog, Myers explained, "On March 16, 1993, at 6:30 p.m., my father succumbed finally to a long and dreadful illness. In the waning hours of that day, we waited with him for the moment of his death to arrive. In that single moment his essence vanished. . . . A certitude about the ultimate cohesion between permanent and transition ruptured and escaped."[14]

Myers's work has been exhibited in museums and galleries across the country and internationally. She taught at Douglass College during the spring semester in 1977 and was artist-in-residence at the Mason Gross School of the Arts in 1987. She also taught at Cooper Union and the University of Hartford. In 1983 Rita Myers was recognized as a member of the Douglass Society for Distinguished Achievement.

2.39
Mimi Smith in her studio, 2011.
Photo: Catherine Czacki.

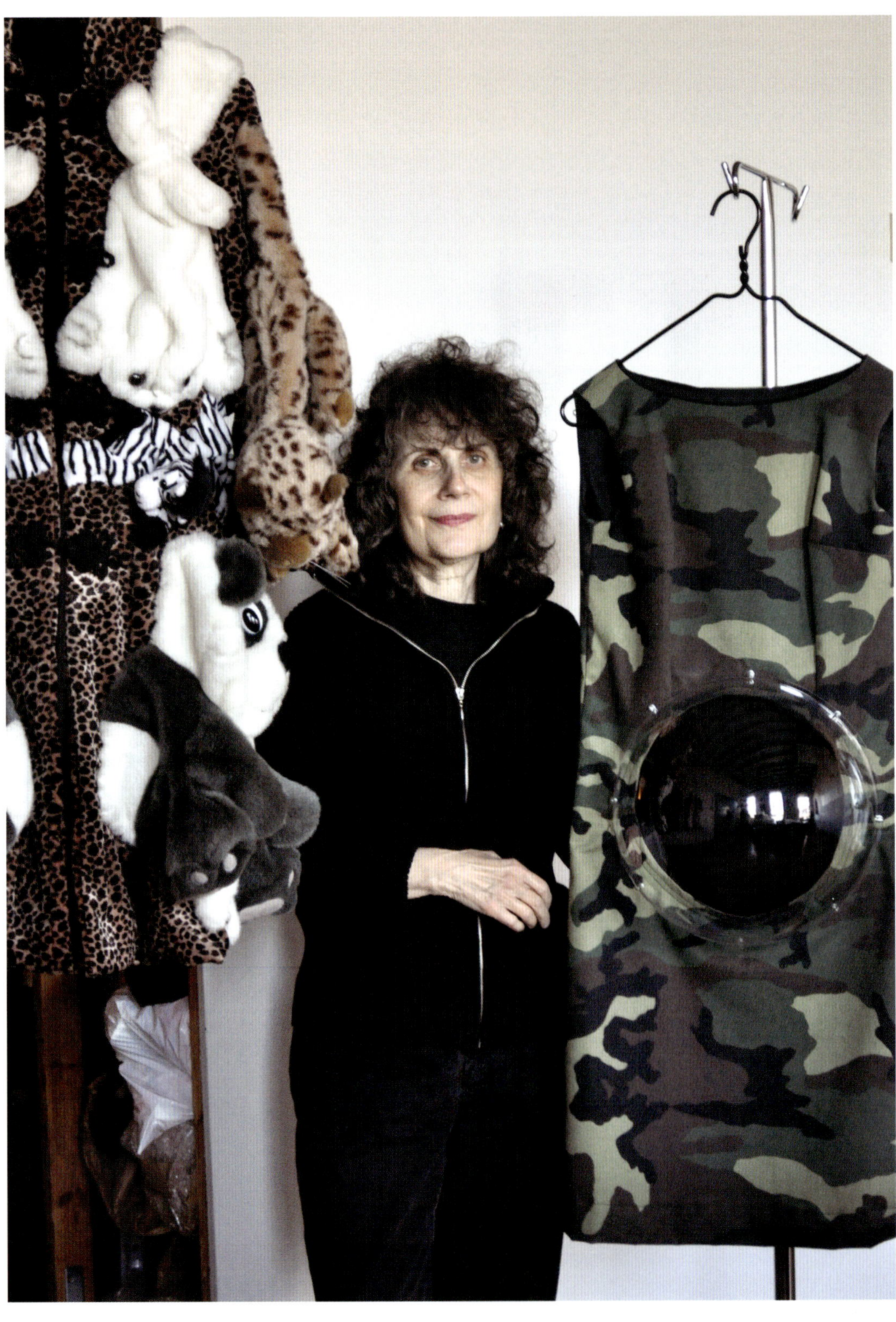

MIMI SMITH

When Mimi Smith emerged in the Pop Art era, she presaged the feminist art movement with her wearable art created from domestic objects. She is a unique, innovative force who came to her artistic maturity just as the dictum about the proximity of "art and life" continued to gain momentum. Smith appropriated the visual rubrics of popular culture and combined Pop imagery and materials with aspects of her personal life.[1] In Smith's production, art did indeed relate to life, but more importantly, to her life—her art is autobiographical. And Mimi Smith's life was that of a young married woman who became pregnant with her first child as she was completing her master of fine arts degree. Smith's projects of the 1960s take their place among the few viable Pop Art objects created by women, while also forecasting feminist art of the 1970s. From the 1960s on, Smith fashioned clothing as an art form and made installations with topical and personal resonance.

At Douglass College, where the Rutgers MFA program was located in the 1960s, Smith had the good fortune to work with instructors who were involved with the burgeoning Pop Art and Fluxus movements. The 1960s was filled with the spirit of Pop Art, and Rutgers was part of this development. Roy Lichtenstein had been on the faculty for three years, beginning in 1960; Allan Kaprow's ideas were a constant presence; and Smith admired works by Claes Oldenburg and Andy Warhol that she saw in New York galleries. From faculty members Robert Watts and Robert Morris, she learned that "anything could be art," and Smith's favored materials became steel wool, plastic bags, fabric, doilies, and tablecloths. She considered the works she fashioned from these nonart materials as avant-garde sculpture at a time when formalism still dictated that art should not have an emotional or personal valence.

Mimi Smith began her art studies at the age of twelve when she attended a Saturday class at the school of the Museum of Fine Arts in Boston. Having learned to sew from her grandmother, she was drawn to costumes installed in the period rooms at the museum.

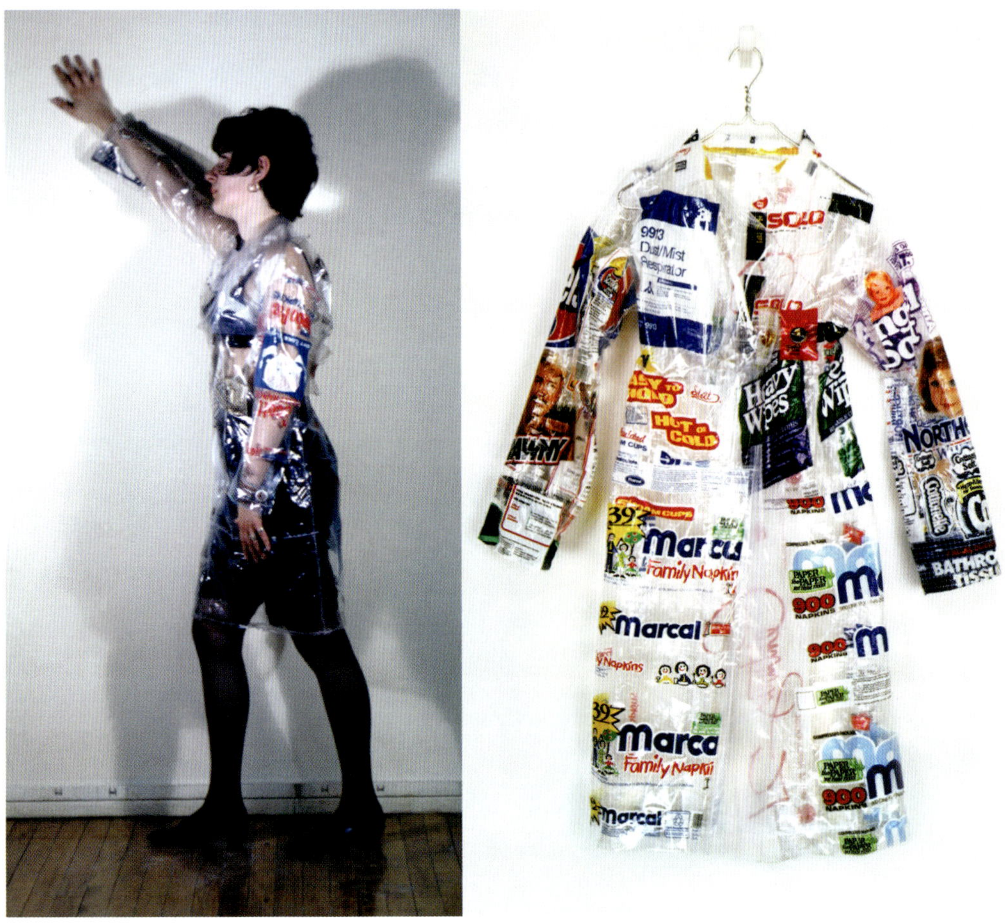

After completing a bachelor of fine arts in painting at the Massachusetts College of Art, she moved to New York City. Smith came to graduate school with skills in crafts and sewing that would become integral to her art production.

Among her earliest works that answered the call for joining popular culture with the personal were *Girdle* and *Recycle Coat*. Using household items, such as rubber bath mats, Smith created *Girdle* (1966), a disturbing, shapeless undergarment with attached garters. Girdles were out of fashion in the 1960s, as women sought less restraint in their apparel. The laces in the front of *Girdle* are reminiscent of the corsets of the past, and the scale of the garment makes the object unwearable. Yet the bathroom references are amusing, and the use of garters alludes to the strictures that women endured to hold up their stockings and appear fashionable. Smith described *Girdle* as "one of the most frightening items of clothing that I can imagine . . . an uncomfortable torture. It doesn't let air in or out."[2] Through her use of mundane products of the home, while referencing "women's work" in the fashioning of her sculpture, Mimi Smith makes a cultural critique of great importance. In 1965 she made her *Recycle Coat*, constructed of plastic bags from everyday products, such as paper napkins and bread; bottle caps were used as buttons. She wore the transparent coat in a photograph made at the time of its creation. For her MFA show in 1966,

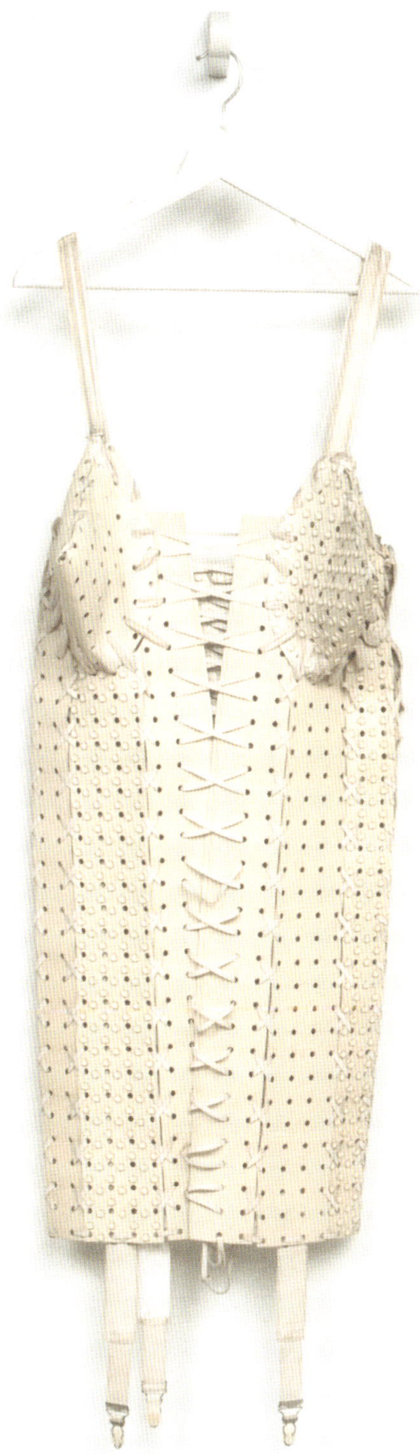

Mimi Smith fashioned a 12- by 12-foot box of plastic sheets for *Wedding* installation. Inside the box she included a transparent gown, plastic flowers, and a thirty-foot train made of plastic carpet runners. Smith noted that the train related to the "woman who would be trod upon and would be endlessly cleaning, cleaning."[3] Before feminist art was seriously defined, Mimi Smith arrived at a protofeminist ideology that was based solely on the desire to connect her art with women's lives.[4] She said, "It was meant to be a giant photo album. You could peak in and see the wedding. Like a frozen event. It was like a lie to me. I had already been married three years."[5]

Mimi Smith resolved to continue making artworks that related to her life as well as a being a barometer of the experiences of women. In the 1970s she introduced life-sized drawings of household interiors and furniture, but fabricated with knotted threads. Commenting on social issues affecting women in the next decade, she created a series of clocks with collaged elements that directly address women's work, poverty, and women's right to choose. Telephones and televisions also appear in this period, alluding to the pervasiveness of new technologies and the increasing invasiveness of the news media. As a feminist, Smith was committed to the issues that face women in American society. As a humanist she focused on the environment, gun violence, threats of nuclear annihilation, the abuse of women, and other causes. Over the next decades, she expanded her oeuvre to include sculptural installations and drawings.

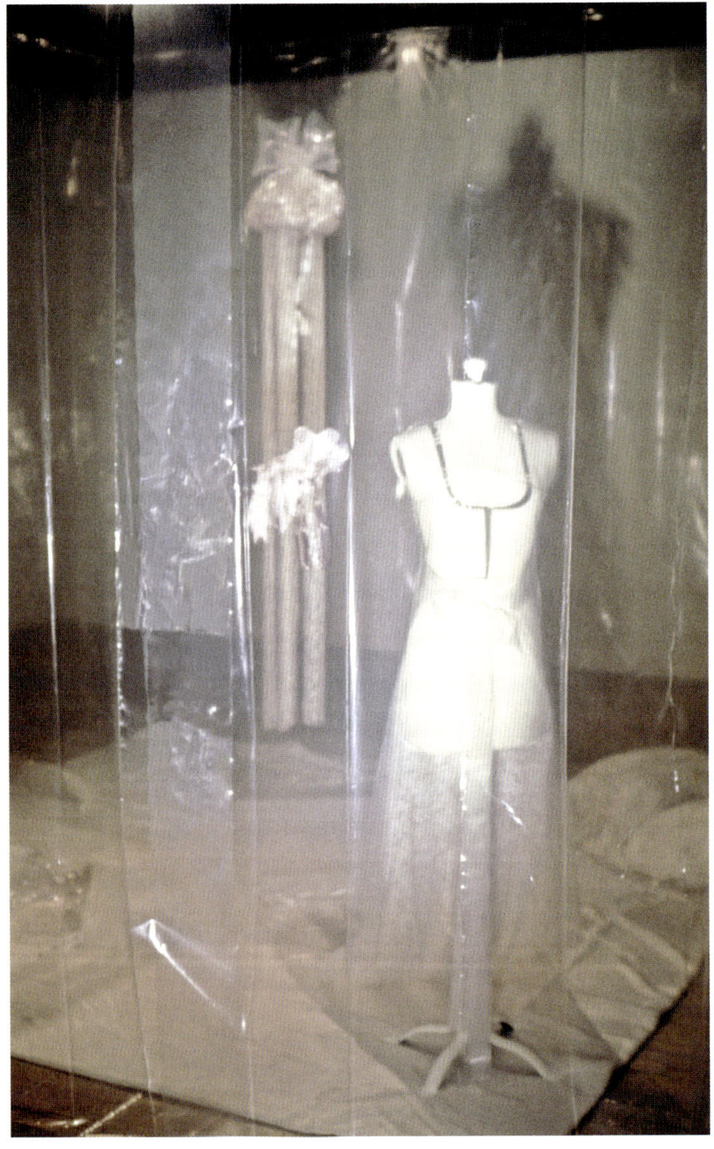

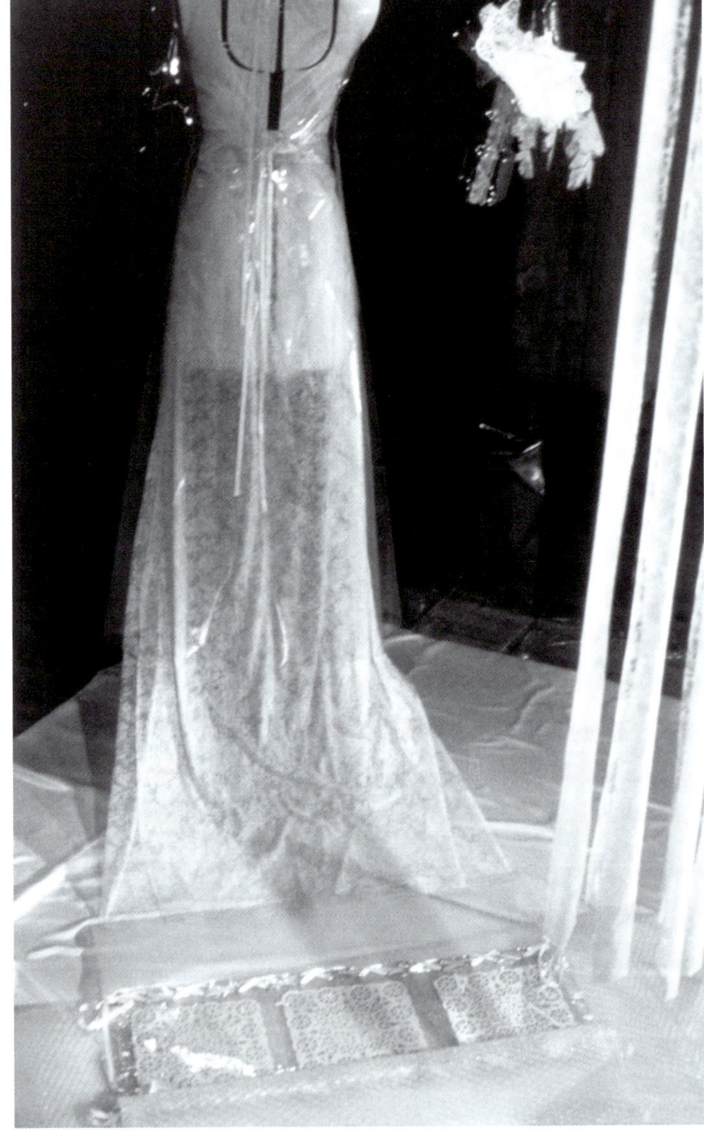

   WOMEN ARTISTS ON THE LEADING EDGE

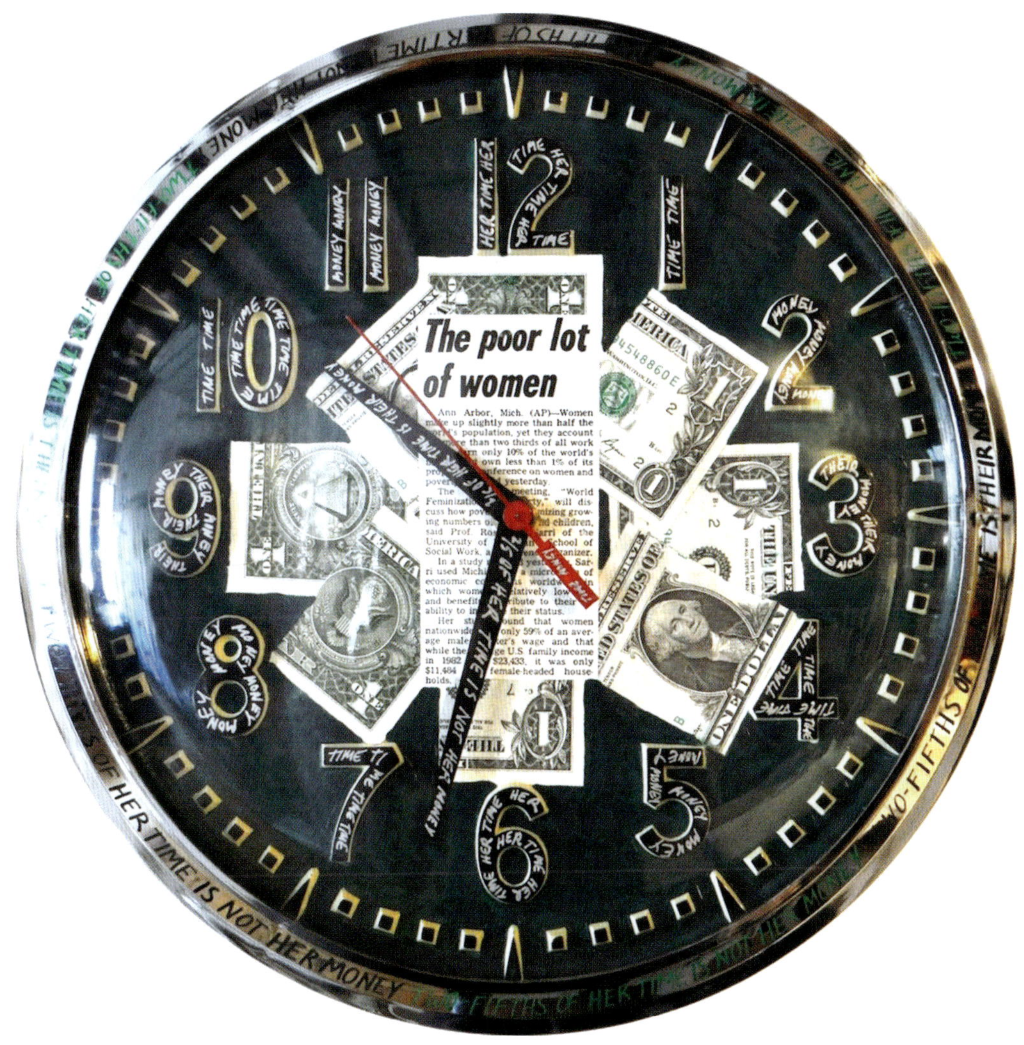

Certain themes related to gender recur in Smith's art, such as protecting a woman's rights. For example, almost four decades after creating the 1966 *Maternity Dress*, which features a transparent dome in plastic that would highlight the expanding belly of the mother-to-be, she made *Camouflage Maternity Dress* (2004). The earlier *Maternity Dress* related to her experience of pregnancy, and her desire to see the baby grow.[6] By transforming her garment into a material associated with the military, is Smith commenting on the difficulties pregnant women face if they are military personnel? In addition to the difficulties of pregnancy in combat zones, women can be threatened with discharge and denial of benefits. In the business world, Smith identifies the ongoing situation for women with regard to working conditions and equal pay in *Her Time, Their Money* (1986). Smith has also commented on gun violence as a threat to women.

In recent years, Smith has continued to explore the personal and the political in her art. Her new works acknowledge that she is advancing into another age group, with drawings and objects that document the changes in wardrobe for a middle-aged woman. In the

"Timeline" series begun in 2000 to the present, shoes become more serviceable, underwear changes from skimpy to large, and there is a renewed focus on age disparities. Now, too, there are grandchildren to consider, and in *Flower* (2010), for example, Smith created a child's dress and placed it inside a green cage. Like a plant carefully nurtured and then secured within an enclosure from outside interference, Smith wonders about the safety of our young as terrorism threatens.

Among Mimi Smith's innovations are the creation of clothing items that embody both form and content. She anticipated the involvement with clothing as an art form as practiced by a number of feminists. Reflecting the uncertainties of contemporary life, Mimi Smith seeks to remind us that women continue to struggle for agency and parity with their male counterparts.

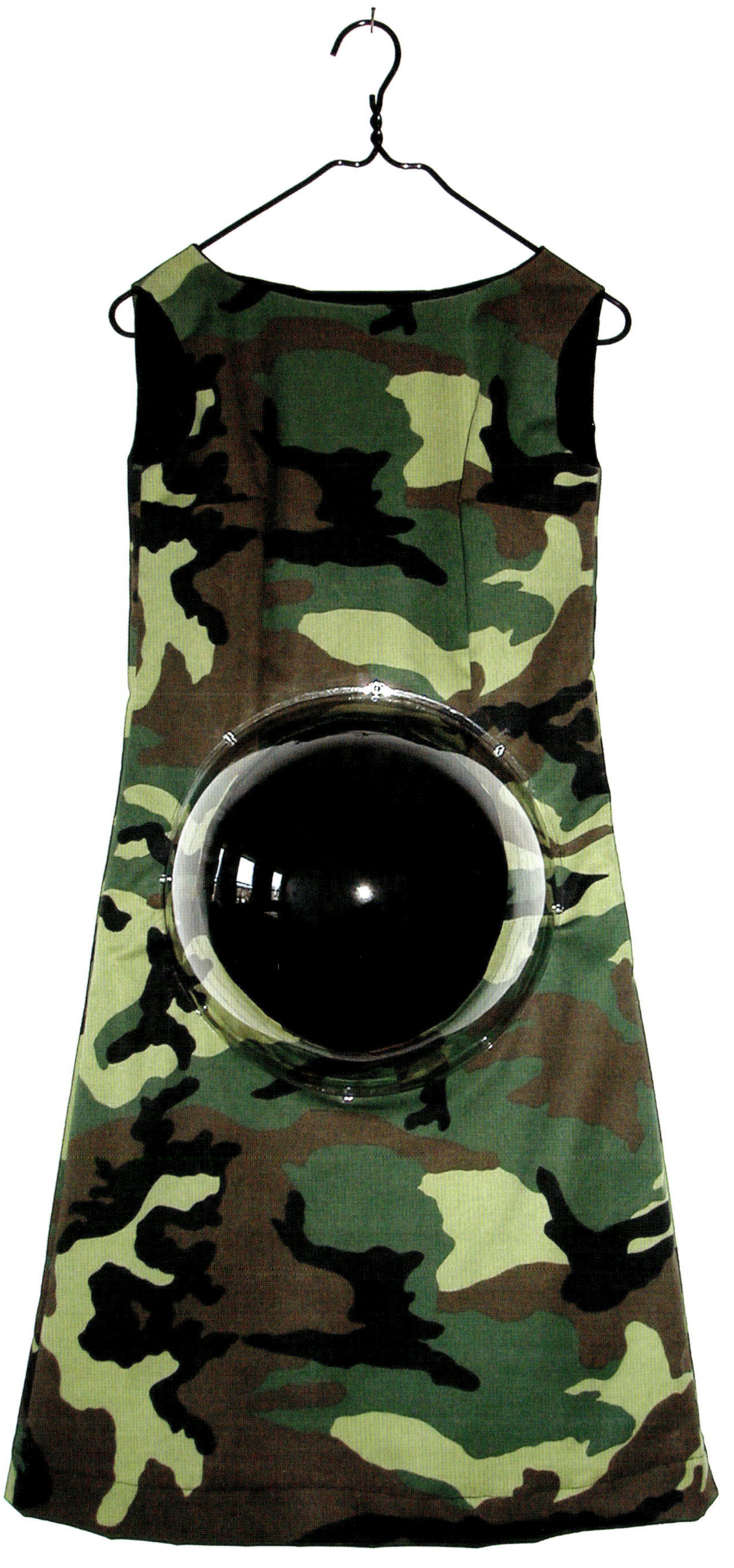

MIMI SMITH

91

2.46
Joan Snyder in print studio, 2016.
Photo: Jennifer Marshall.

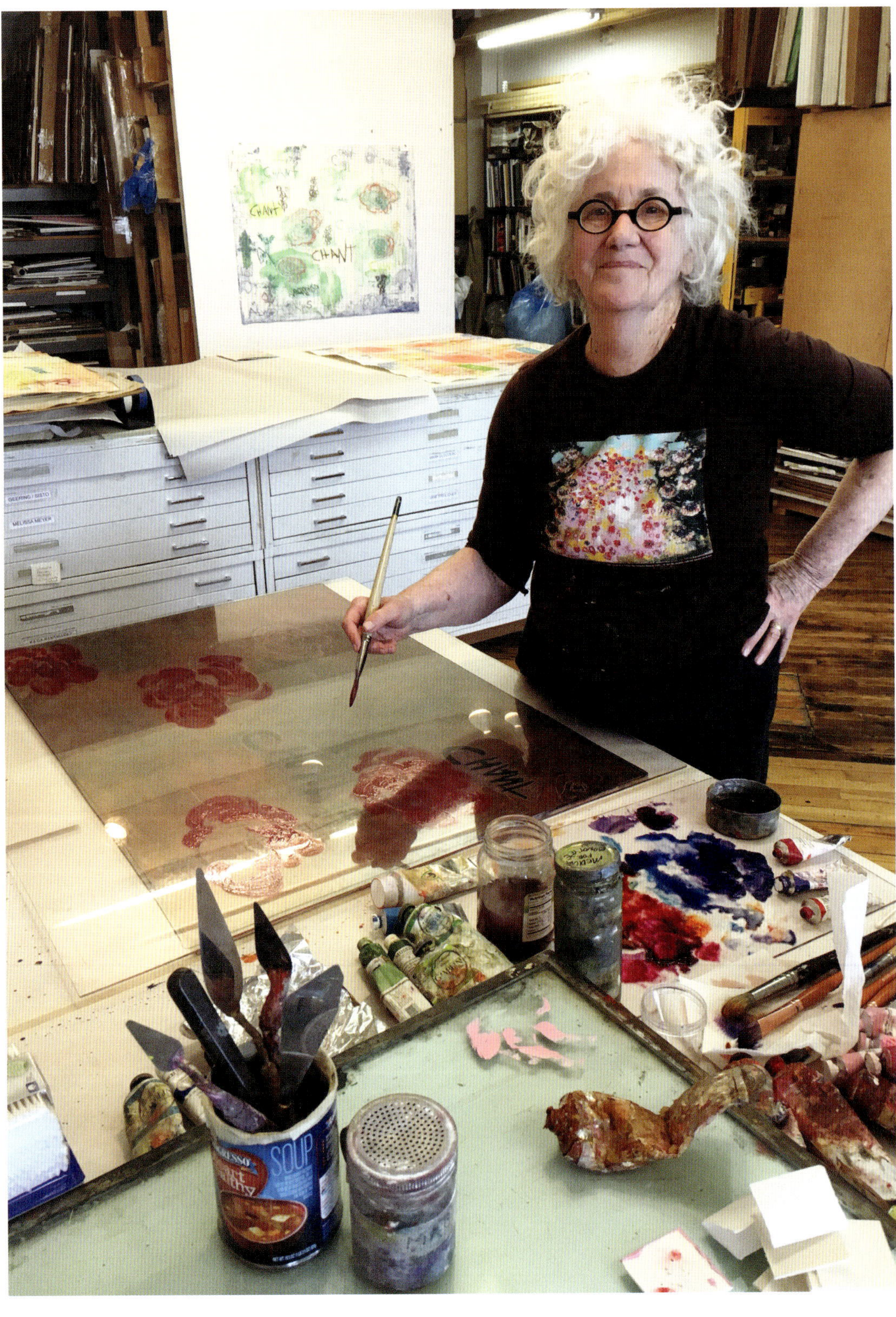

JOAN SNYDER

Sometimes I am sure I know what my work is about—at other times it is a mystery to me. I am happy when I am working and understanding. My work is a language I create—coming from somewhere in my guts, brains, eyes. It is about different things—each painting is different and the same. It's about life and art—my life, my art, other lives, other art. What else can I say?
—JOAN SNYDER, 1974

Joan Snyder made a unique contribution to Douglass College and to gaining recognition for women artists. Through her provocative paintings, drawings, and prints, and the extraordinary legacy of the Women Artists Series, Snyder has been a stellar member of the Douglass alumnae. Acknowledging the centennial year, Snyder noted, "As for Douglass College, I love that it has become such a vibrant and diverse campus."[1]

Joan Snyder was born on April 16, 1940, to parents of Russian/German/Jewish heritage. She grew up in Highland Park, New Jersey, near the Douglass campus. Since both of her parents worked, there were always chores to do at 512 South Second Avenue, and her maternal grandmother, Dora Cohen, was a great comfort during her childhood and teenage years. Snyder attended public schools in Highland Park, and learned to paint by copying reproductions from magazines. While she was in high school, before taking any art instruction, she made portraits of family and friends and was astonished to create a likeness.

In the fall of 1958, Snyder enrolled at Douglass College. She continued to live at home during her undergraduate years. Inspired by the sociology courses taught by Professor Emily Alman, Snyder became a sociology major and envisioned a career as a social worker. She had wanted to study anthropology, but that curriculum was not offered at Douglass.

In her senior year Snyder enrolled in her first art course. Billy Pritchard, an African American artist and educator, was impressed with her work and encouraged her to continue.

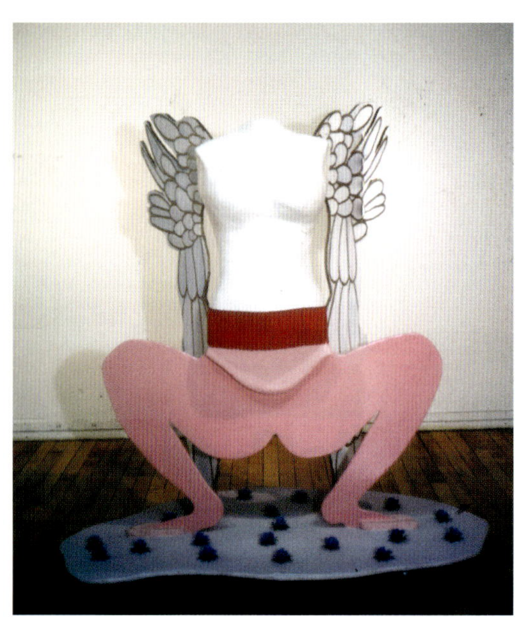

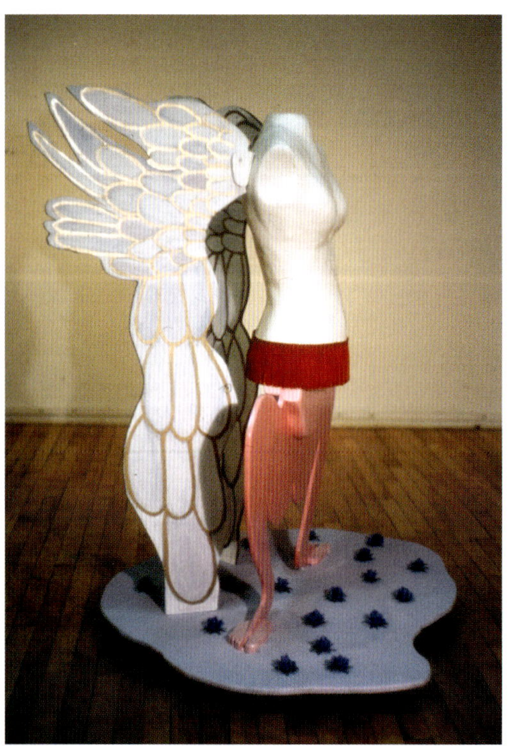

Snyder credits Pritchard as the person who made a huge impact on the direction of her career.[2] After seeing a portrait that Snyder made of her brother, Pritchard recognized a strong expressionist sensibility and showed her reproductions of works by Alexei Jawlensky and the German Expressionists. Snyder was amazed that she had found a way to "talk about my feelings." Her earliest paintings and woodcuts show a connection with these German Expressionists; she had found a direction for her work.

After graduating from Douglass in 1962 with an AB in sociology, she worked at a summer camp, where she met Jona Mach, an Israeli painter, who urged her to continue making art. The following year Snyder rented space for a studio in New Brunswick at the Middlesex Marina on the Raritan River. Feeling ready to leave home, she arranged to live with Emily Alman and her family in Englishtown, New Jersey. Professor Alman had been an important mentor, and their friendship would last for many years.

Rutgers was developing a new MFA program, and in the fall of 1963 Snyder applied. With little formal art training and no courses in art history, she was admitted as a nonmatriculated student and given a chance to prove herself. Mark Berger, who taught art history, encouraged her artistic development. She discovered such artists as Wassily Kandinsky, Paul Klee, Emil Nolde, and Maurice de Vlaminck. Hans Hofmann, who had come to the United States and was an important teacher to some of the Abstract Expressionists, also attracted her interest. She began to make prints, using the facilities at Douglass College. Some of these works on paper were woodcuts of people that she knew, including Jenny, a daughter of the Almans.

In the fall of 1964, Joan Snyder was officially admitted to the MFA program. She found the experience "nurturing" because of her fellow students, who were "amazing" people, working very hard. Among them were Jackie Winsor and Keith Sonnier. "We were all supportive of each other. Seriously it was really an amazing atmosphere. For me, it wasn't because of any faculty members."[3] Even so, she added that Mark Berger was "one of the most important teachers I had. He was the adviser for the thesis course."[4]

She recalls a sculpture she made in Robert Morris's class of an angel with a plaster torso, fringe around the waist, pink plywood legs, and purple plastic roses. "Everyone in the class was making little gray boxes."[5] "I took Morris's silly minimal boxes and made them as crazy and decorative as I could. I put a breast in them, [had] things hanging off them, boxes in landscapes, trees and grass in boxes, pieces of bodies in a box under the ground."[6] For her MFA thesis Snyder created *Angel*, a mixed-media sculpture that included plaster, fringe, plastic flowers, and wheels. She related this life-sized crouching nude female with wings to an altar. In her thesis she wrote, "On a very individual level, there is within each person an altar upon which rests a hierarchy of values, powers, loves, needs. A sort of inner temple to which we are constantly adding and subtracting parts of the landscape from around and outside."[7]

Snyder completed the MFA degree in May 1966 and continued to live on George Street in New Brunswick until the following year, when she moved to New York City. She shared a rented factory building on Mulberry Street with fellow MFA graduates Jackie Winsor, Keith Sonnier, and Mark Berger, her art history professor from Douglass College. She met Larry Fink in 1968 and credits his involvement with classical music and jazz with her attraction to music as structure and emotion. Often her titles for paintings and prints had allusions to music. They were married in October 1969.

This year was important because she reached a personal breakthrough in her art by introducing a series of "stroke paintings." Painterly surfaces and a vivid palette were combined with the structural grid. *Lines and Strokes* (1969) features Snyder's attempt to use a horizontal grid. The strokes of luminous pigment are close to 50 inches wide. She told an interviewer,

> When I started doing the stroke paintings in 1969 I suddenly discovered that paint and marks could be subject matter. . . . I was on a very sophisticated journey into abstract art. . . . What I wanted to do in the stroke paintings was to have a painting that was not only multilayered, but that also had a beginning, middle, and end. A lament, a resolution. . . . Some have very sensuous feelings, also longing, grief, joy.

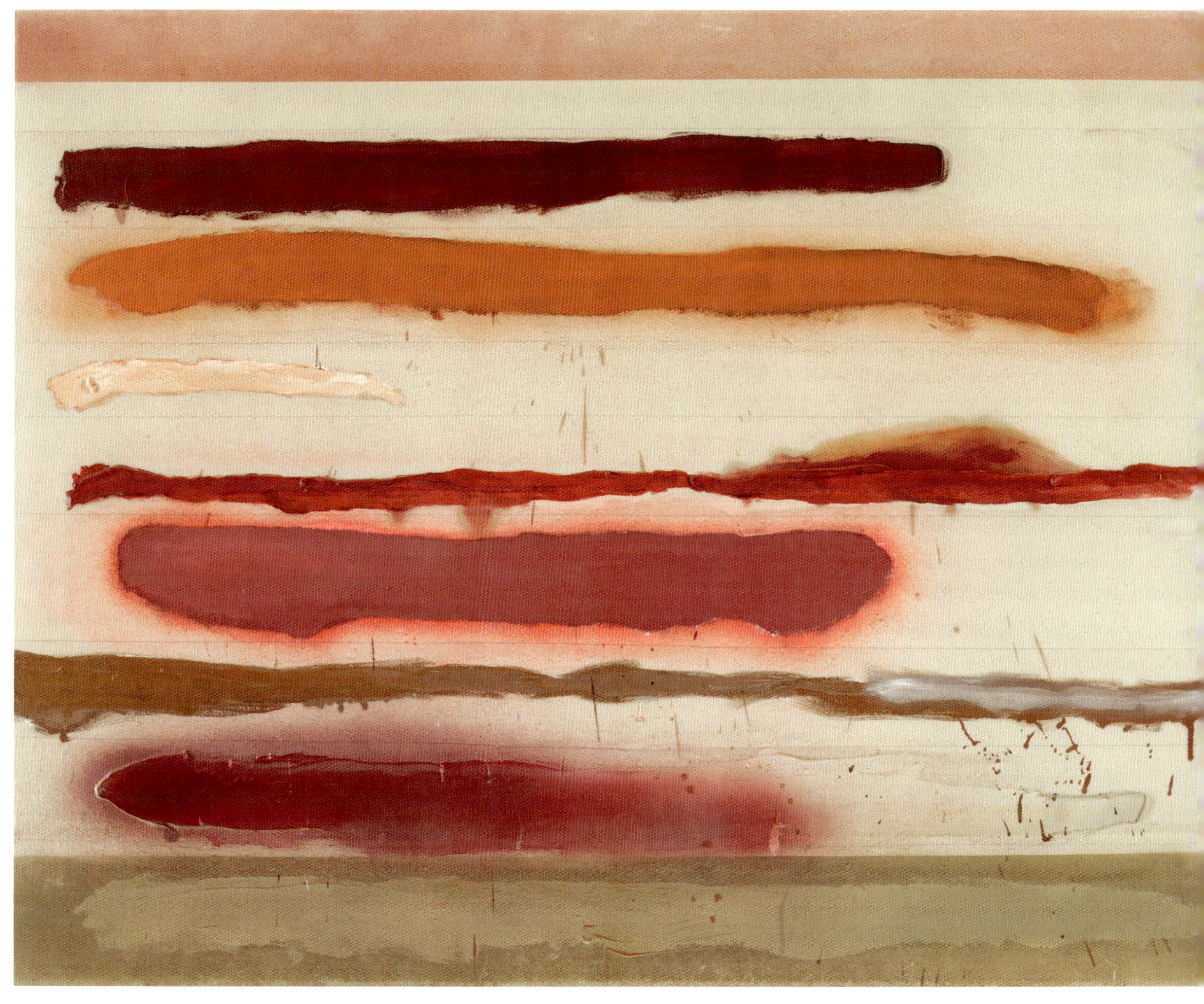

Even though I was going deep into myself about things that were painful for me, there was a lot of optimism in those works.[8]

Lines and Strokes is based on a horizontal grid, and includes bands of color of varying dimensions. Pencil marks are visible and indicate the process involved in the creation of the work. Snyder would continue to include marks, even words, in her future paintings. In this work, luminous bands of color result from variations of media—she used oil paint, acrylic, and spray-on enamel for the broad strokes of color.

Having produced a body of work in this new mode, she had the first solo exhibition of her new paintings at New York's Paley and Lowe Gallery in 1971. This show was a critical

　　　　WOMEN ARTISTS ON THE LEADING EDGE

success, and all of the paintings sold. Among the important collectors who made a purchase was Vera List.

Soon, however, Snyder's involvement with the women's movement would steer a steady direction in her art, and it would keep her connected to Douglass College. From 1971 to 1974 she was involved in a consciousness-raising group that met on the Douglass campus. She attempted to introduce a feminist sensibility into her work.

She joined the dialogue among feminists about a "female aesthetic." Snyder noted the following: "Female sensibility is layers, words, membranes, cotton, cloth, rope, repetition, bodies, wet, opening, closing, repetition, lists, lifestones, grids, destroying them, houses, intimacy, doorways, breasts, vaginas, strong, building, putting together many disparaging elements, repetition, red pin, black . . . stuffing, sewing, fluffing, satin, hearts, tearing, typing, decorating . . . seeing through the layers."[9]

In 1971, with the support of the head librarian, Daisy Brightenback, Snyder initiated the Women Artists Series in the Mabel Smith Douglass Library. At a time when no women were teaching in the visual arts program at Douglass, this series was created to provide opportunities for students to see the work of women artists. She noted in the first year of the series: "Women had been an almost untapped source in the creative arts. . . . We find emerging a new strength, a new vocabulary. . . . Women are emerging from history because history needs them to show the way to peace and the way to another kind of strength and reflection."[10] Initially Snyder was the curator of the series, but in subsequent years, other women on the library staff administered the exhibitions, while a jury of women faculty selected the artists to be included.

Snyder participated in many group exhibitions in New York during the early 1970s. In February 1971 she was included in a group show at Bykert Gallery. In 1973 she exhibited in *Women Choose Women*, a pioneering feminist show at the New York Cultural Center. This idea of women selecting the work of other women had been the underlying principle initiating the Women Artists Series at Douglass College.

Notable changes in her painting were the addition of writing that became an outlet for her need to communicate personal concerns. In October 1974 Snyder began work on a triptych entitled *Small Symphony for Women*.

Inspired in part by a program connected with the Women Artists Series that she had arranged, she commented in a handwritten list on a "female sensibility." But more

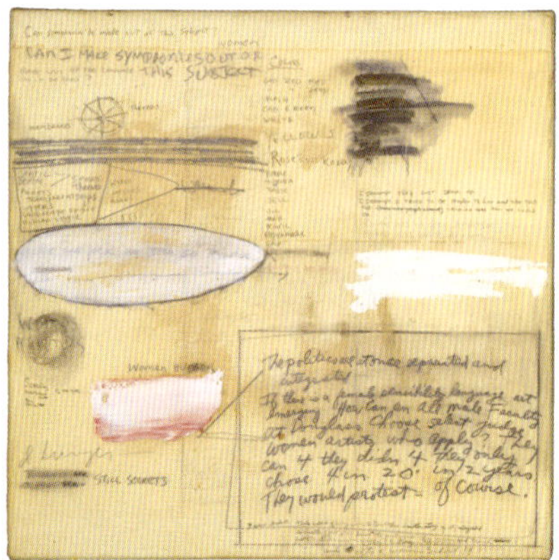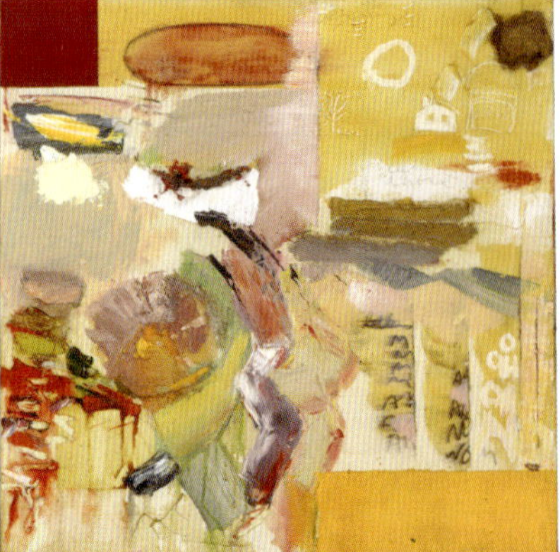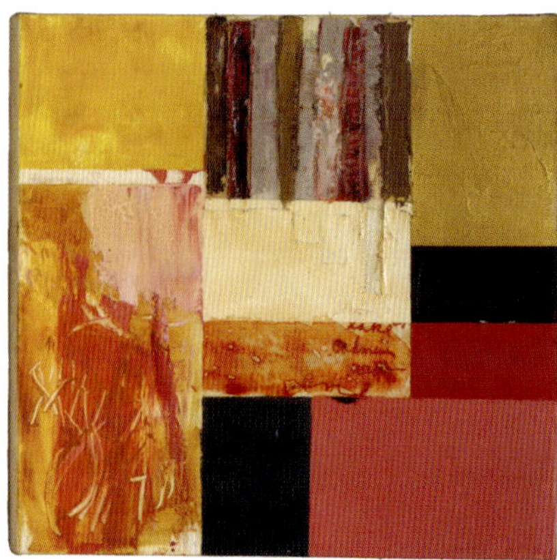

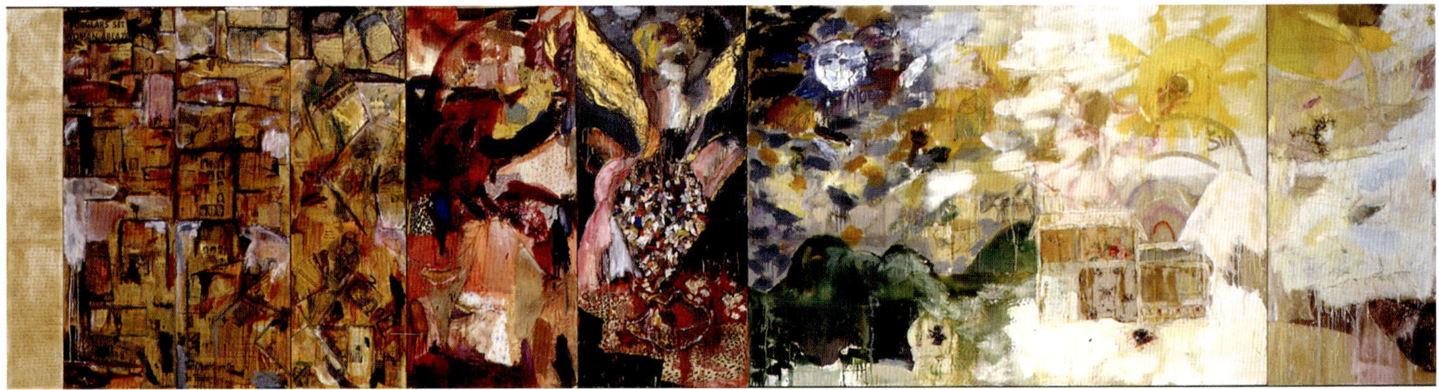

explosive commentary was her handwritten commentary on Douglass College and its all-male faculty. On one of the panels she wrote:

> Can I make Symphonies of this subject. . . . If there is a female sensibility, language, art emerging. How can an all male faculty at Douglass choose select judge women artists who apply? They can't they didn't they only chose 4 in 20 in 2 years. They would protest, of course.

Joan Snyder was a founding member *of Heresies*, a feminist collective and participated in the first issue in 1977. Members of the collective met regularly to determine future themes for issues. At the time Snyder was teaching an advanced painting course at Princeton University and had begun work on a major painting in her Martin's Creek studio.

The 26-foot work, *Resurrection*, was created using oil, acrylic, fabric, wallpaper, newspaper, and tissue paper. Comprising eight panels, the painting was inspired by Snyder's collection of newspaper articles about rape and murder victims. This painting became her "epic" feminist statement of the decade, with references to violence against women. This monumental painting features her remarkable choice of materials to convey a profound statement about women.

Events of Snyder's life, such as the birth of her daughter in 1979, found expression in her use of Jungian symbols, and images derived from nature. Her imagery often included autobiographical references. Words combined with shapes were meant to allude to herself and to elicit an awareness of her personal experiences. Her ultimate goal was to focus on the lives of women as political, sexual, and creative beings.

In 1991, the twentieth anniversary of the Women Artists Series (renamed the Mary H. Dana Women Artists Series in 1987) was celebrated at Douglass College. In an essay for the Rutgers University Libraries journal, Snyder celebrated the women of the Series:

> I believe that women artists pumped the blood back into the art movement in the 1970s and 1980s. At the height of the Pop and Minimal movements, we were making other art—art that was personal, autobiographic, expressionistic, narrative, and poetical—using words and photographs and as many other materials as we could get our hands on. This was called Feminist Art. This was [what] the art of the 1980s was finally about, appropriated by the most famous male artists of the decade. They called it neo-expressionist. It wasn't neo to us. They were called heroic by bringing expression and the personal to their art. We were called Feminist (which was, of course, a dirty word).[11]

The Mabel Smith Douglass Library proudly displays *Our Foremothers* (1995) by Joan Snyder, a print commissioned by the Jewish Museum in New York City. This color lithograph, etching, and woodcut includes the names of every women mentioned in the Old Testament, Jewish and non-Jewish women alike. The names, in varying colors, are presented in a random, nonhierarchical composition that seems to resemble a wall covered with graffiti. Snyder described her motivation for the work: "I would say this is a feminist piece (made by a feminist, a Jew, and an American). The histories of the woman in the Bible were nothing if not those of women ferociously pioneering for the rights of females."[12]

Snyder has never stopped making art. In 2007 she was awarded a John D. and Catherine T. MacArthur Foundation Fellowship. She has also maintained her connection with Douglass and Rutgers. Early in 2010 she began a collaboration with Anne Z. McKeown, master papermaker at the Brodsky Center for Innovative Editions at Rutgers. She produced a first series of paintings created from pigmented paper pulp. Her art is represented in museum collections, such as the Museum of Modern Art, New York; the Museum of Fine Arts, Boston; the Metropolitan Museum of Art; and the National Museum of Women in the Arts.

Joan Snyder founded the Women Artists Series at Douglass College in 1971, before any of the feminist exhibitions and projects arose on the West Coast. Since then (now as the Mary H. Dana Women Artist Series) it continues. Snyder recently reflected on the Series: "I like the idea that it is still going on, still being taken seriously, still a living thing. There is a glass ceiling in the art world that gets splintered only occasionally and slowly . . . but it remains. I experience it and it's tough for me and I know how hard it is for other women artists as well.[13]

2.51

Joan Snyder. *Our Foremothers*, 1995.

Color lithograph, etching, and woodcut,

24" × 34". Courtesy of the artist.

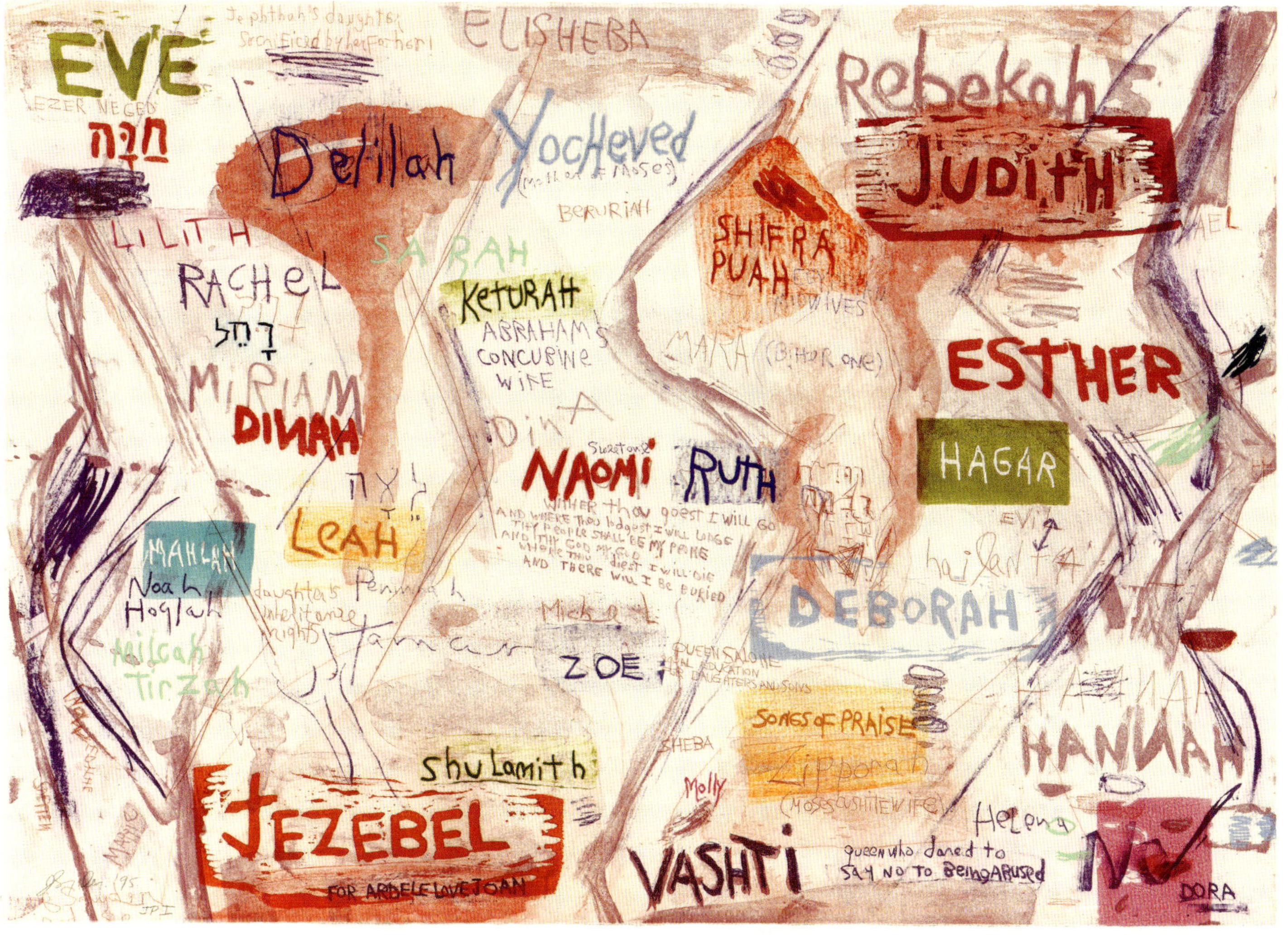

2.52
Ann Tsubota, 2018. Photo: Bill Macholdt.

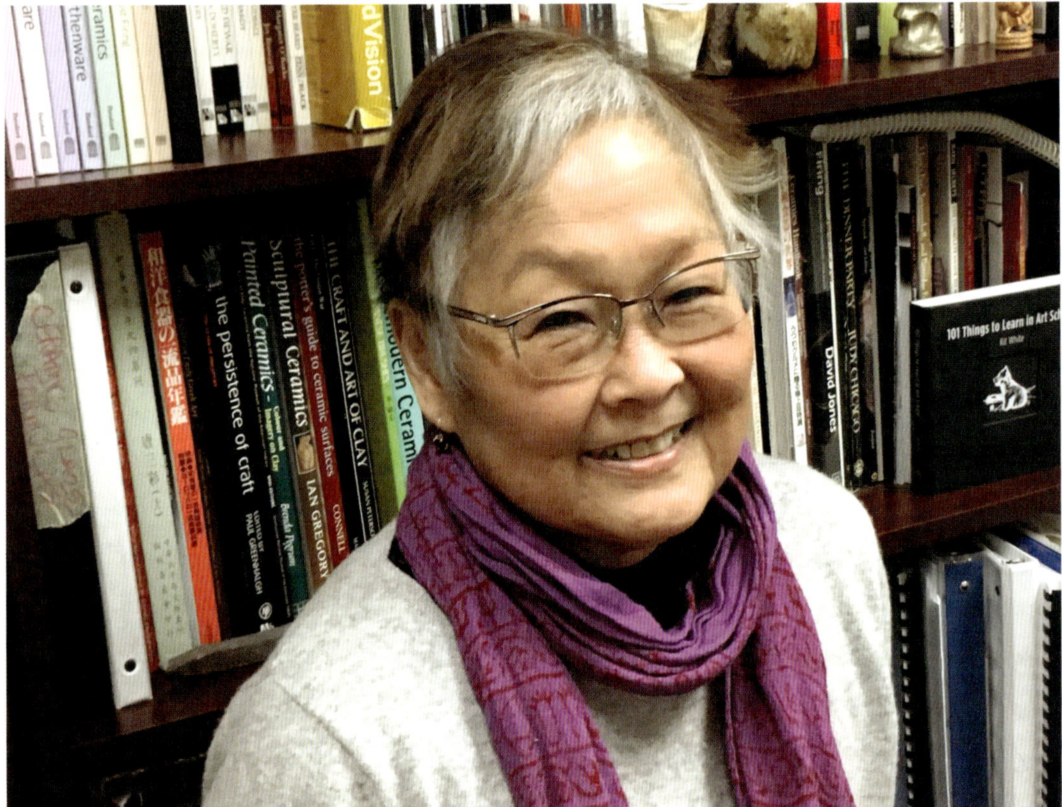

ANN TSUBOTA

Ann Naoko Tsubota was born in St. Paul, Minnesota, and lived abroad in Germany and Japan before coming to New Jersey for study. She came to Douglass College in 1963. She returned to Rutgers in 1972 to pursue the MFA after working at New York's Baldwin Pottery School for two years, beginning in 1968, and at Greenwich House of Pottery in 1969. She taught at Livingston College from 1970 to 1972, and at Douglass from 1972 to 1975. During the summer of 1973 Tsubota studied at the University of Hawaii. She completed the MFA in 1974. After teaching at Rider College and Middlesex County College, Tsubota taught at Raritan Valley Community College as an adjunct until 1979, when she was made a full-time instructor. In 1985 she became the chairperson of the Visual and Performing Arts Department, a position she held until 2002 and again from 2008 to 2014. She has been head of the ceramics program since 1979. In addition she taught the Portfolio Development course for the past twenty years.

Initially Tsubota majored in history, and then in American Studies.[1] She found Douglass very competitive, particularly in the history department. It was "admirable" that all of these women students were so smart.[2] There were virtually no women teachers. She took three or four art history courses with Mark Berger and noticed that there were no women on the art faculty. Ka Kwong Hui became her primary mentor, when she became deeply interested in ceramic sculpture. While she was an undergraduate, Tsubota was aware of the link between the philosophy of Black Mountain College, and certain faculty at Douglass, such as Robert Watts and Geoff Hendricks. Aside from similar interests in ceramics, both Black Mountain and Rutgers faculty explored connections between art and life. At Douglass, Tsubota learned a conceptual basis of art practice based on ideas of John Cage, Allan Kaprow, Claes Oldenburg, and Peter Voulkos, among others.[3] By the time she was a graduate student at Rutgers,

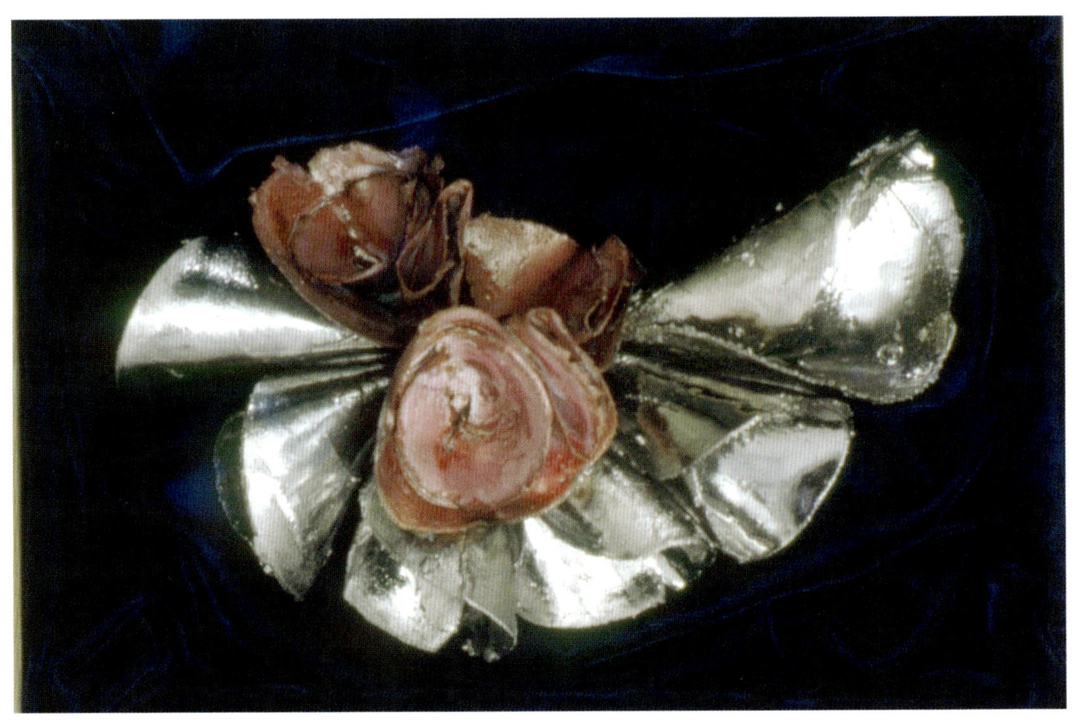

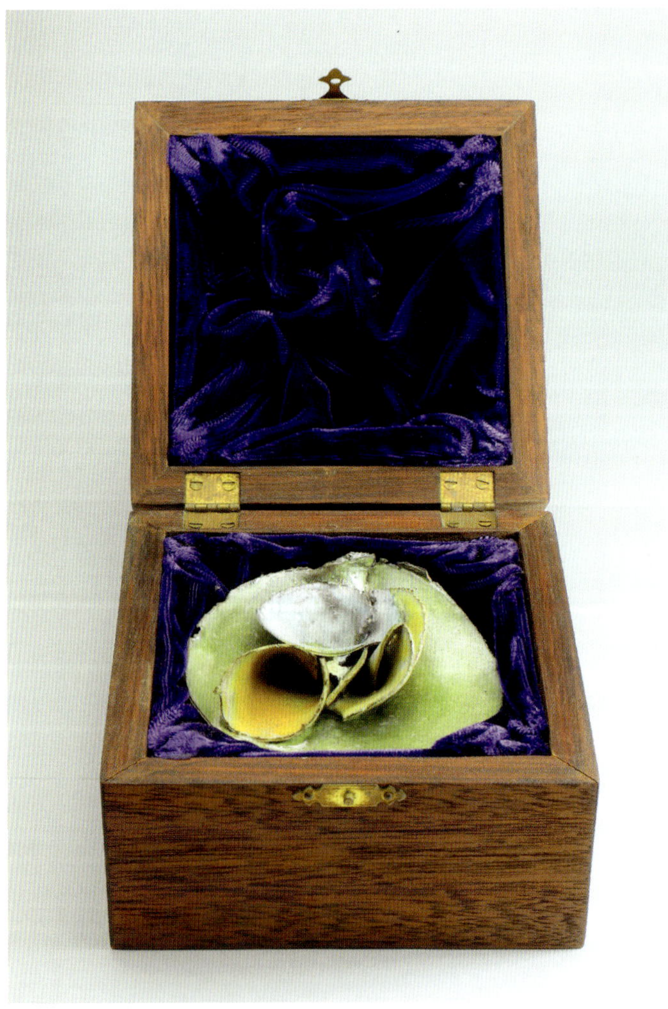

  WOMEN ARTISTS ON THE LEADING EDGE

she had determined to push the boundaries of clay as a medium, and to make connections with the everyday world.

Tsubota continues to work in ceramics. Her major work is sculptural in nature. She is constantly challenging the limits associated with creating sculptures in clay. As a result, her sculptures are innovative and defiant. She challenges the function of clay by expanding its limitations.[4] Using traditional Japanese raku, Tsubota has made works that seem connected to Surrealism or Dada.

As an MFA student Ann Tsubota continued her study with Ka Kwong Hui. She was also in class with Joan Snyder and Jackie Winsor. Tsubota recalls that she studied with Gary Kuehn and Peter Stroud. Other MFA students were sculptors, painters, and photographers. For her, the importance of John Cage, and Robert Rauschenberg, remained dominant. Her MFA thesis project in 1974 featured thin sheets of clay formed into floral arrangements. Some examples could be related to flowers in seventeenth-century paintings from Holland or Victorian jewelry.[5] Her thesis had to do with making these sculptural ceramics and connecting these works with imagery of jewelry or costumes and accessories for women.[6] Sculptor Gary Kuehn became one of her instructors who critiqued her work effectively and "understood what clay was about."[7]

From her graduate school study, Tsubota created objects in porcelain, and used various glazes. Some of these pieces were presented in small boxes, and resemble miniature floral arrangements. Subsequent works became more varied in materials and methods.[8] *Song of the South* (2009) is an exquisitely colorful work in high-fired porcelain with overglaze painting. *Shelter* (2017) exemplifies the direction of her current work using porcelain and other materials to form a series of objects.

Tsubota has devoted herself to her work and to teaching ceramics for decades. From 1994 to the present, she has been involved in raku workshops as a demonstrator and workshop leader around the United States. She has received awards and a fellowship from the New Jersey State Council on the Arts. Her works have been shown at galleries in New York City and New Jersey, and she had a solo exhibition at Douglass College in 1975. Tsubota's ceramics have been included in hundreds of group exhibitions in the past forty years. Her ceramics are in the collection of the Zimmerli Art Museum, Rutgers, and various corporate collections, including Fuji Television Corporation in New York, and Johnson & Johnson in New Brunswick. Ann Tsubota is represented by Sara Gallery and Azuma Gallery in New York City.

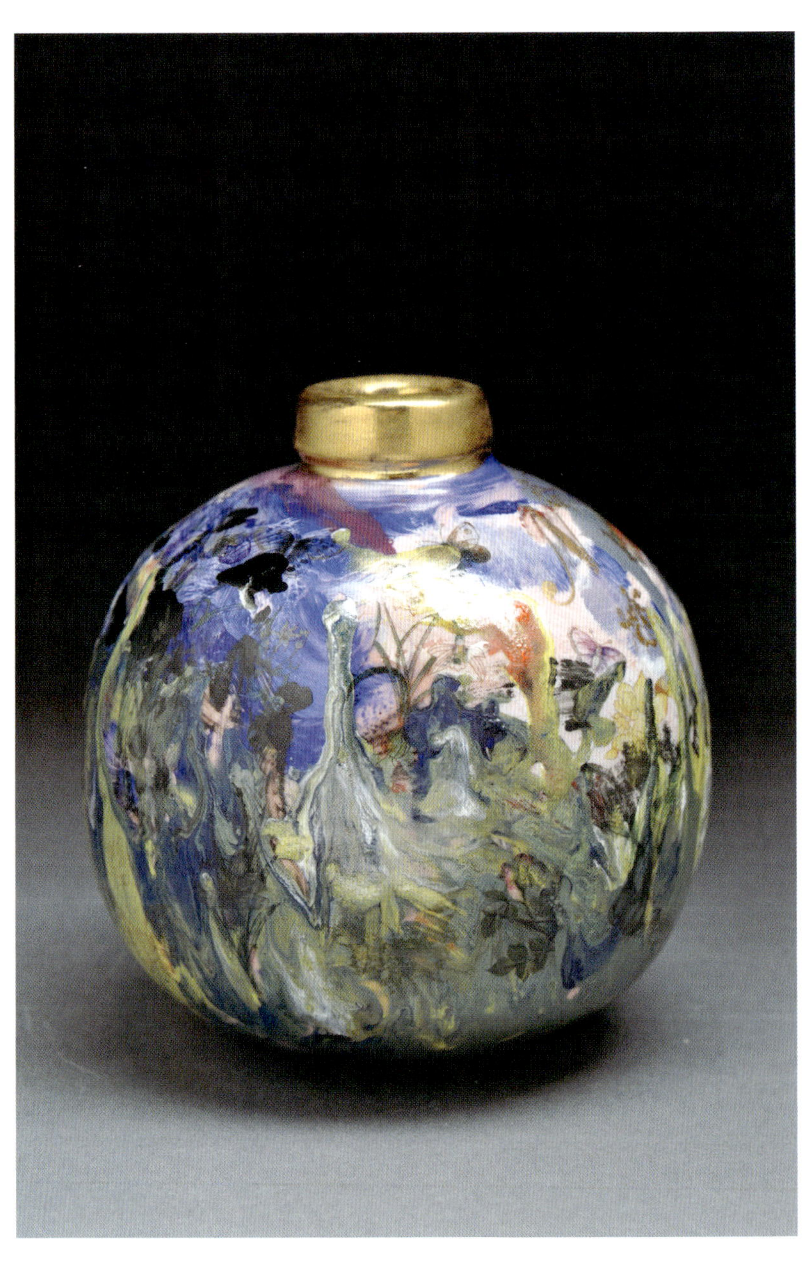

2.55
Ann Tsubota. *Song of the South*, 2009.
Porcelain with multifiring, high-fired
porcelain, overglaze painting, gold luster,
4˝ × 3.5˝ Photo: Craig Phillips.

2.56
Ann Tsubota. *Shelter*, 2017. Porcelain,
soda/wood high fired, each house
6˝ h × 4˝ w × 3˝. Photo: Craig Philiips.

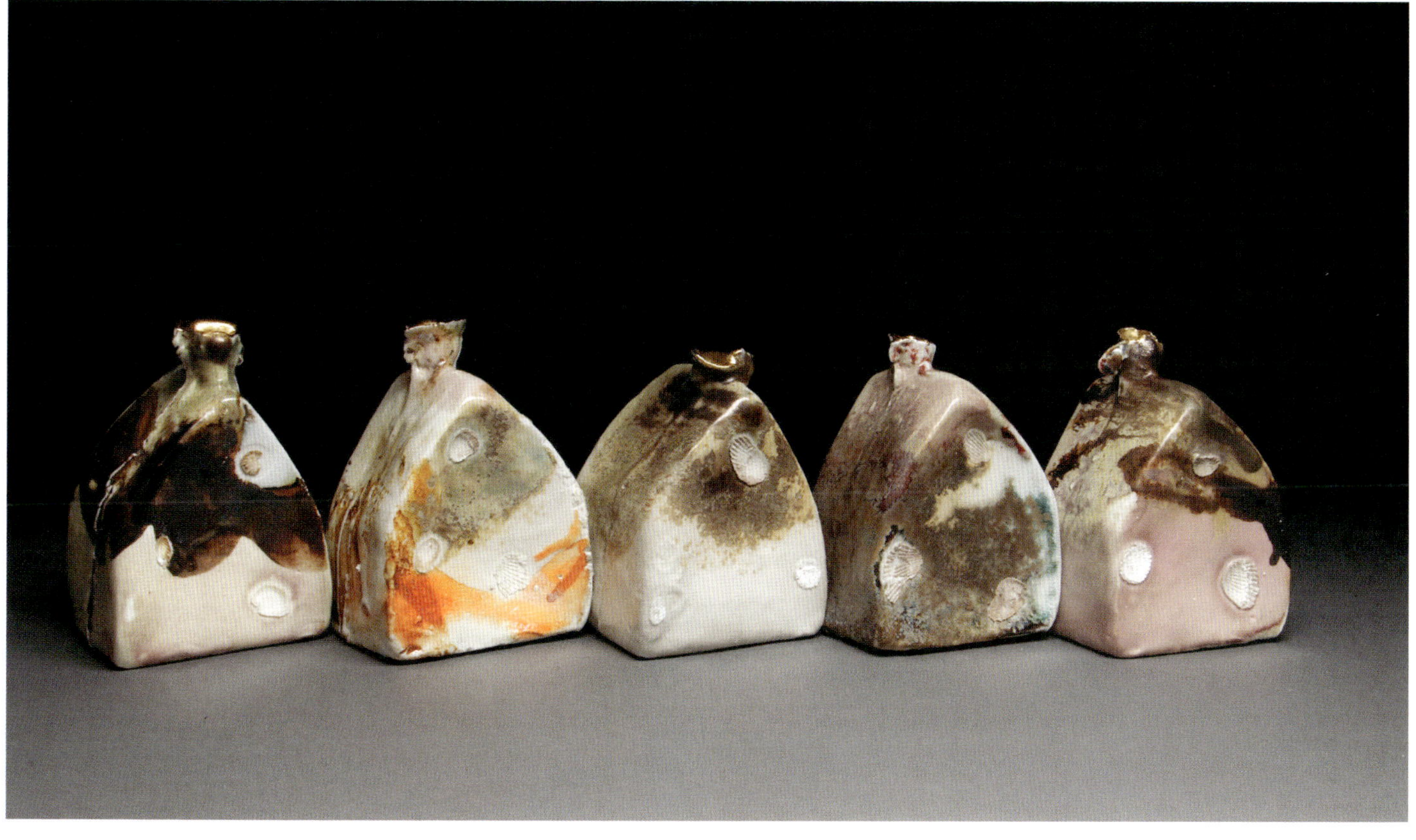

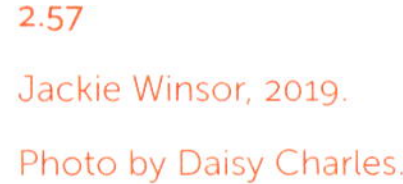

2.57
Jackie Winsor, 2019.
Photo by Daisy Charles.

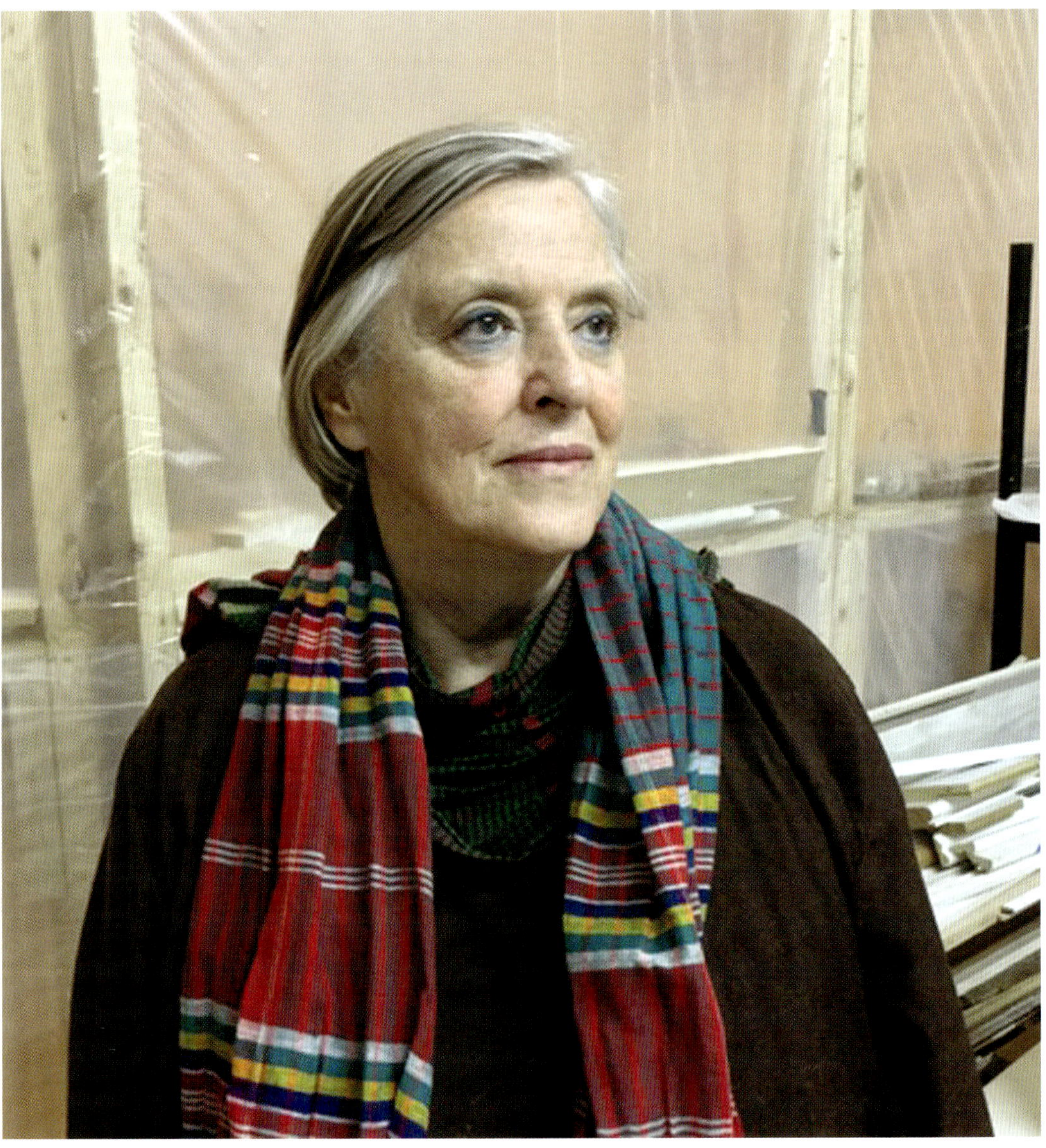

JACKIE WINSOR

Born in 1941 on Saint John's, Island, Newfoundland, Vera Jacqueline Winsor grew up in Newfoundland and New Brunswick, Canada, before moving to the United States in 1952. While living in Boston, Winsor missed the rural setting close to the ocean she had experienced as a young child. She returned to Newfoundland in the summers after her move to Boston. When she started taking art classes in high school, she was given the opportunity to enroll in an art program at the Museum of Fine Arts, Boston. During the summer of 1964, Winsor attended the Yale Summer School of Art and Music in Norfolk, Connecticut. She engaged in landscape painting and photography during her time at Norfolk. After completing a BFA degree at the Massachusetts College of Art in 1965, she chose Rutgers for the MFA. Winsor came to the Douglass campus because it was close to New York City, and the work produced by graduate students appealed to her. After arriving at Douglass College, she found links to avant-garde developments connected to Fluxus in the work of faculty. Winsor had studied painting at Massachusetts College of Art, and at Rutgers she registered for painting and drawing courses with Ulfert Wilke and Reginald Neal. Her instructors encouraged Winsor to explore new directions.[1] The experimental approach to artmaking at Douglass enabled her to combine various media. After working with collage, and cut-up photographs combined with black and white paint, she decided to experiment with sculpture.

Mark Berger, who taught art history and painting, was a favorite teacher. Winsor remembers fondly the camaraderie of the graduate students at Douglass.[2] She completed the MFA in 1967. Keith Sonnier and Jackie Winsor married before moving to New York City. Mark Berger and Joan Snyder shared their converted industrial building on Mulberry Street in Lower Manhattan. In her own work, which continues to advance, Winsor shows the impact of the exploratory, improvisational approach that was espoused by the faculty at Douglass.

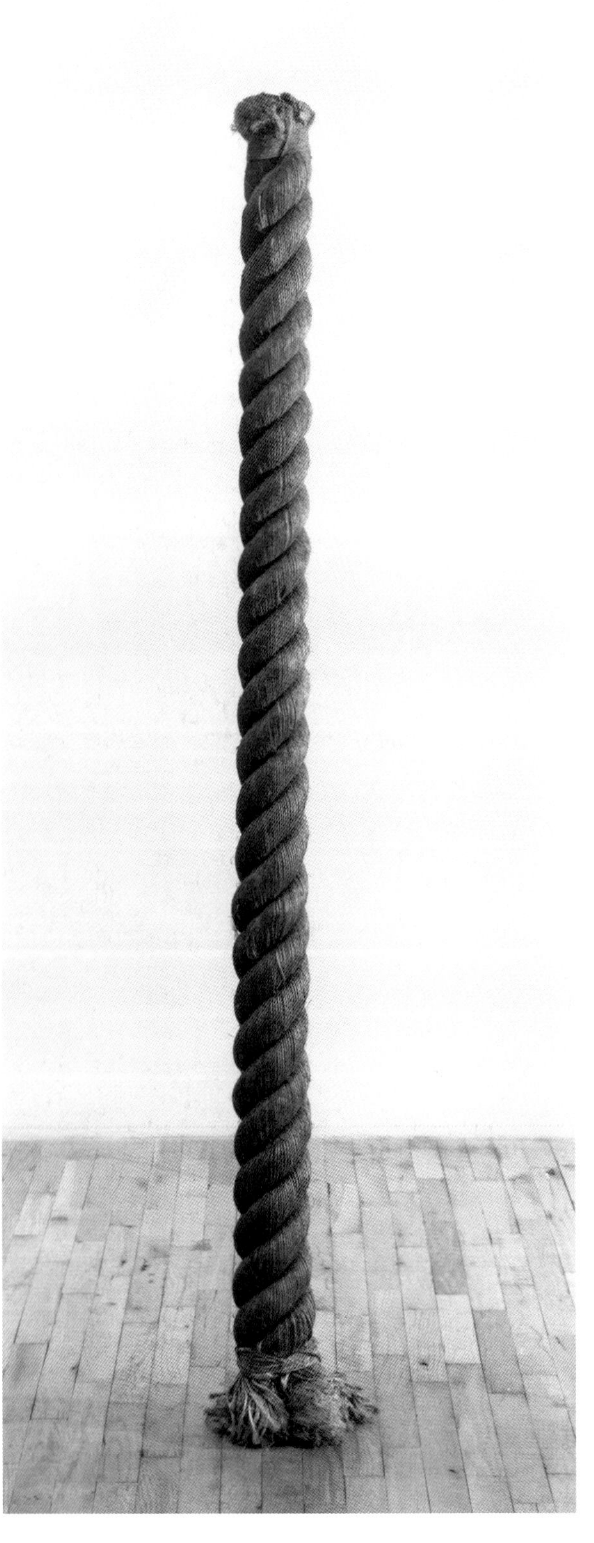

When I was first making sculpture, I just dove in and made
full-scale sculpture right off the bat with no transition
from being a painter. As a painter I was very interested in
drawing, so when I was working on sculptural shapes I was
thinking of them as drawings, you know: a line goes around
and around and around. Part of how I thought of these
early pieces is you must make the form full and fatter and
fatter and fatter until you've built a shape, much like we
build a house: more bricks, more bricks, more bricks. . . . I
suppose I'm very interested not in new, different decorative
material, but in the substance of what you work with and
working with that. Very often what I've done is worked it
to its bitter edge. I burned one of the early cube pieces and
exploded another one.[3]

Her early works in three dimensions were made of cast polyes-
ter resin. When she discovered that this material was dangerous to
her health, she began working with pieces of heavy rope used in
mountain climbing. Winsor viewed her earliest rope sculpture as introducing many lines—like a drawing. *Rope Trick* (1967–68), for example, does not reveal the metal armatures that hold it in a vertical
position to a height of 6 feet. Although her works at times resemble
Minimal art, her approach incorporates more personal elements and
processes than Minimalism. She was dedicated to working her own
materials, with energy and determination. Although Winsor's sculptures have some visual similarities to Minimalism and Post-Minimal-
ism, her works are firmly connected to her personal experience.

Winsor acknowledged the importance of dance to her own work,
and specifically Yvonne Rainer's art as a dancer, choreographer,
and filmmaker. Rainer experimented with the body and its links
to abstraction. Winsor found a connection with Rainer's pursuit of

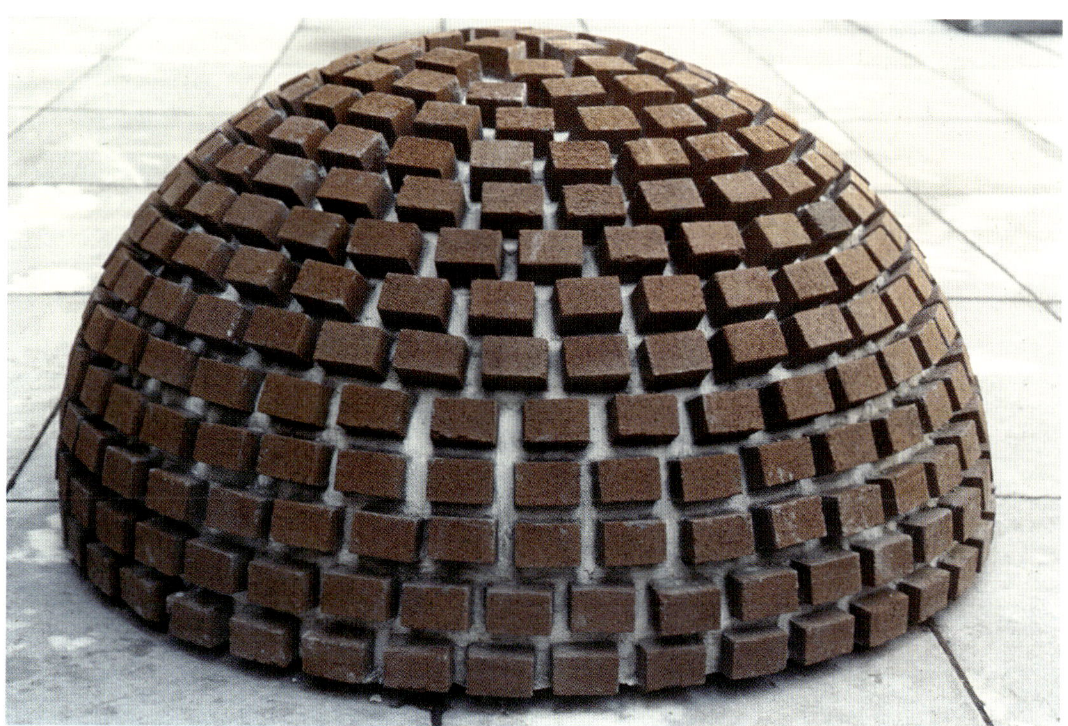

certain actions or tasks, and her own approach to creating sculptures. Her tasks involved joining materials, wrapping and nailing—a kind of choreography of the body at a slow pace, seeking perfect results.

Peter Schjeldahl observed, "Jackie Winsor is the dancing master of American sculpture, severe in the disciplines of grace. She is the most exacting and refined of the several major artists—including Bruce Nauman, Richard Serra, and the late Eva Hesse—who have extended and modified the aesthetic revolution of Minimalism since the late 1960s. . . . Each of her pieces is unique in conception, form, and character."[4] In 1971 she made *Brick Dome*, which was installed outside the Mabel Douglass Library. This sculpture was rebuilt in 1991.

Winsor's sculpture is innovative and deeply involved with process. She is known for the use of geometric forms, particularly the cube and sphere. Her early sculptures created in New York City are associated with "anti-formal" materials, such as rubber, cement, and cord. In the Museum of Modern Art's collection is *Burnt Piece* (1977–78). Winsor wrote, "I wanted to push it to its structural limit to where the concrete was actively, dangerously responding to the heat but was not overwhelmed or destroyed."[5] Winsor's preference for

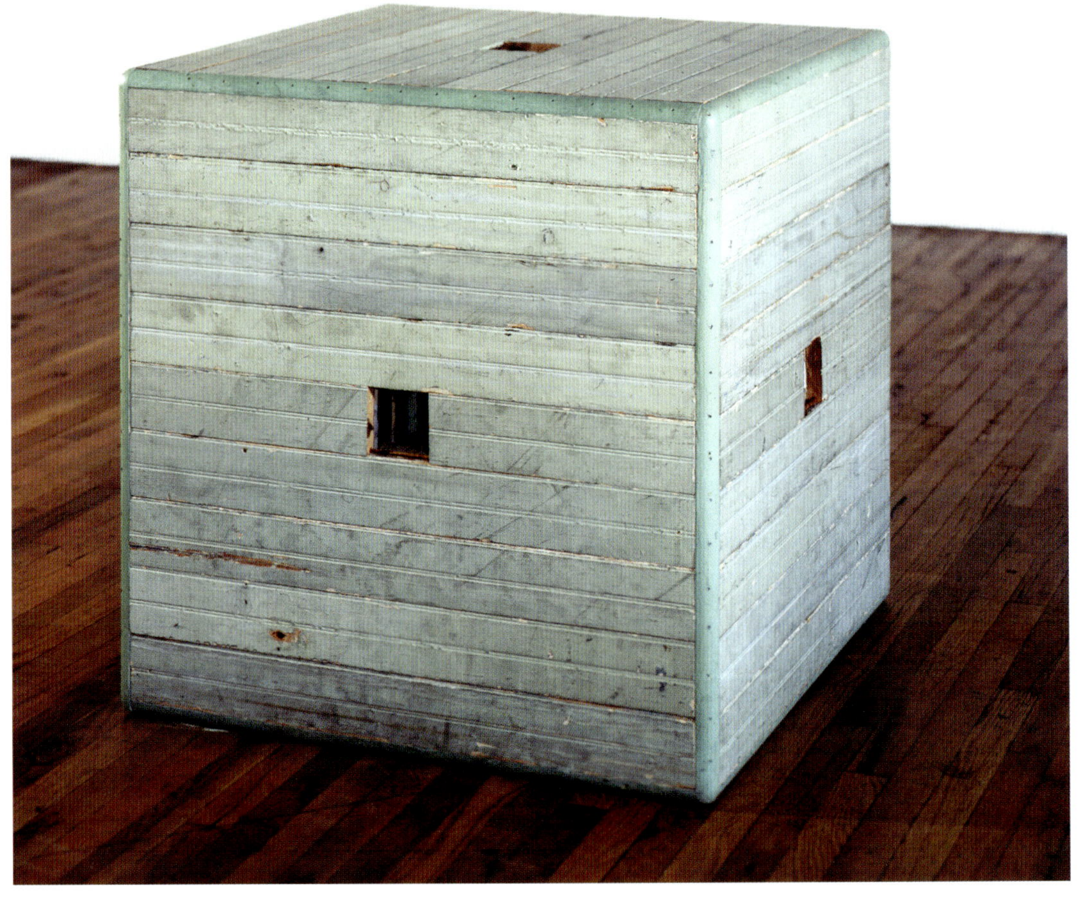

 WOMEN ARTISTS ON THE LEADING EDGE

2.60

Jackie Winsor. *Green Piece*, 1976–77.
Painted wood, wire, and cement,
32 ½" × 32 ½" × 32 ½". Courtesy of
the Paula Cooper Gallery.

2.61

Jackie Winsor. *Burnt Piece*, 1987. Concrete,
burnt wood, and wire, 36" × 36" × 36".
Courtesy of the Paula Cooper Gallery.

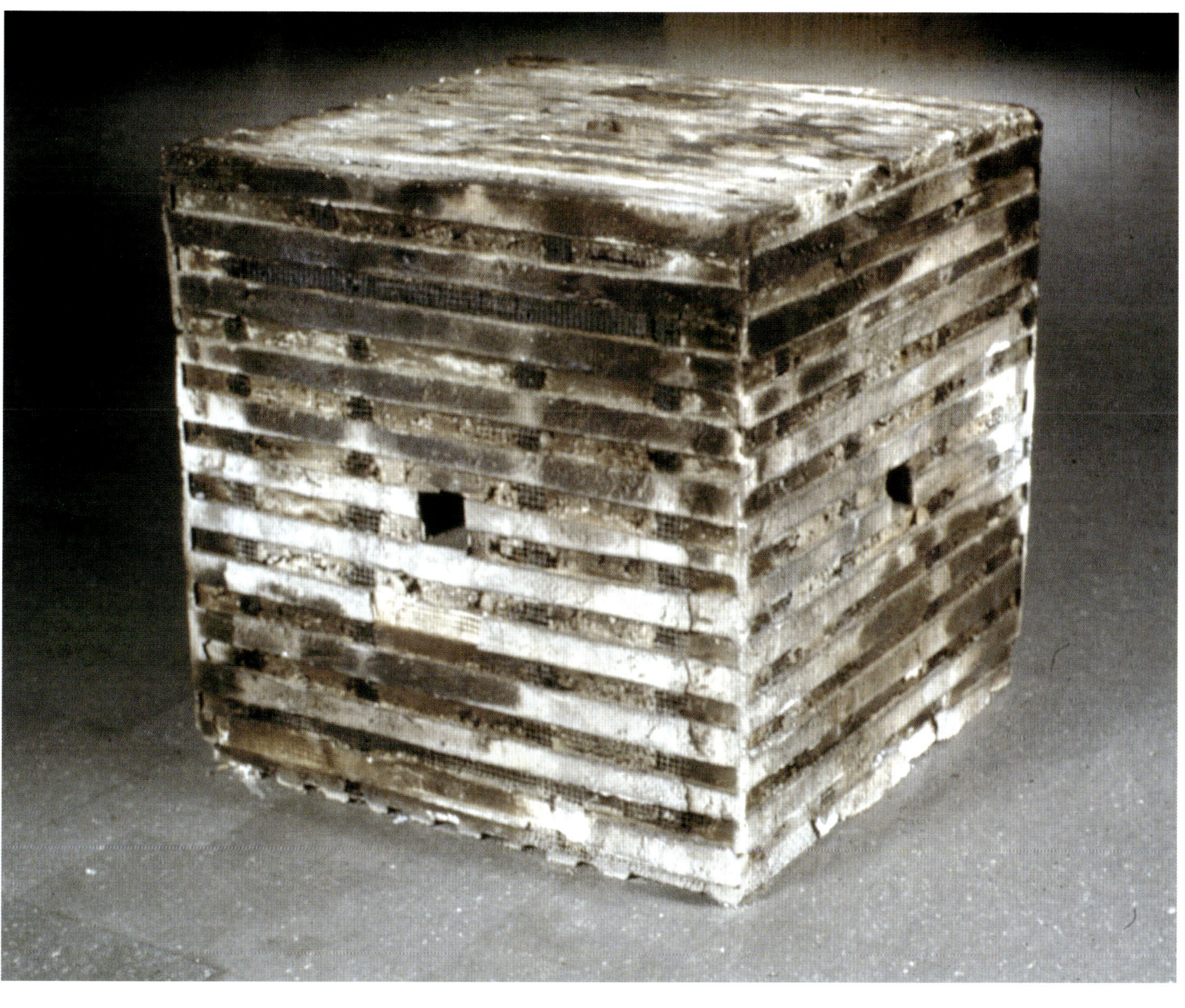

the cube can be seen as related to Minimalism of the 1960s. But she undermines this basic form by setting the cement, wood, and wire structure over a bonfire and burning the cube for about five hours. The artist explained:

> A cube is known, it's knowable, it's a measurement, basically. I wanted to bring the materials that I'd gotten to know together with the unknown. What I used as unknown was the fire or the force of explosives, which I didn't know anything about. It was my own personal unknown. I wanted to make those qualities go into the material so they imbibed it. So we had an event—the explosion, the burning—and there was a lot of unknown in that. The events had consequences, as nature has its consequences.[6]

Dean Sobel observed:

> A purely formal reading of Winsor's work might give the impression of an artist whose interests in material, repetition, and process are brought about by a mechanistic or cerebral approach centred around a physical activity. Winsor's actual approach has always been emphatically based on intuition and inspiration. . . . Winsor's commitment to her work is the result of her unending spirit coupled with her desire to bring human elements back into abstract sculpture in the same way that dance and performance art of the early 1960s attempted to bring the artist's gesture away from the limiting canvas.[7]

Consistently Winsor's art demands time and determination. There are repeated wrappings, nailing, painting. She sees her art as a reflection of her inner self.

Winsor taught at Hunter College, and then was hired at the School of Visual Arts as the first woman faculty member. She has taught at SVA for more than thirty years, and she continues to exhibit her work in various museums and galleries.

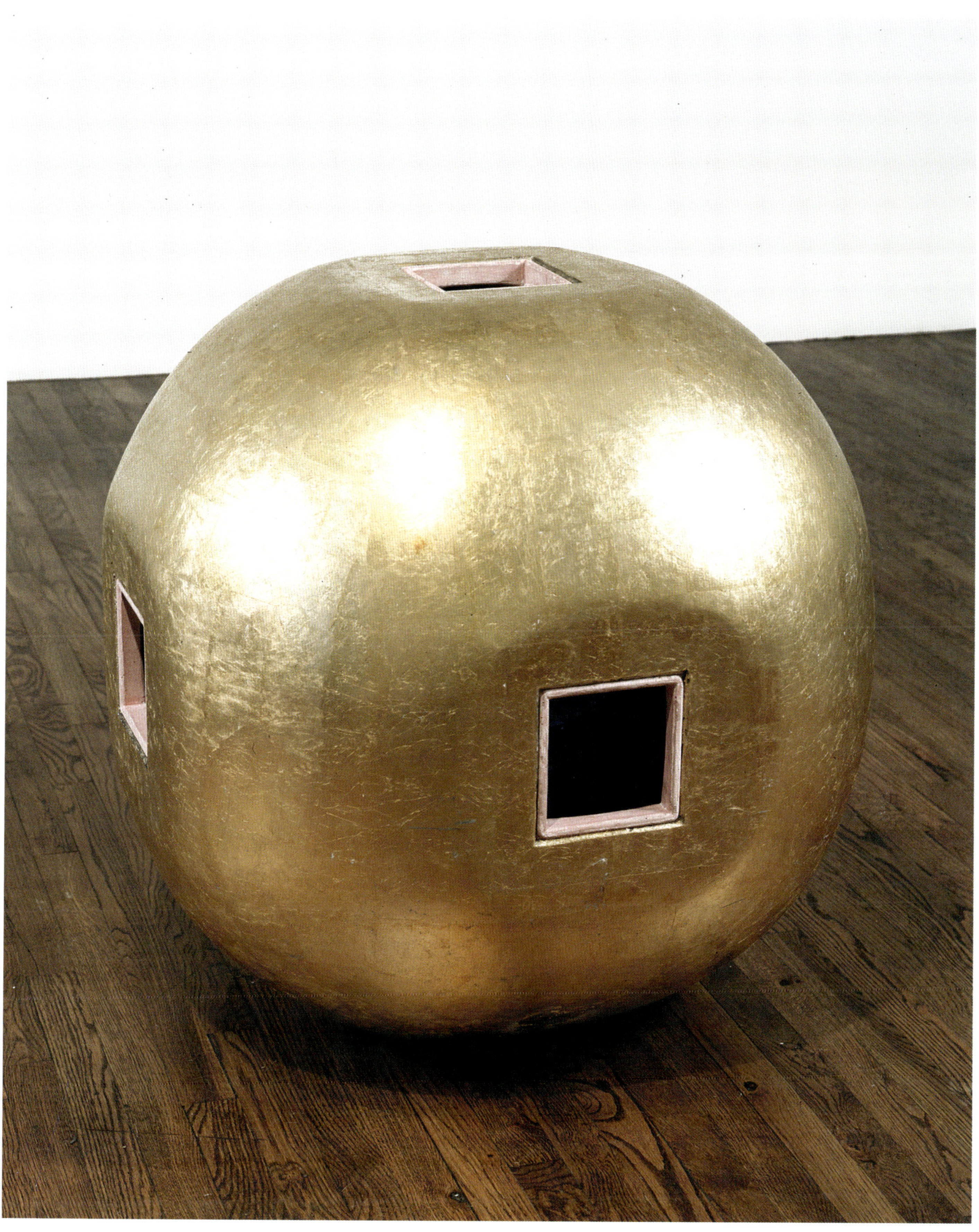

INTERVIEW WITH ALICE AYCOCK

JM Douglass College had become involved with empowering women in the 1960s. What was the focus of your undergraduate years in the 1960s at Douglass—within the art program? You were enrolled in an experimental workshop in art? Was it with Bob Watts?

AA I did study sculpture with Bob Watts, but initially, I took a two-part course (art history and studio) with Sam Weiner. He is somewhat underappreciated at Douglass, I think. I was always interested in art, but I was also very academically oriented. In high school I was in an academic program. Those interested in art were in the same curriculum as typing, etc.—not college bound. I was secretly making paintings in the basement before college, and I started playing with architecture from the time I was very young with my father. But I thought I would become a writer because I thought that had more "intellectual" prestige. I was also a big reader. Curiously, in my senior year of high school I wrote my history paper on Winslow Homer and George Inness. I didn't quite understand until I got to Douglass that I could be an artist and be interested in ideas.

When I got to Douglass, a highly selective wonderful liberal arts school, I was in a very competitive environment of young women. You had to have really good grades. Many of the women were going to be doctors or professionals. Some of them joined the Peace Corps. They were people who were going to do something with their lives, in any field. It was rigorous. The entire school was rigorous. I never met anybody who didn't want to get straight A's.

JM Did this motivation come from the dean? Did the dean present these ideas?

AA No, we gave it to ourselves. As freshmen, the seniors were mentoring us. During exams, it was quiet like a wake. Not a single person was not studying. No one was running around to parties. I mean, that's the way I remember it. I remember a highly competitive intellectual environment. I remember professors in all the fields being hard, teaching to the highest standards of excellence, and they did not teach down because we were "girls." If you were taking a philosophy course, it was tough. If you took biology or physics, it was tough. I was minoring in sociology for a while, and I had fantastic teachers. For example, we were studying the Berkeley riots, Hannah Arendt, George Herbert Meade, Rudolf Arnheim, etc. Amazingly good teaching. We didn't want to take courses at Rutgers College because we had really great faculty.

JM Interesting that Rutgers College was not considered that serious.

AA No, it was just not as selective, I think, but it was a good school. We may not have been Wellesley or Radcliffe, but we sure thought of ourselves as right up there. My sophomore year I was taking a very hard biology class. Back then chemistry and biology were in the same building as art. The labs were there. The basement was art and the attic was art, and there was one art history room.

I was taking a course in creative writing. And the creative writing teacher wasn't very impressed by my writing. She was giving me tough critiques and very little encouragement. I was getting very frustrated. I was a tremendous reader. Books were my solid ground. And I kept a little journal with every hour accounted for. I was so obsessive. Studying all the time, I dreamt *King Lear* for eight nights in a row. No one wanted to room with me. I became anorexic for a year or two. Anyway, I took an art course to fulfill a humanities requirement because I thought it would be easy and would give me a break.

I walked into class and there was Sam Weiner, who was supposed to be "Art Ed," but Sam's class was really so much more than that. Picasso's *Girl Before a Mirror* was projected on the screen. I took one look and thought, "I am out of here." And then he began to speak about Freud, World War I, Einstein and relativity, and that cubism was a compositional system that replaced Renaissance perspective with the notion of simultaneous points of view. I walked out of class and changed my major to art. His class exposed me to Panofsky, Kenneth Clark, John Cage and *Silence*, all the contemporary critics: Meyer Schapiro, Harold Rosenberg, etc., as well as the psychology of perception. He introduced me to contemporary art. It was Sam Weiner who was the intellectual educator. I wrote great papers with him. He encouraged me, mentored me, and he was why I changed my major. Sam was putting everything in the context of ideas. I took art history with Mark Berger as well. I took as much art history as I could. Also I loved history. I had Dr. [Daniel] Horn—who was a fabulous teacher, brilliant. I minored in history and art history. And all those things came together: the reading, the making. There was also John Goodyear who was a great teacher. Truthfully, the artists/faculty were not so interested in teaching skills, but were interested in teaching ideas. That was okay for a while because I was looking askance at artists as craftspeople anyway. But my skill sets were not all that great and I knew the faculty at Douglass wasn't going to teach me how to draw. I wanted to learn various ways of drawing so I took a great course at NYU one summer. I found there wasn't one academic way of learning. The instructor would say, "draw like the Impressionists, draw like the Pop artists, draw like Jackson Pollock." Once again, I was taught drawing by somebody who believed there wasn't one academic way of learning. There was a series of possibilities. That was the summer between my sophomore and junior year, when I had changed my major to art and I decided "let's get on with it." Later in graduate school I bought a book and taught myself to draw isometric projections and plans and elevations to scale like an architect.

Because of the excellence of the Douglass faculty and the students, we did not just sit there like a blank slate and have things thrown at us. We were critical and proactive in our education and understood what we needed to do. We did not just sit and wait. I was a good student in that way. John Goodyear was a great teacher—he was teaching painting and photography. I took sculpture with Watts. But Sam Weiner, John Goodyear, and Mark Berger were my main people, as well as Geoff Hendricks.

JM	What kind of work were you doing then?

AA	I made these horrible trees that were just monstrous—painted pink, gold, and green. And then I would leave them to be thrown out. I stopped painting fairly early on in my junior year, and started cutting out wood and Masonite forms that I assembled in high relief and painted. Then I moved on to building three-dimensional geometric shapes in wood. I became engrossed in minimal art. In a painting class I painted a garbage can. Then I thought, "Why don't I just make a garbage can?" I then asked the graduate students how to cut right angles and how to make three-dimensional hexagonal shapes in wood.

Graduate students were teaching assistants, and of course, they were just a few years older. They thought they were a lot better than us and they were. Jackie Winsor was a few years older, and she was a role model for me because I admired her from afar and I liked her work. Charles Simonds was there—we had a more competitive relationship. Rita Myers was a close friend, a year younger than me. Rita and I were pals, and as far as I know, Rita and I were the two little stars of the undergraduates—the little pets. There were others, of course. For example, Ted Victoria mentored me. Keith Sonnier was there as well.

JM   What about John Goodyear's work at that time?

AA   John Goodyear was making paintings related to Op art, and Richard Anuskiewicz was his friend. He was an excellent teacher. I never got the sense that the faculty felt that because they were teaching women they were not taken seriously.

JM   The New Jersey College for Women seemed to have been based on the model of the "Sister Schools" that opened dynamic possibilities for women.

AA   It did.

JM   The graduate art students were encouraged to be professionals. They were encouraged to come to New York City and see Rauschenberg shows.

AA   So were we. I attended the MFA critiques with Bob Watts. If the graduate students were going somewhere, I took advantage of that and New York City to see the museums, galleries, and dance performances (Cunningham et al.). I moved into the city every summer. I did an internship at the Guggenheim Museum between my junior and senior year. Douglass and its proximity to New York City was a constant exposure to the avant-garde, but you had to be proactive with your education. We were invited to go to Billy Kluver's "Nine Evenings." I was encouraged to go to shows and see Eva Hesse as well as the minimal artists; I wanted to live in New York. Watts was there in the background, encouraging the Happenings.

JM   But there were a lot of people coming to campus—John Cage and dance groups like Paul Taylor's.

AA   Douglass was very New York oriented. I took dance there. We had master classes with major avant-garde dancers, so it was constant exposure. If you wanted it, "here's the avant-garde, if you want, just go for it."

JM When you went to Hunter, Robert Morris was involved in performance art as well as minimalism.

AA Sam encouraged me to go to Hunter. Tony Smith was there, and so was Robert Morris. Had I gone to Wellesley, Sara Lawrence, or Radcliffe, I would have lost years to nonsense. In every case, I was where I was meant to be. Being at Hunter with all those art historians like Leo Steinberg. When I got to New York I was very influenced by conceptual art. And I stopped building things for a few years.

I had a group of friends that stimulated one another. My husband Mark Segal, Michael Chisholm, and Rita Myers . . . it was a perpetuation of energy. We all moved to New York together. We were involved with 112 Greene Street, the first artist-run co-op. In the beginning of my junior year, I met Mark Segal at Rutgers, and we married after my graduation from Douglass. He worked at MoMA.

I know that from early on and up to the present time, there are things I haven't been able to do or places I haven't been invited to because of my gender. But I thought I was special from the time I was a tiny little girl—and I didn't understand that people couldn't see that. It didn't mean that the barriers weren't there. But I did not dwell on it when I was in school or throughout my career as an artist. I had to keep my focus on my art and not on the obstacles in my path.

JM Even now it's a man's world. Whatever measure there is of success.

AA Regarding Mark Segal, this is important to say…no person other than my parents gave me the unconditional, total support that he did. He provided a safe, solid zone to protect me as a young artist in the New York art world during our ten-year marriage. He also provided a solid intellectual repartee.

JM I think of your work—it has a lot of personal aspects, devoted to humanity.

AA When I was around eleven years old, my father bought me fifty books, and told me if I read them he would buy me fifty more. He encouraged me to read and think widely. His mother, born in 1883, studied math in college. She taught school. She was a painter, writer, mathematician, and she tutored her children and grandchildren. She was the woman I tried to emulate all through my childhood. My own mother gave me unconditional support for my life as a creative person. It wasn't as though I had to learn that a woman could be what she wanted to be. It was unquestioned.

INTERVIEW WITH LETTY LOU EISENHAUER

Letty Eisenhauer was an undergraduate at Douglass College from 1953 to 1957. In 1961 she joined the Graduate Program in the visual arts, and also served part time as the art department secretary. Later she worked as an artist, art educator, and art historian. She is also known for her performances in Happenings by Allan Kaprow and Claes Oldenburg. More recently she was a professor and counselor at the Borough of Manhattan Community College.

LLE   I wanted to go to Bennington, but it was a lot of money in those days, a very exclusive school. I was a scholarship student at Douglass, and a New Jersey resident. I had very good grades in high school and I got a state scholarship. I loved the idea of being with women. I think the atmosphere at Douglass was unusual for its time. It was a school that was really focused on academics.

I always worked with Bob Watts. When I was a freshman at Douglass, I went to my first art class. I remember coming back to the dormitory and saying, "I have a real artist for a professor." Somehow I was totally taken. Watts had that effect on his students. There was something charismatic about him. Watts got me interested in all of art history. We were encouraged to experiment with artmaking, but Watts had a very rigid rule. The correct tool for the job. . . . He was very fussy about tools, and using them correctly.

What really happened was faculty like Bob Watts and Geoff Hendricks opened the door to experimenting for us. Anything you wanted to try, you could try. Watts also had this great sense of joking. You could never tell, but 90 percent of what he was saying was like a joke. And you could never tell when he was joking and when he wasn't joking. That was the difficult part of being around Bob Watts. After a while you got the sense that everything, his entire house that he lived in, became like a great artwork and a joke, where there were funny things. There was always that quality of playing with you all the time in the work. . . . I think Watts had subtle influences on people that no one was aware of. There's that charismatic part of him, or that part that is the engineer, always playing, out there doing something weird.

JM   What was the reaction of the students to the work of the faculty? When Kaprow arranged a Happening at Douglass what prepared the students for that? Was there some kind of seminar?

LLE   I think in Allan's case there would have been a very nontraditional approach to materials. There always had been. There's this weird dichotomy that I can think of. In the classroom also, Watts would be very traditional. Then he would take us to New York to see Rauschenberg's painting that you had to water because it was made of grass, on view at the Stable Gallery.

LLE   I graduated in 1957 and came back as a graduate student in February 1961. It was the first year Roy Lichtenstein was there [Roy Lichtenstein arrived in September 1960]. I came back as a graduate student, and as the department secretary. That was the deal. I would get to be a graduate student if I would be the departmental secretary. That was the most interesting year. Ronnie Stein came to the graduate program, and George Segal. Allan Kaprow had already gone. So there were some interesting people around in the graduate program, but most everybody was doing their own independent thing.

What really happened in the 1960s is I met Roy Lichtenstein at Rutgers. He was the funniest man I ever met. He used to come by my desk and tell jokes. I thought he was so funny. For Roy art was much more under the control of the artist. Watts was saying that anything could be art. I think that Roy turned out to be much more Zen than Bob Watts in the long run. Art and life are two separate things. Watts was saying that they are the same thing, which is what Kaprow said. Anything I do, anything I see in the world is grist for the mill and is art and can be art. I always saw Rutgers as the follow-up to Black Mountain College. This is what happened: it was this wonderful place, and there were ideas churning about. And everyone has to understand that Bob Watts was really an engineer to start with. He was always reading *Scientific*

American. He was always looking into engineering magazines that must have had an impact on what he finally decided to do.

JM What about Allan Kaprow's *Spring Happening*?

LLE Bob and Allan came to me with this idea. So you're caught between believing in what they're doing and fear for yourself. I think it had to do with the rites of spring, that we were going to re-create some kind of imagery of rebirth and growth. Allan used interesting imagery in describing things to me. "You're Dixie Dugan, you're the Statue of Liberty, you're Miss America, you're the Great Mother Earth."

Every performance I did for Allan had a definite plan based on an idea that he wanted to communicate. Usually there was a great catharsis in the work. The performance at the Mills Hotel [Courtyard] where I had to climb the mountain, it was almost like a reverse birth image. I climb up there, and then the other mountain comes down. Allan says, "It will kiss you." Well it kissed me. It put me back into the earth. I got planted again. So I always saw it as a death image: Innocence dies to be planted and reborn.

JM Did you attend the Happenings at George Segal's farm?

LLE I went to the events on the chicken farm. Oh sure. There were always things going on out there. And Allan and his wife Vaughan would often have parties, and we would go back and forth between the two places. This was prior to the serious "getting into the art world." It was very low key. It was more like a family of artists buzzing around exploring new ideas together in their own individual styles. At the moment it did not feel competitive. We all knew each other. That's the amazing part. Everyone did the separate thing in their own way, but we all knew each other.

INTERVIEW WITH MIMI SMITH

JM   What was your experience at Douglass when you enrolled in the MFA program in 1964?

MS   I came out of Boston and Mass Art, where I was used to drawing from casts, and lots of drawing from life. I was a painting major when I came to Rutgers. The two main people I took classes with at Rutgers were Bob Watts, who taught sculpture and an experimental workshop, and Mark Berger, who taught the art history classes. I also took a class with Robert Morris, which was an incredible eye-opener to me. This was all within a two-year period. They took us—more than what they taught us. They took us to places that just blew my mind. The classes were moved to the evening. We went to many Fluxus events. Bob Watts took us to "Six evenings at the 92nd Street Y," that had Buckminster Fuller and Marshall McLuhan speaking. We spent a very long time reading Marshall McLuhan. We spent practically a year reading John Cage. We attended a lecture on Rauschenberg's *Bed* by Leo Steinberg at the Met Museum. Robert Morris took us to the Green Gallery in 1964 to see the Lucas Samaras show of his *Room #1,* which was very amazing to me.

We also went to Happenings, I remember seeing one by Alison Knowles where she made a big salad in a garbage can. At some point Watts decided he wanted to start an Institute for Advanced Studies patterned after the one at Princeton. But he wanted it in *art,* not in science. He got a grant. This must have been 1965 or '66. He picked eight or ten students, half were graduate students and half were undergraduate. He got some money. We all went and all got equipment and we made video loops. For Watts's Experimental Workshop, he took us to Nam June Paik's studio on Canal Street. Paik had us each make a two-minute video with the Porta-Pac video camera. We each did a Happening in front of a video camera. Other things that happened at that time were Lucinda Childs and James Byers visited one night. They did a beautiful performance for us. It was just incredible. It was in the Douglass Art Gallery—the gallery where everyone did their MFA thesis shows. Lucinda Childs just walked around under this huge bare lightbulb. They both had costumes on. It was an incredible event. We were also invited to a party at James Byers' place, where he was staying, which was a hallway on the upper West Side. We all had to bring something. There was a whole focus at the time about these events. As I interpreted it, the whole Fluxus thing, with people doing everything, made me feel that anything you did could be art. It was an extremely exciting time.

Then there was Robert Morris. He had a seminar I took. He had us talk about art in an incredibly intellectual way.

JM Do you think Morris was hired to be a seminar person?

MS It was a seminar. We talked about art theory. We didn't make art in the class. Morris also thought anything could be art, and it seemed there was a theory you could have for it. It was the first art class I had taken in my life where anyone talked about a reason for making art—the things behind making art. I remember Morris saying that it is important to be able to verbalize your work. You shouldn't just do it. You should know what it is about. To me, that was really different and significant.

JM What effect did the Fluxus artists (or the Fluxus aspect of Bob Watts) have on you?

MS I think it made me think I could make work using anything I want about anything I want and it could be art. For me that was new and refreshing. It gave me the license to do whatever I wanted to do.

JM Did you think that the all-male faculty treated women differently?

MS Yes. In the six years I went to art school, undergrad and graduate, I had one teacher who was female. They assumed that the boy students would have careers, but not the girls. You could tell this especially when dealers and critics came to campus to visit and talk.

MS Bob Watts took us to his house and showed the Experimental Workshop students his work, including the stamps and stamp machines. The classes in the MFA program were open ended. We were taken to many lectures in New York, and to exhibitions in galleries and museums.

PART THREE

THE WOMEN ARTISTS SERIES AT DOUGLASS COLLEGE

In 1971 when Douglass alumna Joan Snyder (class of 1962) conceived the idea that exhibitions of women artists' works could be shown in the Douglass Library, she opened the door to creating a landmark series with a lasting impact. The Women Artists Series is the oldest continuous exhibition program devoted to emerging women artists.[1] The artists who participated, the students who saw the exhibitions, and the administrators who helped to organize the shows experienced a transformation of their assessment of women artists. At this date more than five hundred women have been included in exhibitions at the Mabel Smith Douglass Library.

Under the able direction of Lynn Miller in the early years, and other coordinators, including Evelyn Apgar, Beryl Smith, and Ferris Olin, the Series has continued to flourish. In 1987, the Series was renamed the Mary H. Dana Women Artists Series, endowed by Professor Emerita Nellie Smither in memory of her friend Mary H. Dana (class of 1942). And since 2006, the Series continues as a program of the Center for Women in the Arts and Humanities at Rutgers. How and why was this Series launched?

Joan Snyder visited Douglass College in June 1971 and saw her former professor and friend Emily Alman. In an interview Snyder recalled, "Somehow or another I said to her it would be good if we could have some women's shows on this campus. And for some reason she said to me, 'Why don't you talk to Daisy Brightenback' [later Shenholm], who was the head librarian. . . . I went to Daisy and she was excited about the idea and immediately supportive.[2] The idea, of course, was that at that point there were no women teaching studio courses in the art department at Douglass. And I felt like the women students needed to see some art work by women."[3]

When Douglass College approved the inauguration of the Women Artists Series on September 13, 1971, Joan Snyder was asked to serve as curator of the series. The artists she selected for the first two years included artists Mary Heilmann and Pat Steir. Snyder recalled, "At first I wanted to show women that the students would love to see, who would be important for them to see. Then I wanted to show women who needed a break, who were wonderful artists, but hadn't been showing their work."[4] The series preceded other feminist ventures. For example, on the West Coast Judy Chicago and Miriam Schapiro began teaching feminist art, but the Women Artists Series predates *Womanhouse*, their major project, shown in 1972. Lynn Miller initially was handling the calendar and publicity, but soon she became the curator of the shows with the assistance of a jury of artists and art historians.

Solo exhibitions in the Women Artists Series have included some of the most acclaimed women artists as well as many promising talents. There was consistently a balance between including well-known feminists (for example, Miriam Schapiro, Nancy Spero, May Stevens, and Faith Ringgold, among others) and artists with limited critical exposure at the time of their selection. The creative potential recognized in these younger artists was affirmed by their subsequent success in showing their work. The Series also celebrated the achievements of women at various stages in their careers. Artists who had been actively producing for decades, such as Alice Neel and Louise Bourgeois, were honored, as well as young artists, such as Alice Aycock and Bibi Lencek. From the beginning women artists from New Jersey were given recognition in these shows. Group exhibitions of New Jersey women closed the year-long schedule, and women working in the state were selected for solo exhibitions .

The Women Artists Series at Douglass College was a landmark, both in the successful use of an alternative space and in the serious commitment to women's art by an educational institution. From its inception the Series also became an important political statement. In 1971,when the Series was initiated, there were few exhibitions devoted exclusively to women's work. The shows at the Douglass Library antedate such major group exhibitions as *Women Choose Women* at the New York Cultural Center in 1973, and the founding of women's cooperative galleries, such as A.I.R. (1972) and Soho 20 (1973) in New York City. In those years women artists were receiving little critical attention—they were all but ignored in annual exhibitions of contemporary art organized by major museums, and they had only limited acceptance in commercial galleries

Alienated from the art world, the women artists chosen for solo exhibitions at Douglass often reaffirmed their commitment as professionals while showing and lecturing about

   WOMEN ARTISTS ON THE LEADING EDGE

their work. Yearly catalogs included critical discussions about the nature of feminist art. The diversity of images and styles reflected a new set of values and interests among women. For many artists there was an attempt to turn women into proactive subjects in contrast to their more usual depiction as sex objects in the art of men. The range of techniques, materials, and artistic intent indicated that women refused to accept the tyranny of male-dominated criteria for quality.

Even when critics recognized the achievements of women—and some of these artists did find some acceptance in commercial galleries and museums—the Women Artists Series had an important role. The representation of women artists in important art collections and in public institutions has not held fair measure with their accomplishments. The Series helps to document the contributions of women to contemporary trends in art. Women's unique approach to artmaking and consciously feminist work account for only one portion of their artistic production. Women encouraged eliminating the distinction between "high" art and traditional women's art forms—stitching, quilting, weaving, china painting, and so forth. The interest in autobiographical issues, overtly sexual imagery, and the involvement with pattern and decoration also finds root in the influence of women artists.

It is evident that the artists have benefited from their exhibitions at Douglass. For some, inclusion in the series was their first opportunity for a one-person exhibition. Even for well-established artists, participation in the Series on a college campus proved to be an exciting stimulant. At Rutgers, the artists were able to reach a different audience from that which frequents New York galleries. Installed in the lobby and circulation desk of the Mabel Smith Douglass Library, the exhibitions were made accessible to students, faculty, and staff—including those who did not visit art galleries on campus.

Intitially the Women Artists Series provided a source of role models for aspiring female art students at the university. This situation has changed for the better over the past decades. Within the Visual Arts Program of the Mason Gross School of the Art (which assimilated the Douglass, Livingston, and Rutgers College art programs as of 1981), there are at least seven women artists on the faculty. Among these women are ardent feminists who have long been active in the women artists movement.

At Douglas College, the Series continues to be a model of support for women by women. For many years a jury selected artists for the yearly calendar. Student interns visited artists' studios and helped to prepare the annual catalogs and install the exhibitions. The

Series has been an overwhelming success. No longer the only venue bringing attention to women artists, the Series now operates in conjunction with dynamic, accomplished women who have joined the Visual Arts faculty. The search for new forms of artistic expression and the burgeoning feminist consciousness to be discovered in these exhibitions can now be nurtured by the women artists teaching painting, drawing, sculpture, printmaking, and photography at Rutgers. The Douglass Library has dramatically renovated the spaces where the Series was installed. The Mary H. Dana Women Artists Series proudly continues to celebrate the achievements of women.

3.1

Women Artists Series, 25 Years,

1971-1996, cover of catalog.

Collection of the author.

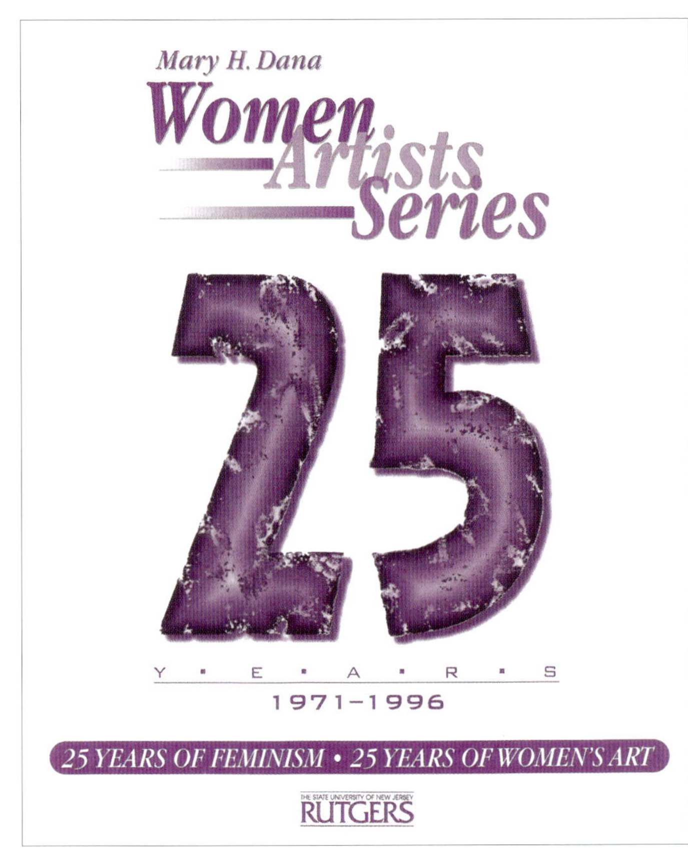

THE WOMEN ARTISTS SERIES AT 25 YEARS

Ages of Discovery, The Women Artists Series: My Memories,
by Joan Marter

When I arrived at Douglass College in 1977, as assistant professor in the art department, photographer Amy Stromsten was the only full-time woman instructor on the studio faculty. Apparently, for the previous two decades at Douglass, undergraduate and graduate art students had few women artists teaching them, except for the occasional adjunct professor. The exclusively male faculty was surely an anomaly for a women's college—particularly in the visual arts, which had many women qualified to teach. Fortunately for all future students at Douglass College, alumna Joan Snyder had an idea for introducing the work of women artists on campus. Why not a series of exhibitions? She approached Daisy Brightenback, Librarian at the Mabel Smith Douglass Library, who accepted her plan with enthusiasm. Financial support, however, was always a problem.

When I joined the advisory committee for the Women Artists Series in 1977, I discovered that funding for installing exhibitions and publishing catalogs was a major concern. Secondary, but also important, was the selection process. The Series changed from an invitational arrangement in the early years to a jury that selected artists from submitted slides. Formation of a jury coincided with the appointment of distinguished women artists to the faculty, and the intention was to "discover" the works of unknown artists. With that purpose in mind, the Series was advertised through the Women's Caucus for Art. When the number of women sending slides grew to over three hundred in one year, the jury returned to a modified invitational scheme. No individual chose the artists, however. Many women artists on the faculty participated in the jurying process.

The Women Artists Series has included some of the most acclaimed women artists associated with feminist art, as well as many promising talents. Well-known feminists, such as Miriam Schapiro, Nancy Spero, and Faith Ringgold, were early participants. One of the special group exhibitions I will always remember was one co-organized by a group of my undergraduates at Douglass entitled *Modern Masters: Women of the First Generation*. Devoted to women artists over the age of seventy, the show included Dorothy Dehner, Sari Dienes, Elsie Driggs, Perle Fine, Dorothea Greenbaum, Dorothy Hood, Buffie Johnson, Lois Mailou Jones, Esphyr Slobodkina, and Jane Teller. Many of these artists came to the campus in December 1982 and were honored by a reception in the Dean Mary Hartman's residence. The students who had researched their artistic careers and written essays for the exhibition catalog had a chance to meet with wonderful artists.

In recent years many artists with limited critical exposure have exhibited in the Series. Installed in the corridors and reading rooms of the Mabel Smith Douglass Library, the Series has been a landmark, both in the continued use of an alternative space for exhibitions and in the serious commitment to women's art by an academic institution.

The Women Artists Series has provided role models of remarkable women artists for Douglass students and graduate students at the Mason Gross School of the Arts. Initiated at a time when few opportunities were extended to women for exhibiting their work, and critical attention was negligible, the series continued into a period of limited acceptance for women in museums and commercial galleries.

Groups such as the Guerilla Girls and the Women's Action Coalition boldly put forth information about the ratio of women artists to men in group exhibitions or announced that few paintings and sculptures by women were on display in American museums. The rhetoric in catalogs for the Women Artists Series has been less strident, and the shows have been quiet tributes to the accomplishments of women professionals. The Series continues to be a model of support for women by women.

During the decades of my service on the advisory board and jury, a change of purpose evolved for the Women Artists Series. In my opinion, the initial motivation was to fulfill a temporary need: to present the art of women when few other venues were available. However, exhibitions devoted solely to women artists are still important. By organizing solo and group exhibitions of women's creative production, the initiators of the Series have acknowledged the rich diversity of women's creative production. While I applaud the flourishing Women Artists Series, which has survived despite financial crises and changes in staff, I am disappointed that women artists have still not gained the long-sought parity with their male counterparts in the art world. Women are creating some of the best painting and sculpture among all of their contemporaries.

It is my hope that the Women Artists Series will continue for at least another generation of Douglass students. Rutgers now has a Visual Arts Program at the Mason Gross School of the Arts, with a faculty of accomplished women artists, who bring attention to the contributions of women. At Douglass, the Women Artists Series remains the locus for ages of discovery—both young women and those with many years of work bring their paintings, sculptures, book projects, and works on paper to the campus for exhibitions. Affirmation of women as creators continues as Douglass validates gender-specific studies.

From its inception the Women Artists Series has been an important political statement: affirming the mission of Douglass College to instruct and affirm the creativity of women, as well as asserting the importance of women's art to the larger community.

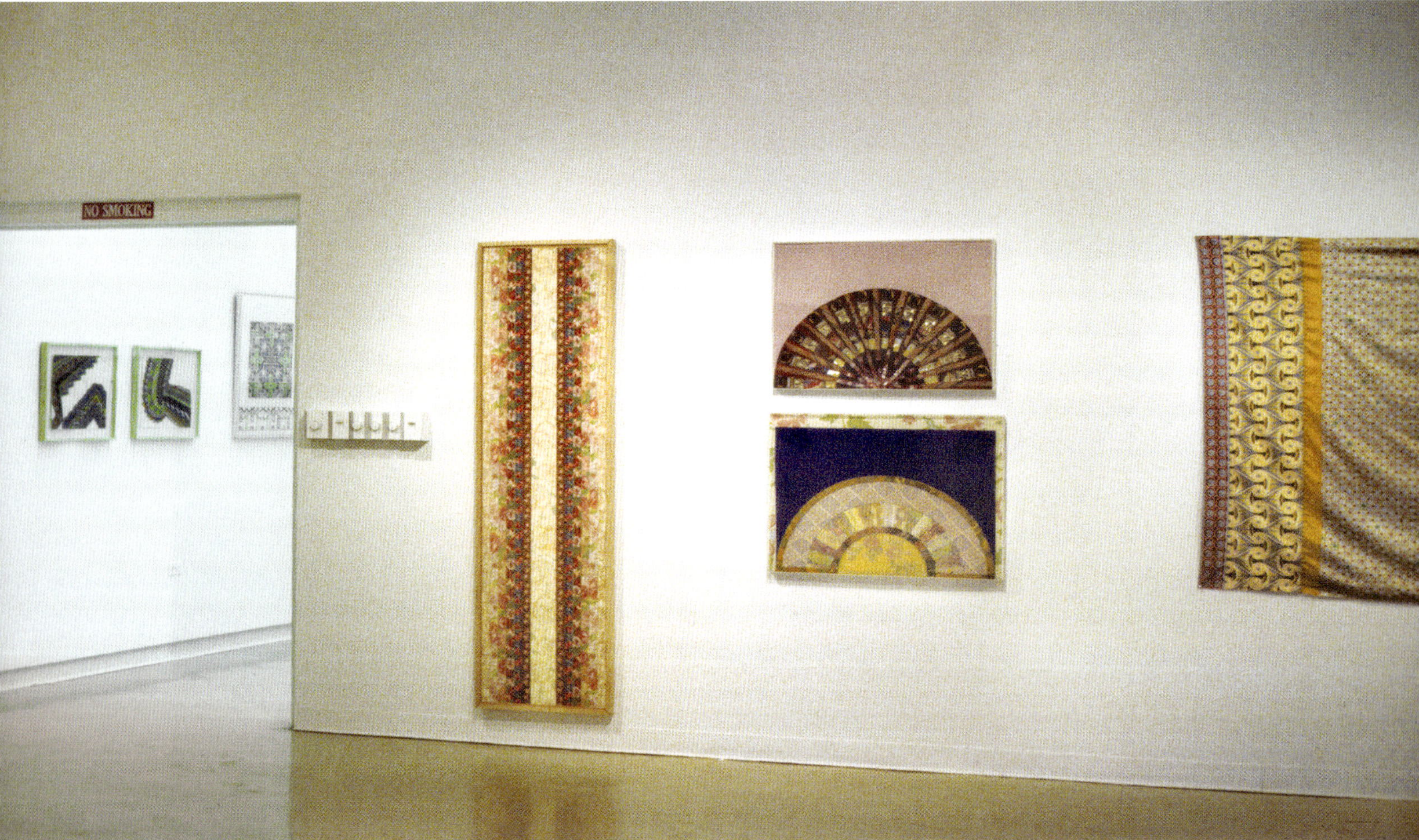

3.2

Installation of *Decorative Art: Recent Works,*

November–December, 1968. Walters Hall Art Gallery.

EXHIBITIONS AT THE WALTERS HALL ART GALLERY, DOUGLASS COLLEGE

Attention has been given to the Women Artists Series in the Mabel Smith Douglass Library. Other art exhibitions took place in the Douglass College Art Gallery in Walters Hall on the Douglass campus. Several of these shows were organized by Professor Joan Marter in connection with her undergraduate course Workshop in Curatorial Practices.

These exhibitions were organized with the assistance of undergraduate students at Douglass College, and offered the opportunity for Douglass women to work directly with women artists. There were a few Rutgers College students who also participated. Generally the students were assigned to visit one woman artist in her studio and to prepare information about her work. The topics were chosen by Professor Marter, and usually the subject also included a series of her presentations in a seminar format. A catalog was printed for each exhibition, and the students had an opportunity to publish essays on their selected artists. Fortunately, the proximity to New York made it possible for these exhibitions to be arranged through the borrowing of works directly from artists' studios. The topics were chosen because they related to ideas currently being explored by contemporary women artists. The truly amazing aspect of these exhibitions was their progress toward completion in a single semester. The topic was defined in early September, students were assigned artists to visit in their studios, and the exhibition was installed in late November. Somehow a catalog was also put together and printed by the time of the opening. Following are titles and particulars on each of these exhibitions.

Decorative Art: Recent Works, November–December 1978

*Foreword by Joan Marter, Assistant Professor, Department of Art,
Douglass College*

This exhibition was made possible by the perseverance and enthusiasm of eleven Rutgers students. A course entitled Workshop in Curatorial Practices was intended to provide these students with practical experiences in organizing exhibitions and writing the accompanying catalogs. The essays that follow are the result of personal interviews with each of the artists included in the show. Individual members of the class conducted the interviews and researched the issues involved in decoration and pattern.

Decorative Art was chosen as the theme for this group exhibition because artists who utilize aspects of the decorative or patterning in their work are now beginning to receive international attention. It is our hope as the organizers of this show that our efforts will make some small contribution to the acknowledgment of this significant development in contemporary art.

Artists

Cynthia Carlson by Suzanne Leeson
Mary Grigoriadis by Angela Mauti
Valerie Jaudon by Christopher Dern
Richard Kalina by Scott Nicol
Jan Kaufman by Maria Pellerano
Gloria Klein by Amy Whitney
Joyce Kozloff by Angela White
Robin Lehrer by Caroline Laccetti
Tony Robbin by Patrick Little
Miriam Schapiro by Marta Rothwarf
Bob Zakanitch by Alison Speckman

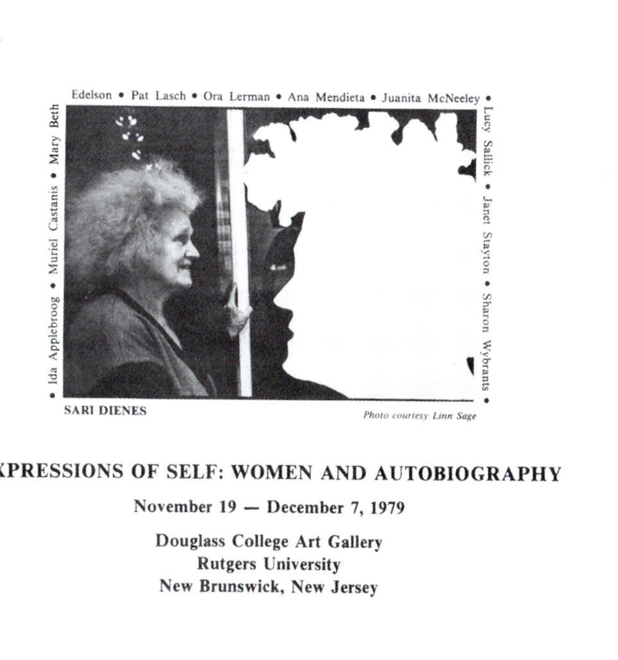

Expressions of Self: Women and Autobiography, November–December 1979

Foreword by Joan Marter, Professor of Art, Department of Art, Douglass College

The class chose Women and Autobiography as the theme, and the artists were determined after examination of slides and reproductions.

Autobiographical interests in the creation of painting, sculpture, and mixed media constructions are found in virtually all works of art, but these featured artists make self-realization and documentation principal aims of their production. Some of these women include references to objects that have special meaning to their lives. Others use events of their past or current activities (rituals) as a form of self-expression. Visual diaries are often created in their search for self. These issues are explored in the following essays.

Artists

Ida Applebroog by Jacqueline Appleton
Muriel Castanis by Lisa Mallers
Sari Dienes by Henry Duffy
Mary Beth Edelson by Ilene Trepel
Pat Lasch by Carolann Dvorak
Ora Lerman by Patricia McDermott
Ana Mendieta by Jan Gura
Juanita McNeely by Mary McNiffe
Lucy Sallick by Fiona Shrodo
Janet Stayton by Andrea Sperling
Sharon Wybrants by Linda Backer

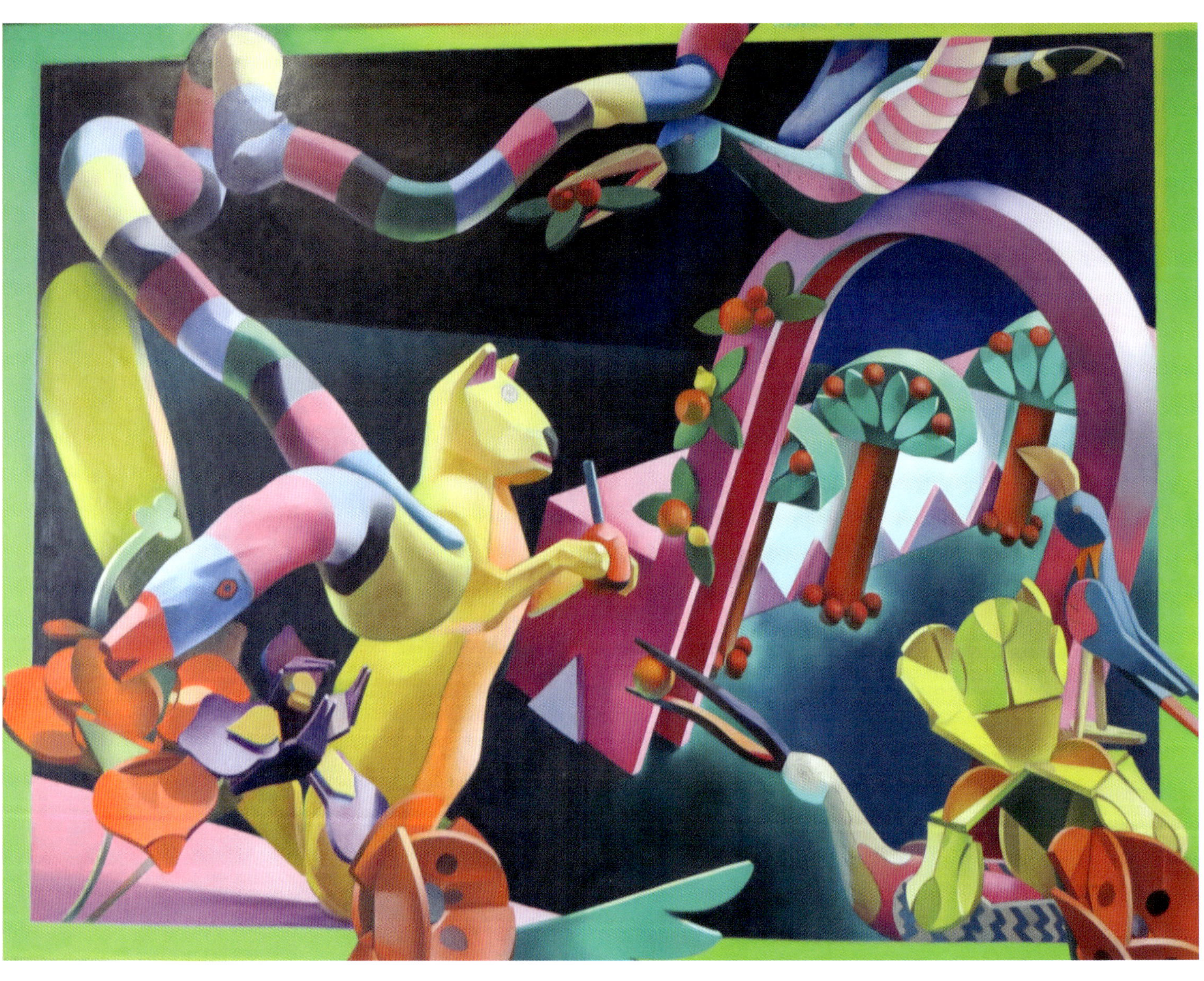

      WOMEN ARTISTS ON THE LEADING EDGE

Ora Lerman by Patricia McDermott

Her work is frankly personal in an age of depersonalization. She feels a necessity to paint, an urgency to communicate a feeling or an idea, an idea resulting from a personal experience. Her body of ideas then becomes her own history.

Those ideas are given expression not only by the objects she has carefully chosen to include in a painting but also by literal expressions in words written on the painting's border. Lerman strives for a balance between verbal and visual expression, between the illusion of three-dimensional space so well handled within the painting and the denial of that illusion by the patterned border, which reinforces the planar nature of the canvas.

Some paintings by Lerman are more overtly autobiographical than others. . . . Self-realization, an important idea in any autobiographical work, implies an understanding of both the beautiful and the ugly aspects of one's personality. . . . . More recent works by Lerman relate to experiences she has had, but communication of the idea within the work is emphasized, not the personal experience. . . . still utilizing toys in a free-fall through space, more explicitly dealing with the division in today's culture between job and recreation. "The Garden of Eden Syndrome" implies a loss of innocence, such as in growing up, making the use of toys in this work all the more ironic.

Ana Mendieta by Jan Gura

Ana Mendieta, a Cuban-born artist whose works exemplify the unification of nature and the woman's body, specifically hers, lived a life mixed with many traumatic experiences. She left her homeland in 1961 due to the political involvement of her father, and came to the United States where she lived in orphanages and foster homes in Iowa. . . . Mendieta, who thinks of the earth as the Goddess, states that the making of her earth-body sculptures is not the final stage of a ritual, but a way of asserting her emotional ties with the earth as well as conceptualizing Cuban culture. For several years Ana Mendieta has carried on a dialogue between the landscape and the mythical female body. She does this by embossing her silhouette on different mediums in nature, whether it be burned into the side of a mountain in Mexico, cut out of a garden of flowers, or fertilized on a patch of grass in Iowa.

In her photographs of the "sculptures" that she has done, the woman's body is intertwined with her obsessions with death, rebirth, blood, skeletons, earth, and religion. These sculptures are done impulsively at the site and left there to become part of nature. It is immediately after the sculptural process that she photographs her new creation. There have been times she has come back to the site to see the piece evolve, grow, and change, as human beings do during the course of a lifetime.

The representation of her life through her art is a unique effort. Each person has had meaningful experiences in his or her life, yet it is this artist's individual way of presenting hers that makes the works so meaningful. All of Mendieta's photographs include her silhouette, nature that surrounds her, and a deep searching into her soul. It is this total synthesis that gives Ana Mendieta's work a mystical aura.

fragments of myself/the women, An Exhibition of Black Women Artists, November–December 1980

Foreword by Joan Marter, Associate Professor, Rutgers University

This exhibition of African American women artists was organized by eleven students enrolled in Workshop in Curatorial Practices. The practical experience gained in the selection of works, installation of the show, and writing of the accompanying catalog should be useful to these women as they prepare for art-related careers. The essays included in this catalog resulted from personal interviews with each of the artists chosen for the exhibitions.

Diversity of expression, imagery, and media can be found in the artistic production of black women artists. This exhibition reflects both the broad-ranging interest of these artists and their shared experiences of being black women in a white male–dominated society. Personal history and current circumstances of life find realization in their works. Some of the artists retain figurative imagery; others explore various forms of abstraction. Different approaches can be found, and the results are powerful artistic statements.

Artists

Emma Amos by Elizabeth Ilona Payleszek
Camille Billops by Laura Gradick
Lula Mae Blocton by Ruth Ann Flaig
Vivian Browne by Cheryl Molnar
Jacqui Holmes by Gail Aaron
Margaret Kelly by M. Marion Clough
Valerie Maynard by Luana Maekawa
Janet Taylor Pickett by Marilyn Voliva
Howardena Pindell by Wendy McNeil
Mavis Pusey by Cettina Maria Cardone
Faith Ringgold by Cheryl King

Excerpts from Sample Essays

Emma Amos by Elizabeth Ilona Payleszek

Amos has become increasingly aware of the African element, and consciously tries to incorporate it into her art. Her interest in Kente cloth for its beautiful colors inspired her to try to weave her own.

Basically, Amos is known as a figurative artist. She was one of the few nonabstract artists in The Spiral, a group of black artists. Amos was the only woman member of the group and was also the youngest. Even though she came in contact with all the major black artists of the time, she continued with her own style.

Examining her work, one finds definite relationships in everything she does, from her use of colors to the style of her prints, to the warmth that radiates from her figures.

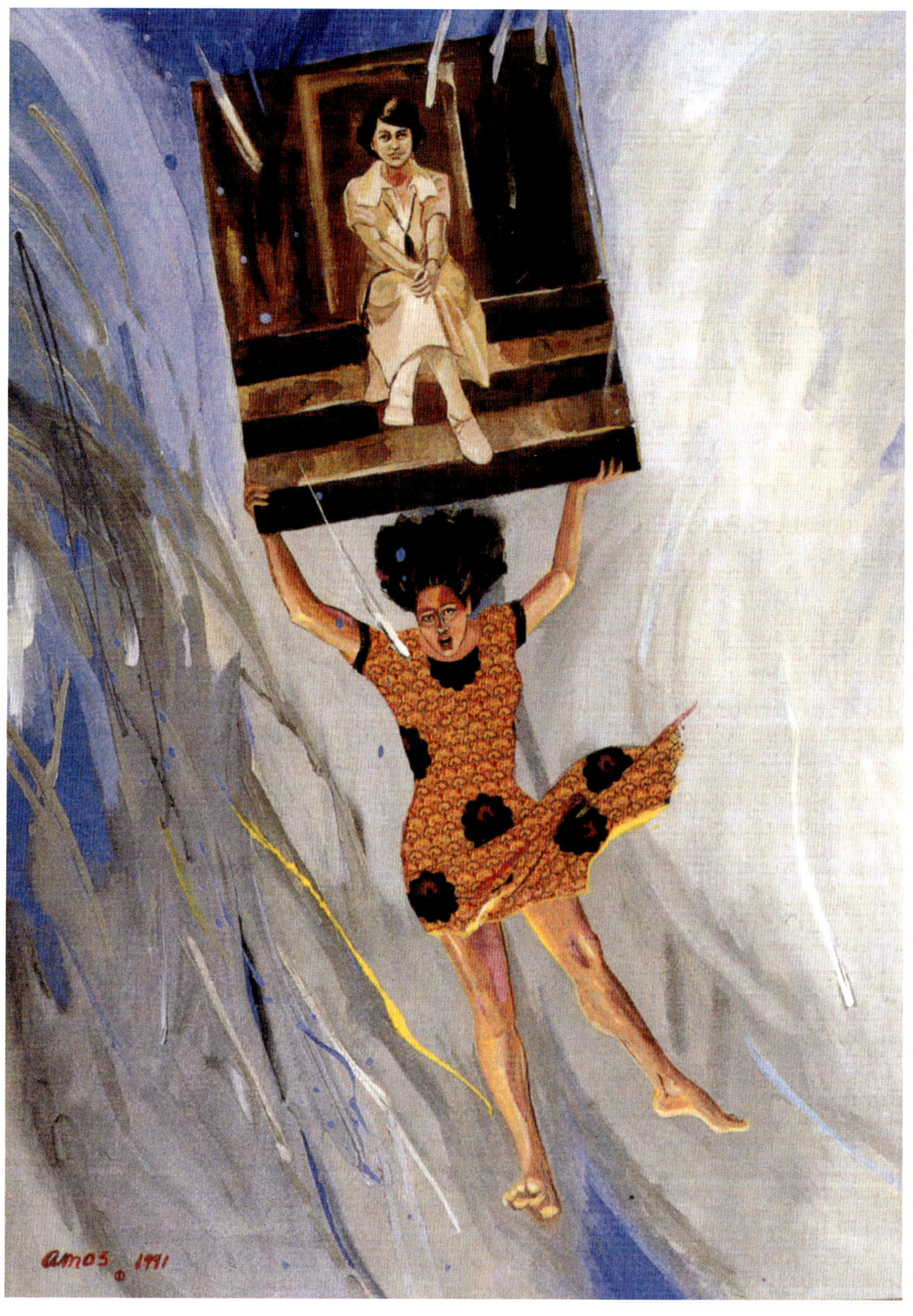

Modern Masters: Women of the First Generation, December 1982

Douglass College, collaboration with the Women Artists Series and Dr. Marter's course: Women in Art

Artists

Dorothy Dehner by Shari Samson
Sari Dienes by Teresa Ferrara
Elsie Driggs by Regina De Rosa
Perle Fine by Shula Bloch
Dorothea Greenbaum by Carolyn Moran
Dorothy Hood by Betty Ann Schoenfeld
Buffie Johnson by Barbara Sanoudis
Lois Jones by Moira Kowalczyk
Esphyr Slobodkina by Kyoko Yamaguchi
Jane Teller by Gitl Jean Bornstein

3.7

Linda Stein. *Hero 590 with Wonder Woman
Shadow*, 2007. Wood and collaged acrylicized
paper with archival pigments. With Wonder
Woman Shadow (printed on vinyl). 78" × 40" ×
10". Kathleen W. Ludwig Global Village
Living Learning Center. Douglass College.
Photo: Courtesy of the artist.

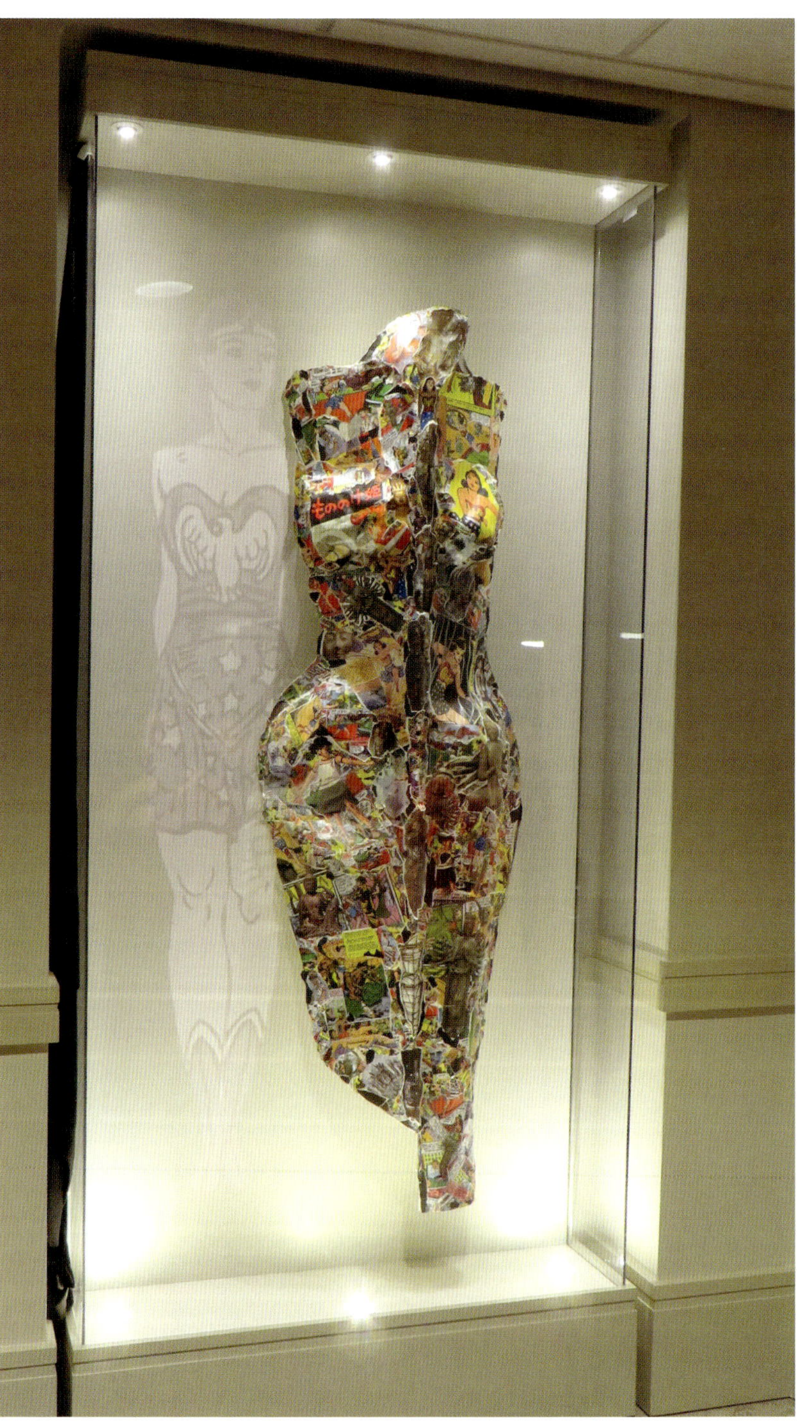

CONCLUSION

More on Douglass College and Women Artists

Since the late 1970s, art students from Douglass College have been taking courses at the Mason Gross School of the Arts. The bachelor of fine arts degree as well as the master of fine arts— initiated at Douglass—continue to flourish at Rutgers. Moreover, Douglass College remains actively involved with the support of art students and women artists in the community. Forty-eight years have passed since the Women Artists Series was established at Douglass. The celebration of women's creative achievements continues through exhibitions, lectures, and the commissioning of new artworks for the Douglass campus.

In June 1984, for example, the National Women's Studies Association held a conference at Douglass College in cooperation with the Women's Caucus for Art of New Jersey and the Women Artists Series. *Representative Works, 1971–1984* was organized under the auspices of the Mabel Smith Douglass Library in the thirteenth year of the Women Artists Series.[1]

The Women Artists Series has been supported by various members of the library staff, and faculty members through four decades. In 1987 a large endowment was offered by Professor Emerita Nellie Smither in memory of Mary H. Dana (class of 1942). Currently the Mary H. Dana Women Artists Series has been transformed into a selection of invitational shows. In addition, an endowment in memory of an artist, Estelle Lebowitz, was established in 1999. The Estelle Lebowitz Visiting Artist-in-Residence program brings a woman artist to campus for presentations, meetings with students, and an exhibition of work by the visiting artist.

Organized group exhibitions of New Jersey women artists and thematic shows still take place in the Mabel Smith Douglass Library. These exhibitions are supplemented by the Virtual Exhibits available online, largely prepared by Beryl Smith (class of 1982). Information about the history of the series, an index of artists who have been included in exhibitions, and bibliographic details are included in this excellent website, partially maintained by the

Center for Women in the Arts and Humanities. For example, women artists can be located by the year of their inclusion in the Women Artists Series. After 2006, when Ferris Olin (class of 1970) and Judith Brodsky co-directed the Institute for Women in Art (now the Center for Women in the Arts and Humanities), and Nicole Ianuzelli became the project manager, a varied selection of exhibitions and publications were organized for the Douglass Library and the gallery at Mason Gross School of the Arts. Rutgers has also become a major center for various feminist archives. For example, the National Women's Caucus for Art and Lucy Lippard donated their archives. The National Association of Women Artists presented its art collection to Rutgers. The Miriam Schapiro Archives on Women Artists is housed in Special Collections, University Archives—Rutgers University Libraries.

Because of the commitment of Douglass College to women artists, the National Association of Women Artists decided to donate their collection to Rutgers: "In 1992, the National Association of Women Artists Collection at Rutgers was established to give a permanent home to a growing collection of art (now comprising over 200 works) that recognizes the achievements of N.A.W.A. and its member artists. The oldest women's art collective still in existence, N.A.W.A. was founded in 1889 to promote high standards for women artists and provide them with the opportunity to display their works."[2]

Other programs continued on the Douglass campus. In the spring semester of 1995, I organized the Douglass Colloquium: Women Artists, Public and Private Spheres. A series of presentations was held at Douglass College and included evenings devoted to the Guerilla Girls, Faith Ringgold, Jackie Winsor, and Pat Adams.

Douglass women artists have created works of art for public view on campus. For example, Jackie Winsor constructed *Brick Dome* for the grassy entrance area to the Mabel Smith Douglass Library in 1971. Ten years later Alice Aycock completed *The Miraculating Machine in the Garden (Tower of the Winds)*, a large-scale sculpture located adjacent to the Douglass Library.

The acquisition of great works of art continues to enrich the campus. The latest addition is Linda Stein's *Hero 590 with Wonder Woman Shadow*. This sculpture was donated by Gloria Steinem under the auspices of Have Art: Will Travel! Inc. The gift was intended to honor the 100th anniversary of the founding of Douglass Residential College, and was installed in the newly completed Kathleen W. Ludwig Global Village Living Learning Center. This construction from 2007 is made of wood with collaged acrylized paper and archival pigments. The shadow of Wonder Woman is archivally printed on vinyl. The sculpture is more than 6 feet high.

Linda Stein recalls:

> It all started back in 2007 when Ferris Olin and Judy Brodsky asked me to be in *Eccentric Bodies: An Exhibition of Work by Artists with a Feminist Gaze*[3] at the Mason Gross School of the Arts Galleries. . . . The three of us began talking about a Stein sculpture being sited at Rutgers. We even chose the larger-than-life sculpture, *Hero 590*. . . . Along the way, Gloria Steinem acquired the piece. Enter Alison Bernstein. . . . she began working on the Steinem Chair, and she wanted very much to have the Stein piece donated to Douglass.[4]

In 2017 the Gloria Steinem Endowed Chair in Media, Culture, and Feminist Studies was established at Rutgers. Linda Stein won the 2016 Artist of the Year Award for Commitment to Arts and Culture by the National Association of Women Artists. *Hero 590* is part of an ongoing series of works by Linda Stein that addresses the role of women as heroic defenders, brave warriors of the modern world. She draws comparisons to Wonder Woman, featured in popular culture. Stein connects her series of female knights to 9/11 and the need for strength traditionally associated with women—nurturing, resourcefulness, endurance.

Douglass College women have supported the arts for many decades. Women artists will continue to have a voice and a presence on the campus, within the university, and in the larger community.

ACKNOWLEDGMENTS

Thanks to Dean Jacquelyn Litt of Douglass College for her enthusiastic support. Also Thomas Sokolowski and Donna Gustafson at the Zimmerli Art Museum have planned an exhibition related to the Visual Arts Program at Douglass. I am grateful to Stephanie Crawford, Kayo Denda, Erika Gorder, and Fernanda Perrone for their assistance with University Archives at the Alexander Library, Rutgers University.

NOTES

VISUAL ARTS FACULTY AT DOUGLASS COLLEGE

1. Mary Ingraham Bunting was the dean at Douglass College from 1955 to 1960, which was a period of innovation and expansion for the visual arts. She encouraged the presentation of new developments in music, dance, and performance art. The MFA program was also initiated under her direction. Geoff Hendricks called Dean Bunting "a breath of fresh air . . . this great spirit." Having come to Douglass from Bennington College, she loved the arts and was a real supporter of the department. Interview with Geoff Hendricks, October 24, 1995.

2. Black Mountain College was founded in 1933 by John A. Rice, initiated at a time when the Bauhaus in Germany had closed and Hitler had risen to power. Refugees including artists and intellectuals came to the United States. Josef Albers, who left the Bauhaus, came to this college in the mountains of North Carolina to teach art. The secluded environment encouraged individuality, experimentation, and a creative spirit. Among the renowned artists who came to work at Black Mountain were Willem and Elaine de Kooning, Robert Rauschenberg, Merce Cunningham, John Cage, Cy Twombly, Kenneth Noland, Susan Weil, and Dorothea Rockburne.

3. Beginning in 1951, Rauschenberg was creating his white paintings, which reflected light and captured shadows cast over the canvas.

4. John Goodyear was born in 1930 in Los Angeles. He studied at the University of Michigan, Ann Arbor, where he received an undergraduate degree in design and a master's degree. Goodyear made three-dimensional paintings in the 1960s and was included in *Art of the Responsive Eye* at the Museum of Modern Art in 1965. In the 1970s he worked with Gyorgy Kepes at the Center for Visual Studies at the Massachusetts Institute of Technology.

5. Geoffrey Hendricks, "Beginnings," in *Critical Mass, Happenings, Fluxus, Performance, Intermedia and Rutgers University, 1958–1972*, ed. Geoffrey Hendricks (New Brunswick, NJ: Rutgers University Press, 2003), 12.

6. Ka Kwong Hui was a native of China. Although he had studied Chinese culture, he considered a new opportunity: manufacturing a new type of ceramic china using Western technology. After spending one year at Wildenhain's Pond Farm Workshop in California, Hui enrolled at Alfred University in upstate New York. He earned a master's degree from this program (renowned for ceramics) in 1952. Because of the Korean War, he was not able to return to China. Hui moved to Brooklyn, New York, and began teaching at the Brooklyn Museum School of Art. After coming to Douglass College in

1957, he sponsored several students in the creation of ceramic sculpture. In addition, during the 1960s, he worked with Roy Lichtenstein in the creation of ceramic tableware. *Ceramic Sculpture by Ka Kwong Hui* (Trenton: New Jersey State Museum, 1987).

7. *Ceramic Sculpture by Ka Kwong Hui.*
8. The text of "Communication" is published (slightly revised) in John Cage, *Silence* (Middletown, CT: Wesleyan University Press, 1961), 41–56.
9. For the interview of Allan Kaprow by Sidney Simon, see Benjamin H. D. Buchloh, Judith F. Rodenbeck, *Experiments in the Everyday: Allan Kaprow and Robert Watts—Events, Objects, Documents* (an exhibition catalogue) (New York: Wallach Art Gallery, Columbia University, 1999), 71.
10. Interview with Letty Lou Eisenhauer, New York City, April 26, 1996.
11. Joan Snyder, *Introduction to Eight Women Artists: A Series of Exhibits at the Library, Douglass College, 1971–72.*
12. Geoffrey Hendricks, "Introduction and Acknowledgements," in *Critical Mass, Happenings, Fluxus, Performance, Intermedia and Rutgers University, 1958–1972*, ed. Geoffrey Hendricks (New Brunswick, NJ: Rutgers University Press, 2003), ix.
13. Amy Stromsten, "Ten Years of Women's Art: An Introduction," in *Ten Years of Women's Art,* ed. Amy Stromsten and Patricia Ann McDermott (New Brunswick, NJ: Rutgers University Press, 1981). Amy Stromsten was born in 1941 in Detroit, Michigan. She studied at the University of Michigan, Ann Arbor. In New York City, she studied at the Cooper Union School of Art in 1969 and took graduate seminars in the history of photography. Her photography can be found in Michael Aaron Rockland, *Homes on Wheels* (New Brunswick: Rutgers University Press, 1980).
14. Interview with Joan Semmel by Joan Marter, August 9, 2017.
15. Interview.
16. Interview.

INTERVIEW WITH ROY LICHTENSTEIN

1. Hoyt L. Sherman, *Drawing by Seeing* (New York; Hinds, Hayden & Eldredge, 1947). Hoyt Leon Sherman (1903–1981) was a professor at Ohio State University, and Lichtenstein was his student in the 1940s. Lichtenstein entered the School of Fine Arts at Ohio State in 1940, and he was influenced by Sherman's systemic analysis of the construction of a painting. Lichtenstein served in the U.S. Army from 1943 to 1946 and then returned to Ohio State where he completed the BFA in 1946 and the MFA in 1949. Sherman's "flash room" was a darkened room where images would be flashed on the screen briefly. Students were told to draw what they saw. Hoyt Sherman did experimental work in the field of optics and perception.

ALICE AYCOCK

1. Interview with Alice Aycock by Joan Marter, April 27, 2017.
2. Aycock's column, called "Melange," appeared from March 1966 to February 1967.
3. Interview with Alice Aycock by Joan Marter, April 27, 2017.

4. Interview.

5. Interview. Aycock mentioned very little about the art she created at Douglass, with the exception of shaped canvases, sculptures of trees painted bright colors, and a garbage can that she constructed and painted. Robert Hobbs does not illustrate her student work at Douglass in his monograph.

6. Robert Hobbs, *Alice Aycock, Sculpture and Projects* (Cambridge: MIT Press, 2005), 6.

7. Christine Filippone, *Science, Technology, and Utopias, Women Artists and Cold War America* (London: Routledge, 2017), 129.

8. Filippone, 128.

9. Mary Tinti, "Celebrating the Public Art of Alice Aycock," *Woman's Art Journal* 29 (Fall/Winter 2008): 6.

10. Tinti, 7.

LORETTA DUNKELMAN

1. Interview with Loretta Dunkelman by Joan Marter, December 13, 2017.

2. Interview.

3. Interview.

4. Interview.

5. Message from Loretta Dunkelman, February 14, 2018.

6. Message.

7. Message from Loretta Dunkelman, February 15, 2018.

8. Message.

9. Loretta Dunkelman, artist statement, February 1973, Loretta Dunkelman file, Women Artists Series, Douglass Library.

10. Elizabeth Gaudino, "Loretta Dunkelman," in *Artists on the Edge, Douglass College and the Rutgers MFA* (New Brunswick, NJ: Rutgers, 2005), 15–16.

KIRSTEN KRAA

1. Interview with Kirsten Kraa by Joan Marter, January 13, 2018.

2. Interview

3. These teaching methods Roy Lichtenstein learned at Ohio State University from his instructor Hoyt Sherman, who was interested in studies of perception. For more information, see David Deitcher, "Unsentimental Education: The Professionalization of the American Artist," in Hand-Painted Pop, American Art in Transition 1955–1962, ed. Russell Ferguson (New York: Rizzoli, 1993), 99–106.

FRANCES TANNENBAUM KUEHN

1. Roy Lichtenstein introduced exercises in perception that he learned from Hoyt Sherman at Ohio State University. For a description of Sherman's methods, see David Deitcher, "Unsentimental

Education: The Professionalization of the American Artist," in *Hand-Painted Pop, American Art in Transition, 1955–62* (New York: Rizzoli, 1993), 99–106.

2. Interview with Frances Kuehn by Joan Marter, January 10, 2018.

3. Interview.

4. Interview.

5. Frances Kuehn divorced George Kuehn in 1980. In the early 1990s she married Ray Hoobler, a mathematician. Kuehn also spent a year in India and incorporated Indian deities into her painting. Florence Quideau, "Frances Kuehn," in *Artists on the Edge, Douglass College and the Rutgers MFA* (New Brunswick, NJ: Rutgers University Press, 2005), 18–20.

6. Interview with Frances Kuehn by Joan Marter, February 6, 2018.

7. Interview.

LINDA LINDROTH

1. Interview with Linda Lindroth by Joan Marter, January 12, 2018.

2. Interview.

3. James Hugunin, "Holly Wright and Linda Lindroth: Notions of Presence and Absence," *Afterimage* 7, no. 8 (March 1980): 14–15. See also James R. Hugunin, *Multiple Dissentions: Linda Lindroth's Embedded Imagery*, 1984. http://lindalindroth.com/wp-content/uploads/Hugunin2.pdf.

4. Message from Linda Lindroth to Joan Marter, February 11, 2018.

5. Email message from Linda Lindroth to Joan Marter, January 12, 2018.

6. E-mail message from Linda Lindroth to Joan Marter, February 11, 2018.

7. Linda Lindroth, "Trickster in Flatland," in *Trickster in Flatland*, photographs by Linda Lindroth, n.p.

MARION ENGELMAN MUNK

1. Remarks of Marion Munk at a panel discussion, "Experiments in Education," Douglass College, March 10, 1999.

2. Remarks.

3. Conversation between Marion Munk and Joan Marter, January 6, 2018.

4. Remarks of Marion Munk at a panel discussion, March 10, 1999.

5. Ka Kwong Hui was born in 1922 in Hong Kong. He was educated at the Shanghai School of Fine Arts and the Kwong Tung School of Art in Canton, China. He received the MFA at the New York State College of Ceramics.

6. Remarks of Marion Munk at a panel discussion, March 10, 1999.

7. Conversation between Marion Munk and Joan Marter, January 6, 2018.

8. Marion Levinston, "The Expression of Organic Form in Clay," (master's thesis, Rutgers University, 1962).

9. Marion Levinston statement in *Ten Years of Women Artists*, ed. Amy Stromsten and Patricia McDermott (New Brunswick, Rutgers, 1981), n.p.

10. Marion Munk, "Letter from America and Czech Republic," *CPA News: The Newsletter of the Craft Potters Association* 35 (May/June 1994), 4.

11. Catherine Hammond, "Marion Munk," in *Artists on the Edge, Douglass College and the Rutgers MFA* (New Brunswick, NJ: Rutgers University Press, 2005), 28–32.

12. Liubov Popova's *Painterly Architectonics* (1918) is an example. Whitney Chadwick, *Women, Art and Society*, 5th ed. (London: Thames & Hudson, 2012), 265ff.

RITA MEYERS

1. Interview of Rita Myers by Joan Marter, January 21, 2018.

2. Quoted from an essay by Diane Ashton in *Artists on the Edge, Douglass College and the Rutgers MFA* (New Brunswick, NJ: Rutgers University Press, 2005), 34.

3. Ashton.

4. Ashton.

5. Ashton.

6. Ashton.

7. Message from Rita Myers, February 13, 2018.

8. Rita Myers, *Body Halves* (1971) shown as a postcard exhibition organized by Lucy Lippard, May 1973–February 1974. Box 10, Rita Myers Archive, University Archives, Rutgers University. Thanks to librarian Fernanda Perrone for assistance with the Rita Myers files, University Archives.

9. Shelley Rice, "Mythic Space: The Video Installations of Rita Myers," *Afterimage* 9 (January 1982), 8.

10. Message from Rita Myers, February 10, 2018.

11. Rita Myers, *Phantom Cities*, University Museum of Contemporary Art (Amherst: University of Massachusetts Amherst, 1990).

12. My thanks to Electronic Arts Intermix for their assistance in viewing early videos by Rita Myers, as well as *Phantom Cities* and *Resurrection Body*.

13. John G. Hanhardt, "Rita Myers," Digital Catalogue. *Twentieth World Wide Video Festival.* World Wide Video Centre, Amsterdam, the Netherlands, May 8–25, 2003.

14. Rita Myers, "Resurrection Body," VIDEOBRASIL (November 1994), n.p.

MIMI SMITH

1. My thanks to Mimi Smith for various conversations about her work, and visits to her studio over the past fifteen years.

2. Mimi Smith, "Girdle," *Heresies* 6 (Summer 1978): 36.

3. Interview with Mimi Smith by Joan Marter, March 30, 2017.

4. Interview.

5. Interview.

6. Interview.

JOAN SNYDER

Epigraph: Quoted by Marilyn Symmes, *Dancing with the Dark: Joan Snyder Prints 1963–2010* (New York: Delmonico Books, Prestel, 2011), 65.

1. E-mail message from Joan Snyder to Joan Marter, January 3, 2018.
2. Conversation with Joan Snyder by Joan Marter, January 4, 2018.
3. Interview with Joan Snyder by Catherine Reed, April 9, 2004.
4. Conversation with Joan Snyder by Joan Marter, January 5, 2018.
5. Interview with Joan Snyder by Catherine Reed, April 9, 2004. Quote is published in *Artists on the Edge, Douglass College and the Rutgers MFA* (Rutgers University, 2005), 42.
6. Quoted in *Dancing with the Dark*, 73.
7. Joan Snyder, "Painting and Sculpture—Philosophy and Technique" (MFA thesis, Rutgers University, 1966), 2, quoted in Symmes, *Dancing with the Dark*, 73.
8. Hayden Herrera, "Joan Snyder [interview] in "Expressionism Today: An Artists' Symposium," *Art in America* 70 (December 1972), 63.
9. The list has often been cited but has been released in facsimile version: Lisa Kirwin, *List: To Dos, Illustrated Inventories, Collected Thoughts, and Other Artists' Enumerations from Smithsonian's Archives of American Art* (New York Princeton Architectural Press, 2010), 30–31.
10. Joan Snyder in *8 Women Artists*, Douglass College, 1971–72, n.p.
11. Joan Snyder, "It Wasn't Neo to Us," *Journal of the Rutgers University Libraries* 54 (June 1992): 35.
12. Joan Snyder' statement on this print is published in Jewish Women's Archive: *Jewish Women and the Feminist Revolution.* https://jwa.org/sites/jwa.org/files/adult_part_2_pdf_material.pdf.
13. E-mail message from Joan Snyder to Joan Marter, January 3, 2018.

ANN TSUBOTA

1. Conversation with Ann Tsubota by Joan Marter, January 5, 2018.
2. Conversation.
3. Ingrid Dahl, "Ann Tsubota," *Artists on the Edge, Douglass College and the Rutgers MFA* (New Brunswick, NJ, Rutgers University Press, 2005), 54–57.
4. Dahl.
5.   Dahl.
6. Dahl.
7. Dahl.
8. See, for example, Glen R. Brown, "Multiplicity, Ambivalence and Installation," *Ceramics Art and Perception* (December 2003): 3–8.

JACKIE WINSOR

1.   Interview with Jackie Winsor by Joan Marter, January 26, 2018.
2. Interview.

3. Interview of Jackie Winsor by Whitney Chadwick, Oxford Art Online, Oxford University Press.

4. Peter Schjeldahl, "The Structure of Who: Jackie Winsor's Sculpture" in Dean Sobel, *Jackie Winsor* (Milwaukee Art Museum, 1991), 13.

5. Excerpt from *MoMA Highlights* (New York: The Museum of Modern Art, 1999), 300.

6. Interview of Jackie Winsor by Whitney Chadwick, Oxford Art Online.

7. Dean Sobel, "Jackie Winsor's Sculpture: Mediation, Revelation, and Aesthetic Democracy" in *Jackie Winsor* (Milwaukee Art Museum, 1992), 43.

THE WOMEN ARTISTS SERIES AT DOUGLASS COLLEGE

1. For a more detailed history of the Women Artists Series, see William Hemmig and Jesse Traquair, "Mary H. Dana Women Artists Series, History of the Series & Chronology of Administration (1971–2011)" (2006), available online as Mary H. Dana Women Artists Series Collection. Also see Beryl K. Smith, "The Mary H. Dana Women Artists Series from Idea to Institution," available online as part of the 40th Anniversary Virtual Exhibit (1971–2011), Center for Women in the Arts and Humanities.

2. Conversation with Joan Snyder by Joan Marter, January 5, 2018.

3. Quoted from Sally Shearer Swenson, "Interview with Joan Snyder [conducted in 1992]," reprinted in *Lives and Works: Talks with Women Artists*, ed. Beryl Smith, Joan Arbeiter, and Sally Shearer Swenson (London and Lanham, MD: Scarecrow Press, 1996), 2: 187. Quoted also in Marilyn Symmes, *Dancing with the Dark, Joan Snyder Prints*, 1963–2010 (London: Delmonico Books, 2011), 76.

4. Conversation with Joan Snyder, January 5, 2018.

CONCLUSION

1. *Representative Works, 1971–1984* [exhibition catalog], Women Artists Series, Douglass College, June 1–30. 1984. Joan Marter was Curator of the Exhibition.

2. Quoted from the Introduction to the exhibition catalog *The Enduring Figure 1890s–1970s, Sixteen Sculptors from the National Association of Women Artists* (Zimmerli Art Museum, 1999).

3. *Eccentric Bodies* was a group exhibition on view at the Mason Gross School of the Arts Galleries from June 14 to August 3, 2007. Seven women artists were featured: Harriet Casdin-Silver, Bailey Doogan, Brenda Goodman, Orlan, Ernestine Ruben, Berni Searle, and Linda Stein.

4. Message from Linda Stein to Joan Marter, March 12, 2018.

SELECTED BIBLIOGRAPHY

Books

Buchloh, Benjamin H. D., and Judith F. Rodenbeck. *Experiments in the Everyday: Allan Kaprow and Robert Watts—Events, Objects, Documents*. New York: Miriam and Ira D. Wallach Art Gallery, Columbia University, 1999.

Denda, Kayo, Mary Hawkesworth, and Fernanda Perrone. *The Douglass Century: Transformation of the Women's College at Rutgers University*. New Brunswick, NJ: Rutgers University Press, 2018.

Hendricks, Geoffrey; Mead Art Museum (Amherst College); Mason Gross School of the Arts (Rutgers University). *Critical Mass: Happenings, Fluxus, Performance, Intermedia and Rutgers University, 1958–1972*. New Brunswick, NJ: Rutgers University Press, 2003.

Herrera, Hayden, with Jenni Sorkin and Norman L. Kleeblatt. *Joan Snyder*. New York: Harry N. Abrams, 2005.

Hobbs, Robert. *Alice Aycock: Sculpture and Projects*. Cambridge, MA: MIT Press, 2005.

Marter, Joan, ed. *Off Limits: Rutgers University and the Avant-Garde, 1957–1963*. New Brunswick NJ: Rutgers University Press, 1999.

Symmes, Marilyn, and Faye Hirsch. *Dancing with the Dark: Joan Snyder Prints, 1963–2010*. New York: Prestel, Delmonico Books, 2011.

Catalogs and Essays

Alloway, Lawrence. "Introduction." In *Women Artists Series, Year Five*. New Brunswick, NJ: Douglass College, 1976.

Beckenstein, Joyce. "Joan Semmel: Naked Came the Nude." *Woman's Art Journal* 36 (Fall/Winter 2015): 3–11.

Conz, Francesco, Geoffrey Hendricks, Larry Miller, and Sara Seagull. *Robert Watts Exhibition*. Budapest: Artpool Art Research Center, 2008.

Gustafson, Donna. *at/around/beyond: Fluxus at Rutgers*. New Brunswick, NJ: Zimmerli Art Museum, 2011.

Lippard, Lucy. "Introduction." In *Women Artists Series, Year Five*, 1–5. New Brunswick, NJ: Douglass College, 1976.

Marter, Joan, ed. *Expressions of Self: Women and Autobiography*. New Brunswick, NJ: Douglass College Art Gallery, 1979.

Marter, Joan. "Introduction." In *Women Artists Year 8, 1978–79*. New Brunswick, NJ: Douglass College, 1979.

Marter, Joan, ed. *fragments of myself/the women: An Exhibition of Black Women Artists*. New Brunswick, NJ: Douglass College Art Gallery, 1980.

Marter, Joan. "Joan Semmel." *Arts Magazine* 53 (November 1978), 12.

Marter, Joan. "Joan Semmel's Nudes: The Erotic Self and the Masquerade." *Woman's Art Journal* 16 (Fall 1995/Winter 1996): 24–28.

Marter, Joan. *Mimi Smith, Constructing Art about Life*. Jersey City, NJ: Harold B. Lemmerman Gallery, New Jersey City University, 2014.

Marter, Joan. "Then and Now: Recognition of Women Artists since 1970." *Journal of the Rutgers University Libraries* 54 (June 1992): 24–27.

Marter, Joan. "Ages of Discovery, The Women Artists Series at Douglass." In *Mary H. Dana Women Artists Series, 25th Year Retrospective*, edited by Marianne Ficarra and Ferris Olin (New Brunswick, NJ: Mason Gross School of the Arts, 1996), pp. 1–2.

Marter, Joan. "Women Artists." *Arts Magazine* (February 1978), 23.

Marter, Joan. "Introduction." In *Artists on the Edge, Douglass College and the Rutgers MFA,* edited by Ferris Olin (New Brunswick, NJ: Mabel Smith Douglass Library, 2005) pp. 3–4.

Miller, Lynn F., and Sally S. Swenson. *Lives and Works: Talks with Women Artists*. Vol. 1. Metuchen, NJ: Scarecrow Press, 1982.

Modern Masters: Women of the First Generation. New Brunswick, NJ: Women Artists Series, Douglass College, 1982.

Nochlin, Linda. "Preface." In *Women Artists Series, Year Four*. New Brunswick, NJ: Douglass College, 1974.

Olin, Ferris. "Thawing the Chilly Climate: Two Decades of Women Artists at Douglass College." *Journal of the Rutgers University Libraries* 54 (June 1992): 28–33.

Smith, Beryl K. "The Mary H. Dana Women Artists Series: From Idea to Institution." *Journal of the Rutgers University Libraries* 54 (June 1992): 4–16.

Smith, Beryl K., Joan Arbeiter, and Sally Shearer Swenson. *Lives and Works: Talks with Women Artists*. Vol. 2. Metuchen, NJ: Scarecrow Press, 1996.

Snyder, Joan. "It Wasn't Neo to Us." *Journal of the Rutgers University Libraries* 54 (June 1992): 34–35.

Sobel, Dean. *Jackie Winsor*. Milwaukee Art Museum, 1992.

Stromsten, Amy, ed., with Patricia Ann McDermott. *Ten Years of Women's Art*. New Brunswick, NJ: Douglass College, 1981.

Wechsler, Jeffrey. *Twelve from Rutgers*. New Brunswick, NJ: University Art Gallery (now Zimmerli Art Museum), Rutgers University Press, 1977.

The Women Artists Series at Douglass College, Tenth Anniversary, Retrospective Show. New Brunswick, NJ: Douglass College, 1981.

Women Artists Series, 1983–84. New Brunswick, NJ: Mabel Smith Douglass Library, Douglass College, 1983.

Women Artists Series 1986/87. New Brunswick, NJ: Mabel Smith Douglass Library, Douglass College, 1986.

Women Artists Series, 1998–1999. New Brunswick, NJ: Mabel Smith Douglass Library, Douglass College, 1998.

Women Artists Series, Year 8, 1978–79. New Brunswick, NJ: Douglass College, 1978.

INDEX

Note: Page numbers in italics indicate illustrations.

ABOUT THE AUTHOR

Joan Marter, Board of Governors Professor Emerita, Department of Art History, was a faculty member at Douglass College beginning in 1977. She organized exhibitions with her undergraduate students on the Douglass campus, and served on the jury of the Women Artists Series for 35 years. Her publications include *Off Limits: Rutgers University and the Avant-Garde, 1957–1963* (1999) and *Women of Abstract Expressionism* (2016), and many essays connected with the Women Artists Series. Currently she is editor of the *Woman's Art Journal*, which has been published continually since 1980.